P9-DHN-016

Accolades for Democracy at the Doorstep, Too! and its Contributing Authors

"Many of us think we've seen it all, and then a book like this comes along that opens our eyes to a whole new world of stories from the frontlines of public management! Mike and Melissa have done a great job with this collection of real stories from women professionals that will inspire us, make us think and also make us laugh!"

Dave Childs, City Manager of Palmdale, California,
ICMA President, 2010

"In these challenging times in local government, it is encouraging to know that professional managers continue to chart the course for many of our cities, counties, and other jurisdictions. Our strength lies in our diversity, innovation, and the passion we hold for the very important work that we do. Never before has this formula been more critical for success in managing the quality of life issues in our communities and for the people we serve. Thanks Mike and Melissa for collecting these stories from such a diverse group of women professionals!"

Darnell Earley, City Manager, Saginaw, Michigan,
ICMA President, 2009

"These stories from women professionals help us understand leadership in times of disruptive change. Rather than admiring the problem, we learn how to seek the solution. Bravo, Mike and Melissa."

David Limardi, ICMA Midwest Regional Director,
ICMA President, 2008

"Mike and Melissa have used the words of many of their colleagues to capture the spirit of local government and the contributions managers and assistants make to their communities. These managers and their assistants tell wonderful stories about why House Speaker Thomas P. "Tip' O'Neill told us 'all politics is local' and about where the rubber meets the road for the citizen. Everyone interested in local government as a profession and in learning 'how things get done at city hall' needs to read their stories."

Ed Daley, City Manager, Hopewell, Virginia,
ICMA President, 2007

"Delivering Democracy to the Doorstep has been a passion of mine throughout my career. I am so pleased to see Mike and Melissa deliver this cadre of stories from women professionals on the front lines that highlight their incredible commitment to public service."

Bill Buchanan, County Manager, Sedgwick County,
Kansas, ICMA President, 2006

"These are the stories of professional local government management women, told by women. They are stories we all need to hear, and to reflect on, as we diversify our profession."

Michael Willis, General Manager, Shellharbour City
Council, Shellharbour NSW Australia
ICMA President, 2005

"Despite all that we learn in the classroom, there are some things that experience alone can teach. Once on the job, we learn some of the most unexpected lessons, and often when we least expect them. The stories that leaders and decision-makers in our profession have to tell are invaluable. With this sequel to ***Democracy at the Doorstep***, we now have two references that give voice and provide valuable insight from both women and men in the local government profession."

Tom Lundy, County Manager, Catawba County,
North Carolina. ICMA President, 2004

"There have been great female managers from the beginning of time whose talents have often been overlooked for just as long. Conduff and Vossmer have assembled stories from women public managers that offer inspiration for public servants of both genders."

Dave Krings, Director, Non-Profit and Local Government
Solutions, TechSolve, Inc., ICMA President, 2003

"Stories represent the chronicles of our lives. Women bring a passion and perspective to stories that can otherwise go missing. Thanks to Mike & Melissa for adding to the collective history of the profession with this volume of stories told by women."

Peggy Merriss, City Manager of Decatur, GA,
ICMA President, 2002

"These reflections of women local government managers exhibit the best of the profession and represent the growing reality of the gender diversity of our profession."

Dave Mora, Life Member, ICMA President, 2001

"Mike Conduff (with Melissa Byrne Vossmer) has once again done an artful job of capturing the stories of some of the most creative leaders in local government – this time from women professionals. This new book, ***Democracy at the Doorstep, Too***! demonstrates his awareness of the value of women to the profession. The stories address the many challenges women have faced throughout their careers and provide wisdom for those who follow in their footsteps. Mike is once again OnTarget with his efforts to share the experiences of all influential thinkers and practitioners in City/County Management. His inclusiveness is evidence of his commitment to the profession. Those who know Mike personally, or have read his books, know that he is one of those people that have truly made a difference in our profession. "

Cathy Holdeman, Assistant City Manager, Wichita,
Kansas, KACM President, 2010

Democracy at the Doorstep, Too!

More True Stories

Democracy at the Doorstep, Too!

More True Stories

MIKE CONDUFF
and
MELISSA BYRNE VOSSMER

© Copyright 2012 by the authors Michael A. Conduff and Melissa Byrne Vossmer, with all rights reserved.

Published by Elim Group Publishing.

978-0-9794875-8-3

All rights reserved. No part of this book may be reproduced or transmitted in any form or by any means, electronic or mechanical, including photocopying, scanning, recording or by any information storage and retrieval system without the prior written permission from the author, except for the including of brief quotations in a review or article.

This book is an amalgamation of ideas, stories and tales from many sources. Every attempt has been made to transmit the information and stories accurately. Permission has been granted for the use of the stories and other material, or it has been obtained through public sources.

This book is intended to provide information concerning the subject matter covered. It is sold with the understanding that the publisher and authors are not engaged in rendering legal, medical, psychological, or other professional services other than those which they are qualified to provide. If legal, medical, psychological, or other expert assistance is required, the services of competent professionals should be sought.

This book is not an attempt to be an exhaustive reference for all of the subjects that lie between these covers. The reader is urged to review all available information on these subjects to receive the broadest and most complete understanding possible.

Every effort has been made to make this book as accurate as possible. There may, however, be mistakes, both of a typographical nature and involving content. Accordingly the reader should use this book with the proviso that it is a general guide and not the ultimate source of information on these subjects.

Since the purpose of this book is to educate and to some degree entertain, neither the authors nor the publisher has any liability or responsibility to any person or entity with respect to any loss or damage caused, or alleged to be caused, directly or indirectly by the information contained in this book.

While the publisher and author have used their best efforts in preparing this book, they make no representations or warranties with respect to the accuracy or completeness of the contents of this book and specifically disclaim any implied warranties of merchantability or fitness for a particular purpose.

Contents

THE STATUE OF LIBERTY

"GIVE ME YOUR TIRED,
YOUR POOR,
YOUR HUDDLED MASSES
YEARNING TO BREATHE FREE,
THE WRETCHED REFUSE
OF YOUR TEEMING SHORE."

The people of France gave the Statue of Liberty to the people of the United States of America in recognition of the friendship established during the American Revolution. Over the years, the Statue of Liberty's symbolism has grown to include Freedom and Democracy as well as this international friendship. The Statue was officially dedicated on October 28th, 1886.

The robed female figure represents Libertas, the Roman goddess of freedom, who bears a torch and a tablet evoking the law. A broken chain lies at her feet. Artists of the period striving to evoke the concept of freedom commonly used representations of Libertas (Liberty.) A Liberty figure adorned most American coins of the time and representations of Liberty appeared in popular and civic art, including Thomas Crawford's Statue of Freedom (1863) atop the dome of the US Capitol.

President Grover Cleveland, the former New York governor, presided over the dedication of the Statue of Liberty.

Interestingly from our context in ***Democracy at the Doorstep, Too!*** no members of the general public were permitted on Bedloe's Island during the ceremonies, which were reserved entirely for dignitaries. In fact, the only women granted access were the designer's wife and the committee chair's granddaughter. This restriction offended area suffragists, who chartered a boat and got as close as they could to the island. The group's leaders made speeches applauding the embodiment of Liberty as a woman and advocating women's right to vote.

We chose The Statue of Liberty as also embodying our themes of Democracy delivered to the doorsteps of our communities and the many roles that Professional Women in Local Government fill in delivering it.

Foreword

"DEMOCRACY at the Doorstep" is a phrase I first heard from Bill Buchanan, former ICMA President and still County Manager of Sedgwick County, Kansas. It is a simple phrase that so appropriately describes the work professional local government managers bring to their communities. Of course, while the phrase is simple the work is not.

When Melissa Byrne Vossmer first asked if I would be willing to find the time to write the Foreword for this showcase of stories by women in local government management, the conversation went something like this: "Hey, Bonnie, congratulations on being elected to serve as the next President of ICMA (International City/County Management Association)…I know you are going to be really busy as you take on this position…Mike Conduff (author of ***Democracy at the Doorstep – True Stories from the Green Berets of Public Administrators)*** and I were talking at a TCMA (Texas City/County Management Association) event and thought that it would be great if you could write the Foreword to the sequel to ***Democracy at the Doorstep*** since you will be the very first woman Assistant City Manager to be President."

I of course was honored to do so, and even more honored to help highlight the incredible contributions of women to local government.

The stories you will read in this great book reflect the journeys or "rites of passage" of women in a profession where balancing work with life is challenging at best. You will learn of the pride women have in being the first female chief administrator or manager in their communities. You will sense the genuine courage, professionalism, and tenacity these women have experienced in their own journeys of delivering democracy. You will learn of the intense delight that women feel when a particular project or achievement was completed and celebrated.

As I reflect on these stories I recall an experience I had at the "Senior Executives in State and Local Government Program" (Harvard Kennedy School – July 2011.) A fellow student asked the instructor how he knew the name and workplace of each student. The instructor noted that he was given the roster of the class participants and that he made time to familiarize himself with the class. He posed the question, "Don't we always make time for things that are important to us?"

Thank you to Mike and Melissa and all of the remarkable and extraordinary women who thought, amidst a multitude of competing demands, that it was important to take the time to share their stories with us. You indeed reflect the tenets of The Athenian Oath, an oath that was taken by the young men of ancient Athens when they reached the age of seventeen.

The Athenian Oath

We will never bring disgrace on this our City by an act of dishonesty or cowardice.
We will fight for the ideals and Sacred Things of the City both alone and with many.
We will revere and obey the City's laws, and will do our best to incite a like reverence and respect in those above us who are prone to annul them or set them at naught.
We will strive increasingly to quicken the public's sense of civic duty.
Thus in all these ways we will transmit this City, not only not less, but greater and more beautiful than it was transmitted to us.

I am pleased to introduce to you the stories of these amazing women who have and are indeed transmitting their communities, not only not less, but greater and more beautiful than their communities were transmitted to them.

As we begin to celebrate the 100 year anniversary of ICMA, I hope you will take time to glance back at the stories of your colleagues in the trenches of delivering Democracy to doorsteps and focus forward on engaging your communities on how professional local government management delivers "Life, Well Run!"

Bonnie Svrcek
President-Elect
International City/County Management Association
Deputy City Manager
Lynchburg, Virginia

Inspiration and Mike's Acknowledgements

MY grandfather used to say, "Mike, when you find yourself in a hole, the first order of business is to quit digging!" He also used to say, "When you finally figure out you have messed up, apologize and make amends as best you can."

Both maxims apply to ***Democracy at the Doorstep, Too!***

The predecessor to this book was ***Democracy at the Doorstep, True Stories from the Green Berets of Public Administrators.*** It is a compilation of voluntarily submitted stories written by local government professionals, largely collected as a result of my Texas City Management Presidential year, way back in 2001. As I recount in that book, the stories lay largely dormant as a result of a job change for me in April of 2001 and a world change on 9/11 of that year. With the support of my incredible spouse ("partner" in the ICMA vernacular) the book finally was released in 2011, a full ten years later than intended.

The ink was barely dry, and the first copies being signed when it was pointed out to me (professionally, but none-too-gently!) that there were no stories by women professionals. "Oops!"

My first response was of course to offer a sincere, humble, long-winded explanation of who, what, when, where, why; "it was ten years ago and there weren't many women, it was voluntary, etc. etc. etc." Body language quickly told me (as we say in Texas) that dog was not going to hunt. And that is of course when Granddad Briggs' first admonition hit. "Quit digging." His second followed very quickly thereafter and I proffered both an apology and a peace offering

– "How about if we do a book of only women professionals' stories?" Making amends.

And so, here we are! ***Democracy at the Doorstep, Too!*** is that book, and it could not have happened without some awesome women.

First of course is my ICMA Board Colleague and co-author Melissa Byrne Vossmer. Her energy and enthusiasm, her intellectual courage and honesty and her feminism (in the best sense of the word) all came to the front in this project. The book simply would not exist without her! Besides, she was the one that accosted me first – no surprise to those that know her!

Next are our cosponsors, Joan McCallen from the International City/County Management Association Retirement Corporation and Tru Dee Bamberg from the National League of Cities Service Line Warranty Program provider Utility Service Partners.

Joan is one of the most articulate and engaging speakers and story tellers I have ever met, with that talent eclipsed only by her financial acumen. I pass along the advice given to me by my mentor, Buford Watson, to every young public service professional I know: "Join ICMA, get active in the organization, and contribute the max to ICMA-RC." I am truly only able to do what I do because ICMA-RC exists and Joan's expertise in that arena is legendary. The value of her support, both emotionally and financially, of this project cannot be overstated. Thanks Joan – you are one of my heroes!

Tru Dee is the iconic female business professional. Her marketing skills know no limits, and when she starts telling stories of her personal journey to the top of the marketing world you simply sit mesmerized. The progress of women in that profession is epitomized by Tru Dee – from an ornament to a fixture, from a go-fer to a go-to, from being window dressing in the building to running the building. Tru Dee, your willingness to support local government in this way is greatly appreciated!

Of course my ICMA journey of now some 35 years has been incredibly facilitated by so many of our talented women staff professionals. Beth Kellar, Betsy Sherman, Martha Perego, Michele Frisby and Rita Ossolinski have all contributed so much to my learning. Uma Ramesh is ICMA's money star and I enjoyed so much working with her when I chaired the Finance Committee for the Board. Sallie Ann Burnett capably coordinates the great meetings I attend (and prints my name REALLY BIG!) Beth Payne ably edits my bimonthly column on governance in ***Public Manager***, and keeps me faithful to just 750 words. Jennifer Kalita helped us coordinate contributors. Gina Anderson-Ford not only keeps Bob O'Neill on the straight and narrow, she tries from afar to do the same for me. This list of ICMA pros goes on and on, and if you want to see a building hum with professionalism, just stop by ICMA headquarters in DC – thanks folks!

When I was thirteen I met the most beautiful young woman I had ever seen. Eight years later we were married, and she has walked beside me on my local government journey for all of the 35 years. We have shared the joys, sorrows, accomplishments, failures, accolades, accostings, hellos, goodbyes and all the moves together. If you want to read a picture of Kathy just go to Proverbs 31. She has taught me to learn to laugh at the days to come, even through tears of current sorrows. Thanks Honey!!

And finally, and most critically, thanks to our authors! Sharing personal stories with others always entails risk. Additionally it takes time, energy and vigor from other potential endeavors. For so many incredible women to invest so much, to risk so much, to share so much is simply inspirational. Authors, thanks to each of you! The profession owes you each a debt of gratitude – as do I!

Enjoy the True Stories!

Melissa's Acknowledgements

IF you read Mike's acknowledgements on the previous pages, you have an idea of how we got to the actual publication of ***Democracy at the Doorstep, Too!*** Mike has been has always been supportive of women managers so I just couldn't believe there were no women in the original book. Fortunately, Mike listened and learned from his Granddad Briggs and quickly offered a solution. It is fair to say that I had no idea the amount of work that would go into pulling the book together. Mike did, and still offered! As co-author on the project, Mike has been both gracious and committed to making the book a reality, all the while being incredibly supportive. Mike has truly been a good friend over the years and I think he has more than made up for his initial oversight! Okay, Mike – you're forgiven!

Acknowledgements are a tricky thing. I always worry about leaving someone out that deserves to be mentioned.

Of course, it goes without saying that the book would still be just a great concept if it had not been for the women who stepped up and contributed a story about their lives and careers in the profession we all love. The one guideline we had was to write a story about an experience you wanted to share that others could learn from. Without exception, every story meets that guideline. Some provide ideas towards better governance, others describe prickly situations with elected officials, staff and citizens, others offer innovative solutions, some acknowledge the generosity of our families, some are stories that share a personal moment and some just make us laugh! It is my privilege to be associated with each and every one of our wonderful authors

– and while there are many I have never met – this book has allowed me to make new, wonderful friends.

Mike does a great job in acknowledging the support ***Democracy at the Doorstep, Too!*** has received from ICMA. Beth Kellar contributed a wonderful story as well as a cover quote and Jennifer Kalita has hit the ground running at ICMA where she will work on issues pertaining to women in the profession in the coming months. Our ICMA-RC sponsor, Joan McCallen was on board immediately after hearing the concept of the book, recognizing it would be a valuable contribution to the profession. And Ross Hoff, as Senior Staff to the ICMA Annual Conference, has been working with us every step of the way in our goal of getting a copy of the book in the Conference Attendees registration materials. Working with Jennifer and others, ***Democracy at the Doorstep, Too!*** is featured at the Women's Luncheon at the Annual Conference.

It also stands to reason that the National League of Cities would find value in supporting the publication of the book, and Tru Dee Bamberg from the NLC Service Line Warranty Program provider, Utility Service Partners, is to be thanked for their generous contribution.

How does one go about adequately expressing gratitude to wonderful, caring and supportive parents? It is never enough, but I am so honored to use this opportunity to acknowledge what my parents have done for me throughout my life and continue to do each and every day. I am extremely thankful. They have nurtured me, supported me and pushed me when they thought I needed it. From the time I was a little girl they made it clear there was not anything I couldn't accomplish if I wanted it enough and was willing to work hard enough. Mom and Dad – though this is not nearly enough – Thank You!!

And finally, I must acknowledge my spouse. When we started dating in 1974(!!) I didn't realize that I had found "The One." Nothing is clear at age 19. But, almost 34 four years later, we are still going strong and have used both the many good times, as well as the adversity we have faced together, to strengthen and deepen our relationship. The story I contributed has to do with the conflict of careers and the unconditional love and support I have received from Mark while I have pursued mine – frequently at the expense of his. Again, a thank you seems so inadequate but I am truly thankful that I have him in my life.

As a labor of love, I am both sad and glad that the journey to publish ***Democracy at the Doorstep, Too!*** has come to an end. I hope that those that read the book will take from it what we meant to be shared, and appreciate these women authors and their contribution to local government management and the positive impact they have had on their communities.

They do indeed bring Democracy to the Doorsteps of their communities!

Introduction

AFTER spending our careers in local government, Melissa and I have a great and enduring admiration for the men and women who serve the public in the villages, towns, cities and counties of our great country. As citizens we often look to the Whitehouse, the Congress or the State Capitol for public policy decisions of import. But the fact is that what happens every day of the year in City Halls and County Courthouses across America impacts us the most.

Some services clearly are national in scope, and while we particularly appreciate the women and men of the U.S. Armed Forces – especially in this anxious time internationally – and intellectually understand the need for federal and state agencies, it is the services that we receive from our local communities that influence our quality of life the most. Think of it this way, dial 911 and you have a public safety response from incredibly proficient professionals in minutes – or less. Start your car and drive on efficient and safe street systems with traffic control devices that function. Flip your electric switch, and see your lights come on, almost all the time. Turn the tap and watch your water flow. Flush and see all that stuff go away. Your local costs for this are very reasonable, especially in contrast to the Federal Income Tax for most of us. Compare the taxes for your local school district and your local government if you want a contrast in cost and benefit.

From an access perspective, if you want to talk to the President or Governor you had best be a big contributor or a sister-in-law. If you have a complaint with a large utility or other provider of service and want to talk to the president of the company or chair of the board you had better own a lot of shares of stock. However, if you want to talk to the Mayor or City or County Manager, just pick up the phone!

Largely because of this access and the accompanying accountability, it is at the local level that Democracy truly thrives.

The Congress and most state legislatures exempt themselves from regulations they promulgate on local governments. They specialize in back room deals and perks. However, open meetings are commonplace in your community and you are most welcome to attend. Want a copy of about anything that exists there? Just ask. Want to get involved? Just volunteer – you will be welcomed with open arms.

Fortunately there are many tremendous local elected officials all across the country. These are folks who give hugely of their time and energy for no more reward than seeing their community improve and prosper. They are rarely paid, almost never thanked, and often maligned. They typically don't get pensions or health insurance. You often have to ask yourself why anyone would even want a job like that, and even campaign to get it. The hallways at a National League of Cities conference are full of stories from great elected officials about the indignities they put up with just to serve.

The Council-Manager form of government clearly puts the elected officials first, and that is how they should be treated and respected. Managers are ethically and professionally obligated to do the will of the majority of the elected officials – even when we disagree with it and have recommended another course. Buford Watson, my mentor, a former ICMA President and long-time City Manager of Lawrence, Kansas used to say to me, "Mike, do what the Council asks you to do. As long as it is not illegal or immoral, do it to the best of your ability. Remember, it is their town, not yours!"

So, while respectfully and sincerely acknowledging the indispensable role of the elected official, we want to suggest that it is the Professional Managers and Administrators in Cities and Counties that are on the front lines of Democracy, and that is what these stories share with us. Like a modern day Paladin or urban Navy Seal, or municipal Green Beret, these folks sacrifice for others, and often at extreme personal cost.

Each of our contributing authors is truly a hero in their own way. We hope you will acknowledge and thank them for helping keep Democracy Strong and for helping create Life, Well Run!

Mike's Personal Note – An Influential Woman

I grew up in an Air Force family, which simply means we lived a lot of different places. While my dad was mostly gone protecting our freedoms and serving the country (Thanks Dad!) my mom raised my sister and me pretty much by herself, militarily removed from family or traditional support networks. She was quite a woman; resourceful, innovative and courageous. Once she put her mind to a task it was all over but the shouting. She rarely encountered a situation she could not master, whether it involved power outages in Indiana winters, or power dinners at the Officer's Clubs. So, when folks ask me where I am from, I say, CONUS (which is military speak for the Continental United States!)

But the whole time we were moving around the country, my mom's mom, my maternal grandmother, lived in the same house. It was my personal anchor to stability, my favorite place to be. No matter how many places I was taken to live, I knew where my grandmother lived. And while much of the charm of that place revolved around cousins, extra freedoms and the rural Southwest Missouri setting that allowed me to roam unfettered, it was my grandmother herself who was the touchstone.

When I was thirteen my folks gave me a great gift and allowed me to spend most of a summer with her. She was an incredible woman, and even as a self-centered teenager I recognized it. Besides her zest for life, her self-sufficiency, her tackle anything and fix anythingness, she simply exuded unconditional love. When you entered her sphere of influence she totally enveloped you in her world. She was the center.

Everything radiated out from her. It did not matter what kind of a car you drove up in, what your job was, how much money you made, how big your house was, whether you were just out of jail or if you ran the jails. At Grandma Briggs' you were family. Her heart influence overshadowed every other factor.

And it wasn't just people. Even stuff listened to her. I protestingly helped her plant a sickly little oak seedling she had me dig up and that I was convinced was already dead from all my hacking at its roots, and watched her tell it, "Now grow, you!" Forty years later that oak is a massive reminder of her. That 13th summer I had a temperamental BB-gun. One day when it had quit me again and again, and all my older cousins had given up on fixing it I told her I was going to just throw it away. She said, "Mike, bring that to me." She held it, pointed it straight up, bounced it in her lap a time or two, spanked it with her hand and said, "Now work, you!" It never misfired again.

That was the summer she taught me to drive, took me strip pit swimming, made me cut my own willow tree switches and provided me the setting to meet the love of my life.

But Grandma Briggs' greatest gift was that she was a consummate story teller. In the cool of the early Missouri mornings we would walk down to the barn to milk Bessie and I would sit mesmerized while she squeezed me a cup of warm milk and told of the early years of her marriage. After a summer and fall of following itinerant welding work on the Mississippi river she and my Granddad would come back to the "home place" with five kids and enough potatoes to see them through the winter. "I cooked fried potatoes for breakfast, potato soup for lunch and baked potatoes for dinner. If there was a way to cook potatoes I tried it. Potatoes, butter and honey we smoked out bees to get make a pretty good desert! We didn't have much, but we had love, and that was enough."

"I remember a time" was the usual start of a great story and generally no matter what I was doing as soon as I heard it I circled over, plopped down on the floor or the grass at her feet and listened to times when people helped each other through the depression and big deals were done on a handshake, when one year there was only enough winter money for a single hundred pound sack of potatoes, about a time when the snow was so deep Granddad and Emory, Jr. had to walk and break trail for the Model A while she drove to get back home, when...

Even as I attended the University of New Hampshire I continued to come back to Grandma Briggs' each chance I got, once driving 24 hours straight to get there in time for home cured bacon and fresh backyard eggs cooked on a cast iron skillet.

I spent two summers working for the Missouri Highway Department in Nevada, Missouri while living with her. Our wedding reception was in her front room. For the ten years I worked in Pittsburg, Kansas I mowed her yard, helped with her chores and honked goodbye each time I left her driveway. Every holiday for years was at least partially spent at her table and the day we buried her I stood underneath that oak tree in her backyard and knew that my heart had seen love as pure as it was meant to be.

Grandma Briggs was an influential woman and a storyteller, and from her I learned that stories tie us together. I hope you enjoy these – I know I did!

Denton, TX 2012

Appropriate Quote

"There is a woman at the beginning of all great things."

Alphonse de Lamartine,
French Poet and Statesman

Story One

Sometimes Advice Comes from the Places You Least Expect...And Other Lessons from the Receptionist's Desk!

As told by Cheryl Hilvert

THROUGHOUT my career in public service, I have learned some great lessons that have helped me both in my work, and in my personal life. While I always expected that I would learn a great deal from fellow managers and professional associations such as ICMA, I quickly learned that lessons can come from a wide variety of people and experiences and that some of the best advice we ever receive can come from the places we would least expect!

As city managers, we often think that we have to have all the answers. This is largely due to the political environment in which we work where the pressure to have the answer to any issue or project, or know where to go to get it, is expected. It is also important for us to inspire those that we work for, and with, that we really are the great manager and leader that we hope they believe us to be. And, of course, it is important that the residents and businesspersons in our community view us as intelligent, experienced public servants in which to have extreme amounts of confidence.

Demonstrating a commitment to public service, working hard to do a good job, and inspiring confidence in others is what we all have to do. And, most of us do a pretty good job at it most of the time. But what about those times when we are confronted with a difficult problem or issue that has no apparent basis, we really don't understand, and that we never talked about in graduate school or at the ICMA conference? That's where the story of one of my most important lessons begins. . .

In the late 1980's, I was fortunate to work as an assistant city manager for a progressive, mid-sized suburban city with a wonderful reputation for providing great services. It was a popular place to live, recognized as a highly-desired business location and had good financial resources. The only problem was that for a variety of reasons, it had a number of short-tenured city managers in a relatively small span of time.

As a relatively new employee to this city, I had not previously been asked to serve as "acting" city manager during the search process. Two other department heads had stepped up to serve in this role during the previous searches for a new manager. This time, however, it was my "turn," and, while I was nervous about the "acting" role, I was also excited about the opportunities that were opening for me in my chosen career.

Shortly after taking on the expanded responsibilities, several elected and appointed officials began to "encourage" me to apply for the city manager position. I was only in my twenties and really hadn't thought much about applying for the "big" job. After all, I had only been with the city for a year and a half and always thought that when I finally would land my first manager's job it would be in a very small city where I could learn along with the organization. I certainly did not think I was ready for a position in a progressive, mid-sized city with a substantial budget, city-owned utilities, lots of opportunities for growth and an employee population that was almost completely unionized. However, I got lots of offers of assistance and support and decided to "go through the process" for the experience, never thinking that I stood a real chance of getting the job.

Long story short, after a long process, I was appointed city manager . . . on a less-than-unanimous vote. Unfortunately, I did not have the political knowledge that I possess now and had limited exposure to a network of colleagues that would have helped me to understand the "message" behind the vote on my appointment. Had my vision been 20/20, I probably would have remained as assistant city manager and continued to learn before jumping into the "big seat."

However, like many of us, I saw an opportunity and was determined to make a difference – for the community, and for myself – in spite of the challenges. I committed to learning as much about the job as possible, and talked to a number of colleagues about things I needed to know to succeed. I took advantage of any relevant professional development program I could find and got involved in my local and state associations. I saw our staff as my most valuable asset and worked with, and learned from, them. I tried to get to know the city employees and utilize their talents and skills through teams to enhance city operations. In general, I truly tried to learn the job to which I had been appointed and to make the City Council proud of the decision it had made to give me a chance.

I was lucky to be surrounded by a group of exceptional city council members, department heads, employees, and citizens who supported me in my new endeavor. For those people, I will always be eternally grateful. However, that support didn't come from everyone.

In spite of my hard work and efforts to become a good city manager, there were a couple of council members who had voted against my appointment and continued to feel that I was not the appropriate choice for the job. Regardless of my efforts to work hard and do a good job, their feelings were not changing. I remained convinced that I could eventually win them over. I didn't.

My frustrations were heightened even more because these council members were women. While I have never been one that focused on the differences between men and women's styles, I suppose that I just expected them to support someone (and another woman in particular) who was trying to do a good job.

Some days were better than others in those early days. I continued to try, and felt that I was making good progress in my personal and professional development. However, there were times when I know that my frustration showed through, in spite of my efforts to hide my feelings. (Which incidentally, I have never really been able to do given my high level of expressiveness – not always a good attribute for a city manager!)

On one of those less-than-good days, I was walking down the hall and was more than a little dejected as a result of the latest bad exchange, comment, or council meeting. I wondered what I could ever do to make it different or if I was ever going to be successful as a city manager. I just wasn't sure that I could take the "politics" associated with our work – politics that don't make sense, and surface regardless of how hard you try to do a good job. That's where the important part of this story begins!

That day, I happened to walk past our receptionist's desk, and my face revealed how I was feeling. Like me, "Bitsy" was a relatively new employee in our organization. She was a receptionist. Her former life with her very successful ex-husband had not required her to work, yet provided her with beautiful clothes and a classy style that somehow didn't seem to fit the lowest paid position in our organization. She was a southern "belle" and did a great job with the public, but never seemed like "one of the girls" on the administrative staff.

With that bit of history, "Bitsy" took one look at me and said, "Honey, can we talk?"

I said, "Of course," even though I wasn't sure I was up for talking or another problem.

She began her conversation, which turned out to be more of a lecture, with a question. She said, "Honey, do you know why women don't get ahead in this world?"

Before I had a chance to come up with some type of an

intelligent-sounding response, she answered her own question by saying, "Women don't get ahead because other women won't let them."

I have to admit that I was a bit puzzled by her statement. After all, we all have similar experiences, don't we? At that time, there were few women in local government management and for those who were, they were clearly plowing new ground in our profession. We all support them, don't we? We are all daughters, wives and mothers with all the pressures those situations can bring that sometimes aren't always shared to the same degree by our male counterparts. Aren't we? I was confused.

Bitsy went on to say that, regardless of who or what we are, perceived competition, petty jealousy, lack of understanding, gossip, and other negative behaviors can be pervasive in the workplace. . . and in life. She added that, if I was going to be successful in my career, I better recognize that . . . and deal with it.

That advice was offered to me more than 20 years ago and I have never forgotten it. It went way beyond the simple message that Bitsy delivered to me that day. After all, she didn't dislike other women or think she was better than they were. Instead, her message was that we don't always support, coach and encourage people like we should. She was observant, politically astute and an excellent coach, in spite of knowing absolutely nothing about being a city manager.

So, from that day forward, I developed a new attitude, continuing my commitment to working hard, doing the right thing, and doing the best I could, but I absolutely stopped trying to feel that I was a failure if I didn't please everyone. I think I understood "things" a little more. I also recognized the need to see possibilities and to help others see them as well.

I went on to work for more than 20 years as a city manager and I really cherished the advice that I got that day from a source that I would not normally have recognized as such a wealth of information.

While it has been a long time since Bitsy and I talked that day, there were many lessons that I learned from that conversation that proved invaluable to me throughout my career.

First, I learned that regardless of how much effort and heart we put into our jobs, there still can be obstacles to our success. We may never understand why they exist, but must deal with them all the same. Recognize that, while not everyone will like or support you, you should always take the high road.

Second, I learned how important it is to recognize and respect the diversity and differences that exist between people at work and in the communities we serve. It is also important to recognize how many things we have in common and support, encourage and coach people toward higher success. Make sure that everyone gets a fair opportunity to succeed, regardless of what you may hear about them around the water cooler. We must also ensure that those who work for us do the same. In the end, we are all public servants and are committed to making a difference for the people we serve.

Third, I learned that when people are struggling, it is important to reach out to them. Sometimes, it only takes a smile; other times a listening ear is warranted; and in other cases, a lecture is in order. Coach, mentor, praise and give constructive feedback to people; they need, deserve and will, eventually, appreciate it. All situations and all people are different, but take the time to be a caring local government manager, regardless of how people may treat you. It will make a difference for your staff, your community and most importantly, for you.

Lastly, never fail to recognize that we can learn a tremendous amount from the people in our communities and organizations – like Bitsy – who have so much to give, regardless of their position or experience. Good advice really does come from places we least expect!

And, remember to pay forward your great advice and experience to friends, co-workers and colleagues who need some support and advice from time to time!

Appropriate Quote

> "It is not easy to be a pioneer - but oh, it is fascinating! I would not trade one moment, even the worst moment, for all the riches in the world."
>
> Elizabeth Blackwell (first women in U.S. to earn a medical degree)

Key Insight

As a City Manager it is important to learn all you can from everyone you can. Words of wisdom can come from the most unexpected places, and the most unexpected people.

Cheryl Hilvert is a Senior Consultant with ICMA. She has served as City Manager in Montgomery, Ohio and Fairfield, Ohio. She is on the Board for the Alliance for Innovation and is a past Regional Vice-President for ICMA. She has her BA and MPA from Eastern Kentucky University, and is a Credentialed Manager.

Story Two

It is Important To Be Willing to Share Your Story

As told by Karen Montgomery

OUR life experiences are what make us unique in the way we lead our organizations. Many years ago, I was encouraged to share more of my life experiences with my staff so they could get to know me better and understand what motivated me to say and do the things I did. I think too often we view others through our own lens of experience without taking into account what has combined to make them the person they are. Years later I had no idea that this practice of being transparent and sharing my own life stories might actually help to save the life of one of my employees. But thank God it did.

We were recruiting for an administrative position and in order to provide coverage for the office during that time, offered it to a woman within the organization on a temporary basis. She was having trouble in her current job, and this seemed like a good way to get her out of that situation while also giving her time to figure out what she wanted to do next. I soon learned that part of the reason she was having difficulty at work was because of the trauma in her personal life. Her 5 year old son had died of brain cancer not long before and she was still in deep grief. The little boy's love for Jesus had been a source of great comfort to his mother during his illness, but now with him gone she was having trouble finding any solace.

Other problems in her home life were surfacing as well; she and her husband were growing distant from each other, and their adolescent daughter was asserting her independence which created even more strain on the marriage. The woman's difficulty in managing all of these emotional burdens had caused her to spiral into a deep depression, for which she had been recently hospitalized. Although outwardly she appeared to be handling her circumstances well enough, inwardly she was growing more despondent every day. One day she told me that thoughts of suicide were becoming a frequent occurrence for her. Her disclosure touched a tender place in my own life experience, and I knew that I needed to share my story with her.

In their book, *True North,* Bill George and Peter Sims illustrate how authentic leadership is achieved, as they share more than one hundred stories of leaders in numerous organizations. The editor of the book says that, "one of the revelations of *True North* is how critical these leaders' personal stories are in shaping their leadership. Time after time, those interviewed [for the book] describe a turning point in their lives – a crucible – that transformed them into the leaders they are today. These tales of how they became the people they are reveal their most deeply held values, their most passionate beliefs."

One of those terrible crucibles in my life was in 1986 when my older brother took his life. Mike was a wonderful man, only thirty two years old when things began to cave in on him and suicide evidently seemed to be the only answer. Yet I knew the pain it caused the rest of us which we carry to this day. I hoped that sharing my story would be helpful to my new assistant.

On the day she came into my office and closed the door, her tear-filled story began to unfold. As I listened, I imagined the huge heartache that her death would have on her family. So I told her about the loss of my brother, and the terrible pain his death had caused. She wanted to know how I had managed to live with this pain for so many years. It was then that I was able to tell her what was truly transformational for me: my faith in God. Being reminded that God's love for her is greater than any pain she will ever experience, she began to let go of her fears about the future.

Today this woman's renewed faith in God remains strong. Several months after we met in my office that day, she wrote me a letter. In it she said, "Thank you for everything you have done for me. When you shared your journey with me it allowed me to really evaluate my life and to realize that I can get through this. You have made me look beyond my circumstances and look towards the future to what God has planned for me."

We all have stories to share and when we become accustomed to sharing our stories with others, we find a meaning in our work that goes much deeper than just our job descriptions. We grow, we change and we're transformed for the better, not only for ourselves but for those we serve.

Appropriate Quote

> "Courage is like a muscle. We strengthen it with use."
>
> Ruth Gordon, Actress

Key Insight

Stories resonate with people. We can illustrate our points and highlight our values with them. Arrival in the City Manager's Suite comes complete with stories of our journey. Some of these are professional and some are personal. You never know when your willingness to share yours will impact someone far beyond the workplace.

Karen L. Montgomery is vice president for finance and administration at Texas Wesleyan University where she is responsible for the finance, budget, human resources, facilities and IT services. Prior to that, she served as an assistant city manager in Fort Worth, has served as chief financial officer and finance director for cities and counties, and has held executive level positions in state government. Karen is a certified public accountant, and holds a Master's degree in Public Administration from the University of Colorado at Denver, and a bachelor of business administration degree from the University of Oklahoma. She is an ICMA credentialed manager and was the winner of the 2010 NCTCOG Award for *Women in Public Management.*

Story Three

Grading the PD

As told by Lauren Palmer

IN my first job as a management intern, I was assigned to write the police section of the city's annual performance report. The assistant city manager overseeing the report made clear that this was not a public relations document. In order to maintain credibility with the public, the report had to be strictly honest, exposing both the highlights of our performance and the areas needing improvement. I took this to heart in preparing the draft that I forwarded to the police department for review.

The following afternoon I received a phone call from the chief of police. He let me know, in no uncertain terms, that my report was garbage. He didn't think much of me or my experience (or rather lack thereof) either. He really let me have it. I was shaking like a leaf when I hung up the phone. The chief was one of the most seasoned and respected department heads – and he carried a gun!

Now I had a problem. If I rewrote the report to address the chief's concerns, I would have to sacrifice our commitment to the public to print the good, the bad, and the ugly of our performance. If I didn't rewrite the report, I would risk alienating the entire police department for this and future performance measurement initiatives.

I discussed my situation with the city manager and assistant city manager, secretly hoping that one or both of them would intervene on my behalf and force the police chief to back off. Of course, as any good mentors would, they promptly pushed me out of the nest and told me to go work it out on my own.

I set a meeting with the chief to discuss the report. I was petrified to meet him face-to-face after the tongue-lashing I had received on the phone, but I mustered my courage. I started the meeting by telling the chief that I was very interested in hearing his concerns and working together to make edits to the report that would satisfy the police department and the city manager. I also told him that I didn't appreciate his tone and comments on the phone, and that I felt we would be more productive if we treated each other with mutual respect. I explained that I had a job to do, and I needed his help to do it.

To my surprise, the chief was impressed when I stood my ground. He offered me an apology and we got down to the business of reviewing the report. At the end of the meeting, I had a better understanding of his concerns, and he had a better understanding of the objectives of the report. I wrote a new draft that, in my opinion, was better than the first and received approval from both the city manager and the police department.

I learned from that experience the importance of considering alternative viewpoints and building relationships. When I worked on the police section the following year, I met with department leaders before writing my initial draft, in order to gather their ideas and earn their buy-in for the report. That approach was much more successful.

Appropriate Quote

Communication is a skill that you can learn. It's like riding a bicycle or typing. If you're willing to work at it, you can rapidly improve the quality of every part of your life."

Brian Tracy, Co-Author with Mike Conduff of the Amazon Best Seller, ***Pushing to the Front*** (and many, many other books.)

Key Insight

There is perhaps no greater skill in a city manager's repertoire than the ability to communicate with others – both internal and external to the organization.

Lauren Palmer is Assistant City Manager in Manhattan, Kansas, and was previously a management analyst in Des Moines, Iowa where she was promoted after successfully completing the Des Moines City Management Internship Program. Lauren received her Master of Public Affairs degree from the School of Public and Environmental Affairs at Indiana University. She holds a BA in political science from the University of Missouri. Lauren is a member of the International City/County Management Association and is a graduate of the inaugural class of ICMA's Emerging Leaders Development Program. She is a past Vice Chair of ICMA's Awards Evaluation Panel.

Story Four

Please Describe the Naked Person

As told by Peggy Merriss

AS a new City Manager, I inherited all of the "perks" that the former City Manager had accumulated, including having an emergency dispatch radio in my car (I actually inherited his car, a deluxe 1990 Crown Victoria, which I was never able to parallel park but it had a sweet police V8 engine.) I rarely turned the radio on.

However, one night I was out in town and the radio was on when this call was dispatched:

> Dispatcher: "907, we have a call of a naked person in the middle of South Candler Street." Police Officer: (presumably 907) "Can you give me a better description?"

I actually don't remember if the Dispatcher replied or not because the only thought I had was, "Really, you need a better description? How about we round up all the naked people in the middle of South Candler Street and sort out the particulars later?"

I laughed all the way into the house.

The next morning I called the Police Chief and asked about the "naked person" call on South Candler Street and told him what I heard (trying not to laugh the whole time.)

He immediately went into a long dissertation about the Officer following protocol, and how the Dispatcher needed to be better trained to give proper information.

This started my career-long crusade to make sure that protocol was never substituted for common sense. It also confirmed that this particular Police Chief and I were not going to be a successful team. And, I never had another police radio installed in my car.

Appropriate Quote

> "Purpose and laughter are the twins that must not separate. Each is empty without the other."
>
> Robert K Greenleaf, Founder of the modern Servant Leadership movement

Key Insight

Finding humor in the happenings of the organization helps keep us sane. Surround yourself with others who appreciate it too. If folks don't...remember Jim Collins' advice about the bus.

Peggy Merriss began her career in Decatur, Georgia in 1983 and became City Manager in 1993. She still holds that position. Peggy served as the first woman President of ICMA in 2002-2003, and is a Past President of the Georgia City/County Management Association. A Legacy Leader for ICMA, she also serves on the Board of The Alliance for Innovation. She is the 2010 recipient of the Strategic Leadership and Governance Excellence Award from ICMA.

Story Five

Honoring a Family Legacy of Freedom

As told by Linda Kelly

I grew up in a small pocket of Los Angeles in a town called Maywood and graduated from Bell High School located in Bell, California. Many of you may recall that the City of Bell experienced a public corruption scandal which altered the perception of city managers nationwide. Ironically, my first job in municipal government was working for the City of Bell as a summer recreation aide as a teenager.

My father came to this country following the 1956 Hungarian uprising. He initially worked in farm labor and once he learned English, became a skilled machinist. My mother occasionally took in children to babysit in our house. As a child, my Dad frequently shared stories with us about the government in Eastern Europe, including the violent regimes and the inequitable systems. Early on, I was drawn to gain a greater understanding of how the world works and became very interested in public service.

My father still held on to old world beliefs regarding how children needed to support the household as soon as they were of age. I watched my oldest sister drop out of college to help support our family, and I was saddened and upset by this because she excelled in chemistry and the sciences. I became more determined to have a different future and this also meant distancing myself from my father. Unfortunately, my Dad did not manage money well and was not a mentor to me and my sisters for financial sustainability. My parents never owned a home. I know that my Dad did the best he could with the resources and outlook he had, but he was battling his own demons and in a new country.

My mother supported my decision to continue my education. Mom could not help with her pocketbook, but she always helped with her heart, telling me to get an education so I could have choices in life. She has since passed away, and I miss having my biggest cheerleader on my side.

College became attainable for me through a combination of part-time jobs, loans and financial aid. During this period, I became mostly a work and study "nerd" which I actually enjoyed at the time, since I felt very productive and independent, and was establishing my future.

Following completion of my Master's degree, I started my first full-time municipal position with the City of Pasadena, California, as a rotational intern working in various departments. I remember being told there were 124 applicants for the three intern positions being filled. I was selected partly because of the public sector work experience I attained while attending college (I had worked in a district attorney's office, in the business office at a community college, and tutored English composition while an undergraduate. I was awarded a bibliographer/research assistant position as financial aid for my Master's degree). Only one of the internships in Pasadena was a rotational assignment and that is the one I selected. I wanted the broadest experience possible.

One of my assignments was in the city clerk's office. In this Charter City that ran its own elections by council district, I quickly became the local election expert. Not having a mentor, but still wanting to advance, I became a city clerk and managed my own department in a smaller municipality, the City of La Puente, California, at the age of 27. The virtue and practice of hard work was something I had going for me and was something I could always count on. I was soon to learn that in California, the profession of city clerk still had a glass ceiling stigma, which was unfortunate, because the work is interesting, valuable and essential to the running of a city. In fact, in many small cities throughout the country, the city clerk is the only required staff person – the Keeper of the Records.

As it turned out, the position was female-dominated and not viewed as a track to advancement or to other city departments. Although I had the education and was a department head, I was coached by city managers (all of them male) that I needed to seek out ways to further expand my experience if I wanted to someday be considered for the opportunity to manage a city, which I did. I wanted doors to continue to open, not close because of the "wrong track" I was apparently on. I took a few steps backward to enable leaps forward, completed additional post-graduate courses at night, became an analyst, and then an assistant to the city manager.

The first city manager job I secured was in an environment with quite contentious political issues. On top of that, within my first week on the job, the community had a flood, a naturally-declared disaster by FEMA standards. I was not dissuaded by this and faced the challenge. One of my prior managers actually cautioned me not to apply for this position because it was a community known to have difficult political issues. However, all experience is learning, and as a younger woman starting out as a city manager, it was a chance to get my foot in the door.

I am proud of my circuitous journey and still cherish my city clerk experience as it provided an excellent foundation through working very closely with elected officials, attending numerous council meetings, providing front counter customer service, and responding to the media.

As a result of my experience, I am sensitive to the unique challenges of women in local government. Currently less than 15% of all city managers in California are female, and the number of those with school-aged or younger children is much less (I am married with two school-aged children). I often ponder how we can improve those statistics and make the job more attractive to working mothers.

One of the reasons I chose the public sector as a career was because it seemed that minorities and women could advance based on merit and not on the good-old-boys network or status. For the most part, the merit system has held true in my experience. While not without flaws, the merit system does contain fair and equitable provisions that support the notion of hard work earning advancement.

Women's paths to leadership are more often not linear, and in my experience that has been true. As a group, women are more likely to face challenges based on familial and gender expectations, roles and systemic organizational issues. I firmly believe that moving through women's unique workplace and life cycle issues requires determination, creativity, hard work and a deep belief that what we bring to the workplace is of value to the organizations and communities we serve.

Appropriate Quote

> "Start by doing what's necessary; then do what's possible; and suddenly you are doing the impossible."
>
> St. Francis of Assisi

Key Insight

There is no typical path to the City Manager's Office. Everyone gets there in their own way and in their own time. The key is to arrive with a desire to serve others while ethically making a difference. If you can honor your heritage while doing so you are especially blessed.

Linda Kelly has served as the City Manager of Sonoma, California, since 2008. She previously served as the Town Manager of Fairfax, California. She received ICMA's 2011 Program Excellence Award for Community Partnerships for partnering with a non-profit on a water conservation garden that serves as a sustainable community model.

In 2008, she completed ICMA's Emerging Leaders Development Program. She started her municipal career in the City of Pasadena following completion of her Master's from U.C. Riverside. She holds a Certificate in Human Resources Management, and completed an internship with the Attorney General's Office. She is an ICMA Credentialed Manager.

Story Six

Ask for a Death Certificate

As told by Pam Rambo Sexton

I was several years into my very first local government job out of graduate school and had the opportunity to serve in that "gateway role" of Assistant to the City Manager where so many aspiring city managers find themselves as a young professional. The community was ideal for me. It was not a small town but by no means a huge city; not out in the middle of nowhere, but still an autonomous municipality. It was close enough to a thriving Metroplex to be convenient, but with a well-established and rich history that made it a standalone community with its own unique identity. The residents there, both old and new, cherished that, and (rightly so) were proud of it.

Because I worked for a great city manager, he was always throwing challenges my way, of both the technical and interpersonal type. He decided that the community, with its proud historical lineage, needed a wall with the framed pictures of Mayors and City Managers at City Hall. These pictures would commemorate the great leadership that had come before and would hopefully inspire others to continue to take a long view of shaping the future. I was tasked with the record research and the collection of photographs. It did not take me long to learn that very few of the desired photographs were readily available.

I anxiously began digging through archives in the City Secretary's Office, the public libraries, the County Court House, the community newspaper and the local universities' libraries. As I dug I also started to meet wonderful characters who recounted their endless stories to me and would point me in the right direction on where to look next. Often they could tell me who to go see, or give me the phone number of someone who was a former neighbor of the best friend of a relative that had moved away for which ever mayor's photo I was desperate to get my hands on at the moment. What had seemed early on to be a pretty straightforward assignment quickly turned into a veritable scavenger hunt. After significant sleuthing, I'm proud to say I had an almost entirely complete collection when it was time for the framing and hanging to begin.

A feat so grand was obviously deserving of a celebration (as was recognition of all those former leaders.) It was also time to wrap this project up because I recall thinking sarcastically that the "real work" I'd been neglecting running all over town listening to stories was starting to stack up. So I quickly went about the business of putting together a reception plan and guest list, making sure to invite those living former mayors and managers and the family of deceased former mayors and managers for whom I'd been able to gather contact information during my search.

Arrangements were made, invitations went out, responses came back and the media was notified. I was feeling very proud of myself and even just a bit smug. Everyone was excited and this was going to be quite the event. I of course was providing my best "Level Five" leadership and making sure to reflect all the accolades to the current mayor and manager.

The very morning of the unveiling, the telephone rang and to my surprise a voice on the other end of the line introduced himself as a former mayor, and in a rather gruff voice demanded to know why he had not received an invitation to the evening's event.

As he went on to explain how offended he was and how derelict I'd been, my head began to spin. I quickly scanned my list and there he was, as clear as day, sixth from the top with my hand written note, "DECEASED."

What had I done? I didn't know who, or when or where, but clearly someone along my journey had told me this man was no longer with us. I'd found his photograph and gone on with my hunt not thinking twice about him after that.

His tongue lashing continued until finally there was silence on the phone as the voice demanded I respond.

"Well?" he said.

How do I fix this? What do I say? My mind raced and finally I just blurted out, "I thought you were dead!"

One would think he'd have burst in to laughter or recounted a Tom Sawyer moment, but unfortunately his rant went on as did my endless apologizing. I was finally released from the phone, with his stern promise that both the City Manager and Mayor would be hearing first hand from him about how seriously I'd offended him.

When he hung up, still chastising me, I promptly burst into tears in front of the entire City Manager's Office. I had worked so hard, ferreted out so many trails and solved so many mysteries and now it was all going down the tubes right in front of my eyes. What should have been a triumph was becoming a catastrophe.

That evening when he attended the reception from the neighboring city where he now lived (with me pushing people out of the way to greet him upon arrival to continue apologizing) and had two of his children and several of his grandkids in tow I wondered how he had gotten all of that arranged on last minute notice. I later found out he'd known for several weeks what we were working on and had made arrangements to be there all along.

Both the current Mayor and the City Manager found the entire situation to be quite hilarious and reflective of that thought-to-be-deceased Mayor's style and legacy. Neither held me the least bit at fault, and indeed gave me lots of credit for the overall effort.

I, on the other hand, learned to always document my research and to never underestimate elected officials. Even when they are out of office, you never know when one might pop up and break the arm you're patting yourself on the back with.

Appropriate Quote

> "Pretend that every single person you meet has a sign around his or her neck that says, "Make me feel important." Not only will you succeed in sales, you will succeed in life."
>
> Mary Kay Ash, Entrepreneur

Key Insight

Most elected officials serve for little or no pay and often little or no acknowledgement of their sacrifices and service. When there is an opportunity to provide legitimate accolades for their service it behooves the professionals to do so. Make sure you do this while they are alive if possible.

Pam Rambo-Sexton is currently serving the City of Fort Worth, TX in the Budget Department. She is the past Director of Environmental Grants and Programs for the City of Arlington, TX where she also served as Senior Management Analyst. Pam started her career with the City of Denton after graduating with a Master's degree in Public Service Administration from the George Bush School at Texas A&M. Her BSW is from the University of Texas. Pam is a contributing author to ***Bottom Line Green – How America's Cities are Saving the Planet (And Money Too!)*** and is Past President of The Urban Management Assistants of North Texas (UMANT.)

Story Seven

Delivery of the Council Packet

As told by Cara Pavlicek

IF I had to guess, I would say that virtually every city manager has dealt with the details of delivering the informational packet to council members for an upcoming city council meeting more than they care to. I would also say that in most cases, the smaller the community, the more personal involvement by the city manager there is in this activity.

This was certainly the case in my first city administrator position. It was in a wonderful Midwestern community of 12,000 residents. Summers were hot and humid while winters were cold and snowy. Council members worked as postal carriers, school teachers, union laborers and the like.

Council meetings were held twice a month and were incredibly efficient. They started promptly at 7:00 p.m. and if they lasted much past 9 p.m. it was considered a long meeting. The efficiency of each meeting was completely due to the Mayor, who to this day remains the most skilled elected meeting moderator I have ever worked with. He was a master at running a swift, effective meeting. He allowed discussion, but not pontification. Packets were read in advance. If questions were asked at the meeting, they had already been asked and answered (with copies to the entire council) earlier that day. The only purpose of repeating a question during the meeting, was to share it with the public when necessary. The mayor's ability to run a meeting was second only to his ability to mentor every new elected official (and new city administrator) about what was expected at council meetings.

The preparation and delivery of the council packets was not so efficient. Without iPads, intranet, or even a networked photocopy machine, we spent every other Friday afternoon in the mailroom at city hall photocopying and collating. It had been a major improvement to purchase copy paper that was already three-hole punched. We used navy blue three ring binders with alphabetical tabs for each agenda item. We prepared a binder for the mayor, the eight council members, myself, the assistant city administrator, the eight department heads, the city attorney and two public copies. Twenty-two total packets. Every other Friday. Packet Friday.

Since long before I arrived in town, an on-duty patrol officer was assigned to deliver the packets. On Packet Friday, when the copying was done, after a quick call to the police station, an on-duty patrol officer arrived at city hall to gather the nine navy blue three ring binders for delivery to the nine elected officials' homes.

For at least the first half of my tenure with the city this delivery process worked. That is, until a well-intentioned (but not so well spoken) council member made the mistake of thanking the patrol officer for his efforts one Friday night by stating "Here is my delivery boy right on time," or something to that effect.

No matter the intent, the words "delivery boy" were used and as a result, it did not take long for the patrol officers, male and female alike, to concur that packet delivery was not real police work. After that, it did not take long for the FOP president to meet with the police chief to discuss the officers' concerns. And it certainly wasn't much longer before said police chief was asking me if it would be possible to find another means of delivering the nine council packets.

My decision to stop using police officers and rely upon city hall staff for packet delivery, is where the real story begins.

[On a side note, the chief and I both thought the officers were a bit short sighted in abandoning the opportunity to have one-on-one access to every elected official twice a month, but on the other hand, it made our decision easier to remove them from delivery duty because after some discussion, we thought it probably was a good idea to eliminate the opportunity for officers to have one-on-one access to every elected official twice a month.]

With delivery of the nine navy blue three ring binders now the responsibility of those of us at city hall, we simply divided up the task of delivering the Council packets. On most Packet Fridays, this would fall to the city clerk, the assistant and me. Of course, we would always engage any other unsuspecting department head who happened to wander into city hall late Friday afternoon. This worked fine until I got a bit more than I bargained for delivering one particular packet.

It was late on a Friday afternoon in the middle of summer. It was still daylight and it was hot and it was humid. The last packet I had to deliver was for a council member who lived in a small bungalow home. With the summer heat and humidity, and no air conditioning, I could tell someone was at home as I pulled in the driveway as the front door was open to allow a cross breeze from the screen door through the open living room windows. I walked up to the front porch with the navy blue three ring binder, rang the doorbell and looked through the screen door to see in full view the Council member in his briefs, feet up on the couch watching TV. Yes, he was only wearing Hanes, or Jockeys, or tighty whities or whatever you call them.

Our eyes met for just a moment. A moment that was long enough for him to see me looking at him looking at me, and I am pretty sure the look on my face wasn't pretty.

As quickly as I could, I bent down, placed the navy blue three ring binder on the front porch and yelled over my shoulder as I raced to the car, "I'll leave your packet out here!!"

We never spoke of the incident. In fact we acted as if nothing had ever happened.

I never delivered a packet to his house again.

I can only hope he never sat on his couch again on a hot summer afternoon with the front door open watching TV in only his skivvies.

Appropriate Quote

> "In order for you to profit from your mistakes, you have to get out and make some."
>
> Lily Tomlin, Comedian

Key Insight

Technology has really simplified packet preparation and delivery, and no doubt will continue to do so. It is a truism that iPads and a Dropbox account are much nicer than a hand me down police cruiser and a screen door.

Cara Pavlicek is the Interim Village Manager of Oak Park, Illinois. After graduating from the University of Washington with a BA in Economics, Cara took an internship with the City of Des Moines, Iowa in 1990 while completing her MA at the University of Iowa, spending five years in the City Manager's Office. After getting married and moving to La Vista, Nebraska in 1995, Cara worked as the Assistant City Administrator and then City Administrator until 2005 (and welcomed a daughter during this time.) She then accepted a position as Village Manager in Downers Grove, Illinois. After two and a half years Cara found herself in Transition and came to Oak Park in 2008 as Interim Parking Services Manager where she remained until being named interim Village Manager for Oak Park in March of 2012.

Story Eight

Providing for the "Least of These" in the Community

As told by Dr. Loré L. Chambers

WHOSE job is it anyway?

I have often asked myself this question when it comes to the homeless in our community.

Coming into municipal government service in 2004, as the Director of Grants and Special Projects, I quickly realized that the City of Salisbury was providing pass through funding for emergency shelters for operating expense. The amount being passed through was $3,880 for one service provider. In recognition that the jurisdiction was entitled to upwards of $50,000, I requested that other providers in the three lower counties of the Eastern Shore of Maryland consider applying for funding, as the homeless citizens tended to migrate from county to county in search of assistance.

Setting up a tri-county model was seen as a best practice to provide a safety net of service providers who encountered these individuals and opened up new avenues to resources. Subsequent years' funding steadily increased from less than $4,000 to over $30,000 in 2009. As with any program that shows steady financial growth, the demand grew as well.

Under the administration that existed at that time, the services to this at-risk population were embraced, especially as the recognition was dawning that the homeless population was increasing. The City of Salisbury was also pursuing the coveted title of "All America City," and the homeless initiative was included as one of the projects to show collaboration across organizations. The City became a finalist but did not win in 2009.

Then the elections happened and with them a change in leadership. With anything new comes a learning curve, new directives, and new goals. The least of these was not high on the list of priorities. I was often informed that "we are not social services."

While I whole heartedly agreed with that sentiment, it was difficult to convey that message to the individuals that would come to the Mayor's office in search of assistance. These individuals came in whatever state they were in, hungry, unwashed, carrying what belongings they had, and in some cases, crying. How could I tell them it was not my job and still sleep at night? The short answer...I couldn't.

Unfortunately with the economic downturn in 2008, a massive wave of foreclosures began to occur and the homeless numbers began to escalate. People who never thought that they would be sleeping in cars, living with relatives, or living in shelters, found themselves in that very predicament for the first time in their lives. And although "we are not social services," these individuals turned to the elected officials for help.

In response to the growing need, the federal government, through the Maryland Department of Housing and Community Development initiated a new program with American Reinvestment and Recovery Act (ARRA) funds to provide Homeless Prevention Rapid Re-housing Programs.

The City of Salisbury was fortunate to receive $311,014 and set up a provider network of four agencies to assist with paying rents, utility bills, security deposits, and hotel/motel vouchers. The program that was designed to last for three years saw the funds rapidly dissipate in two. Suddenly, we did become an arm of social services, and were on the front lines of providing resources and connectivity for homeless individuals and those at risk of becoming homeless.

In 2010, the City of Salisbury once again applied for and became a finalist for the All-America City Award. The City included the homeless initiative in the application as a best practice in multi-agency collaboration. However, this time we invited a young lady that had been homeless to accompany us to Kansas City, KS to tell her story on the national level, as we revealed the collaborative efforts we had put in place to assist in sustaining this population. Not only was this initiative applauded by the audience, the judges found our efforts and those of creating more affordable home ownership worthy and conveyed the coveted title.

It is very rewarding to witness resistance melt into cooperation when enlightenment comes, that even though this population may not vote, they are still our citizens. It behooves us to recognize that the weakest link in the chain of our citizenry can also become the most costly.

Ignoring the needs of the least of these increases the demand for all services: public works, to clean up trash and litter that is left in city parks and open spaces, more community policing to cut down on the incidences of vagrancy, free rides to the warmth of the emergency room via EMS, and code enforcement to locate and clean up homeless camps.

Responding in the affirmative of, "yes, this is my job, and yes, these are our citizens and yes, we can help," made a tremendous difference in how we allocated our resources. Working collaboratively with other agencies to build a network of providers served to attract even more financial resources to the region. With more providers on board, services increased and more programs were created to serve meals on a three meals per day, 365 days per year basis. It has also lead to literacy courses being offered both financial and academic. Other services include connection to counseling for mental health and substance abuse, job training, and assistance to get identification cards that opens the door to employment. The City has seen a decrease in crimes of opportunity which allows us to redirect resources to other areas of the city.

The staff has now been provided with resource information to direct citizens in need of services to the appropriate agencies. Other city departments to include police, fire, and Code Compliance staff carry resource information with them to assist citizens they encounter during their daily activities. This interaction increases the awareness of staff of the need and condition of our citizens and makes their jobs more rewarding as they are able to provide information that helps both the citizens and the city. The staff is seen in a positive and caring light, while the citizens are recognized for who they are, past and future tax payers, for the most part.

This experience taught me some very important things about myself. First it has taught me how to take criticism and keep serving anyway. Although "we are not social services" people are being referred to me by the selfsame individuals that denigrated the provision of this resource. Second, it has taught me how to build collaborative teams that cross organizations to find the commonality of interests and the leveraging and sharing of limited resources. Third, it has taught me how to lead from the middle. Although I did not have the support of leadership to administer this program to the degree that it was administered, it was finally embraced and heralded as the city taking care of its citizens.

Now when asked, "Whose job is it anyway?" I can honestly say, "All of ours!"

Appropriate Quote

> "The trouble with organizing a thing is that pretty soon folks get to paying more attention to the organization than to what they're organized for."
>
> Laura Ingalls Wilder, Author

Key Insight

If you believe you are right and there is no legal, moral or ethical impediment to your actions, go for it! Keep always in mind who it is you are working to benefit.

Dr. Loré L. Chambers joined the Mayor's staff of Salisbury, Maryland on October 26, 2004, as the Director of Grants and Special Projects. In 2007 her position was upgraded to Assistant City Administrator for the City of Salisbury. She also serves as the Executive Assistant to the Mayor and to the City Administrator, and is the Performance Management Manager, Continuance of Operations/Continuance of Government manager, and the American Recovery Act (Stimulus) fund oversight manager for the city. Loré has completed the requirements for and graduated May 18, 2012, with a Ph.D. in Organizational Leadership from the University of Maryland Eastern Shore. She has been involved in community service within the City of Salisbury for more than 16 years.

Story Nine

My ICMA Journey

As told by Elizabeth K. (Beth) Kellar

"COMMUNITY Relations" was the title of the ad. My husband and I had just crossed the border into California in July, 1974, driving our Volkswagen Beetle from Ohio. Since I was eager to find a job, I bought a copy of the *San Francisco Chronicle* to look at the employment ads. The community relations ad sounded ideal – a place called Sunnyvale was looking for someone who could serve as a public information officer, write a quarterly report to citizens and an employee newsletter, and provide staff support to citizen committees.

It took almost two weeks before we had found an apartment and I could apply for the job. In the chaos of our first days in California, our Beetle had conked out after a weekend trip to the Monterey Peninsula and as a result the newspaper clipping was lost. Since the Internet was not yet a reality, the only solution was to ride my bicycle several miles to a public library to retrieve a copy of the newspaper.

The delay in applying may have been fortuitous. Over 200 resumes had been reviewed and several candidates had been rejected. My resume came in after the rush. With a master's degree in journalism and political science, plus writing experience for the nonprofit world, my application made the cut. I was invited for an interview with Assistant City Manager Bill Hopkins who decided I should meet with the city manager. Consequently I was formally ushered into City Manager John Dever's immaculate office. The first thing I noticed was a framed copy of the Athenian Oath on his wall.

He asked me if I had any experience and I nervously opened up my portfolio. To my dismay, all of my publications tumbled out onto his clean desk. Fortunately, that was not a deal breaker. After I got the job offer and started to work, I thought I had died and gone to heaven.

Sunnyvale – Where Innovation Was Second Nature

Although I had studied third world and European democracies when I was in graduate school at Ohio State University, I soon realized that the most exciting place to see democracy in action is in local government. Over time, I came to appreciate what a unique opportunity I had to work in the City of Sunnyvale in the mid-1970s.

One of the Sunnyvale's most valuable assets was its leadership. Council-manager government, adopted in 1949, was respected. The community benefited from having particularly skilled city managers and elected officials who supported long-term thinking.

For example, in 1949, when Sunnyvale had a population of 9,000 and was starting to grow rapidly, concerned citizens suggested that the volunteer fire service needed increased professionalism to keep pace with the changing community. City Manager H.K. Hunter thought the timing was right to create a public safety department, building on the 16-man police department. The police union and volunteer fire department opposed the concept, but Sunnyvale Mayor Walt Jones strongly supported it. The city council approved the merger in July, 1950. Sunnyvale remains a model of a successful consolidated public safety department, always tweaking its approach to meet changing needs.

The Silicon Valley influence also gave Sunnyvale additional opportunities for leadership in technology and management. When I was in Sunnyvale, city officials from around the world came to look at our sophisticated information technology and total performance management system. Everyone on the management team was expected to develop a budget that included quality goals, a fiscal year production plan, productivity trends, and cost trends. John Dever ran a tight ship and the budget was the organization's guidebook.

Entering a Male-Dominated Environment

Not only was I lucky to work in a place where cutting edge management was the norm, I also had been hired by a city manager who was committed to developing his young staff. When I arrived in Sunnyvale, the first person to reach out to me was Camille Cates Barnett. She had been hired the year before and we were the two youngest members of the management team.

The first time we had the opportunity to attend the California City Managers' Department meeting in Monterey, we were excited. When we arrived, we were doubly appreciative that John Dever had brought both of us to the meeting. Only one other woman was present – Tina Clifton, then city manager of Rolling Hills Estates. Later, because Sunnyvale had won ICMA awards and John Dever was being honored, we had the opportunity to attend the ICMA Annual Conference in Seattle.

Attending an international conference of city and county managers was an important opportunity, so I carefully reviewed the conference program. I decided to attend a late afternoon meeting of the Women's Task Force and hoped I might meet other professional women. Imagine my surprise when I found John Wentz, a former ICMA President, holding forth as I entered the room. I saw a look of amused patience on the face of Judith Mohr, co-chair of the task force, as the small group grappled with the notion of women entering the profession.

Thinking outside the Box

Reflecting on that era, I am mindful of the thoughtful mentoring that John Dever provided. In addition to giving young staff members the opportunity to serve on the management team, he also gave us supervisory responsibilities and assigned us to staff citizens' committees and to head city-wide task forces. Such high profile opportunities helped me grow and develop skills at an early age.

One way that John Dever pressed the management team to think outside the box was to assign individuals for some period of time to another department. My management rotation was to the nearly all male public safety department. Sunnyvale was just starting to hire women as officers, which was straining the department's culture. I was assigned to sit in the public safety chief's office, which was vacant as we were in the process of recruiting a new chief. Suffice it to say that I was an "odd woman" out in many respects.

To gain a sense of the department's challenges, I decided to ride with officers on all shifts and to spend time in the emergency call center. One night when I was riding with an officer on the graveyard shift, we got a call to respond to a knife fight. The officer got out of the car and tried to subdue a suspect who resisted arrest. My assessment was that the suspect did not understand a word that the officer was saying so I began speaking to him in Spanish. He immediately calmed down. "What did you say to him?" asked the officer.

"I just explained that you were not going to hurt him," I replied. Word got around about my magical Spanish language skills, which led to some useful conversations about how to deal with such situations in the future.

Moving to ICMA

After two years in Sunnyvale, I had to face a common two-career challenge. My husband's post-doctoral fellowship was ending and he needed to find another job. He interviewed for jobs in Houston,

Columbus, Ohio, and Washington, D.C. I had an opportunity to spend a week in Washington, D.C. to write up a case study about Sunnyvale's Total Performance Measurement Project for the U.S. Government Accountability Office. While I was in D.C., the *ICMA Newsletter* published a job ad for a communications director at ICMA. Talk about good timing!

My initial goal was to spend at least five years at ICMA so I could demonstrate career stability. It turned into quite a career opportunity and my journalism skills were much in demand with my initial responsibilities as editor of *PM Magazine,* the *ICMA Newsletter*, and public relations.

There were several reasons that ICMA was such a good fit for someone like me. First and foremost, the profession has an amazing history and set of values. Whenever I was challenged by an overly ambitious workload or competing priorities, I always pictured someone like John Dever and the competing demands that are a city manager's daily reality. While ICMA members have high expectations, they work in real partnership with staff. Nowhere has this been more important than in the ethics education and enforcement area where I was privileged to work with so many smart, thoughtful ICMA members in my 25 years as ethics advisor.

Over the years, I had the opportunity to work in almost all of ICMA's programs and with three very talented executive directors, Mark Keane, Bill Hansell, and Bob O'Neill.

There were, of course, challenging times. When I had my first child in 1978, the organization had no experience with anyone giving birth and then returning to work shortly thereafter. There were adjustments the organization needed to make and it did so over the years.

In the 1980s, the ICMA leadership worried about what women in the profession wanted. I remember one women's meeting that I helped Camille Barnett set up at an ICMA Conference. When some ICMA Board members asked what was going on, I said I thought that the women wanted to get together, network, and talk about issues that concerned them. That's exactly what has evolved over time. Women now often attend the women's luncheon to network and to have good conversations.

ICMA always challenged me intellectually. When Bill Hansell became executive director in 1983, he had a lot of ideas but not enough revenue to pursue all of them. Like all executive directors, Bill Hansell pushed his management team to develop new sources of revenue that aligned with membership goals.

That entrepreneurial spirit gave me the confidence to take the initiative to put together an international municipal development grant to USAID in 1989. It was an incredibly competitive process and I was fortunate that Mike Murphy was interested in returning to ICMA after working for Catholic Relief Services in Central America to become ICMA's first international department director. ICMA's international work continues to flourish today under David Grossman's leadership and a team of highly skilled staff and consultants who have taken on challenging assignments throughout the world.

My wide-ranging assignments and matrix management experience prepared me for my next opportunity to serve as ICMA's deputy executive director in 1990 after Don Borut departed to become the executive director of the National League of Cities.

Work Your Values

Jim Ley, who had a long and successful run as the manager of Sarasota County, said something that stuck with me: "I work for my values now." When everything is in balance in our lives, that's how it feels. For me, that means giving full attention to my family, doing meaningful work, being involved in the community, and in some way, touching other people's lives.

Volunteering for Montgomery County, Maryland, gave me a variety of fulfilling, and sometimes intense, experiences, especially when I was chair of the Montgomery County Ethics Commission. A sniper incident had paralyzed the Washington, D.C. area in October, 2002, and Montgomery County Police Chief Charles Moose had been at the center of a local, state, and federal law enforcement effort that led to the arrest of the two individuals who were later convicted. The Ethics Commission had issued an advisory opinion that winter that concluded that police officials who were invited to speak about the incident could not be paid for talking about a subject that was directly related to their official duties.

However, Chief Moose later asked for a waiver from the County ethics law so he could be paid for book and movie deals while he remained in his job as police chief. The County Executive supported the waiver and the *Washington Post* editorialized that it was a free speech matter. The Ethics Commission determined that it would be unwise to grant a waiver as it could erode trust in government and might lead to employees jockeying for position in high profile situations.

There was a media circus around the Ethics Commission's deliberations with reporters trying to eavesdrop on confidential proceedings. It was a good reminder that so much of what we do in public service puts us in a fishbowl where everyone has an opinion though only a few have the facts. I was glad that the Ethics Commission dealt with the pressure in a thoughtful way that upheld the law and the high standards that have been a tradition in the County.

In 2006, with the encouragement of Bob O'Neill, I began a new phase of my career by leading the Center for State and Local Government Excellence and ICMA's public policy team. This has made me more keenly aware of my responsibility to the next generation: Am I giving growth opportunities to young professionals? Do I take time to counsel young people who are considering a public service career? Are the policies and research that we undertake sensitive to generational issues?

Most of us remember the part of the Athenian Oath that entreats us to "transmit this City, not only not less, but greater and more beautiful than it was transmitted to us." As we consider the generational consequences of today's fiscal and environmental policies, many of us have come to appreciate another strategy embedded in the Oath: "We will strive increasingly to quicken the public's sense of civic duty."

Those of us who care about the future of our communities know that we can't make them better by our own efforts alone. Whatever we can do to energize our employees, residents, and elected leadership about our shared stewardship responsibility is the best investment we can make in the future.

Appropriate Quote

> "Every great dream begins with a dreamer. Always remember, you have within you the strength, the patience, and the passion to reach for the stars to change the world."
>
> Harriet Tubman, Abolitionist

Key Insight

There are lots of (not funny) jokes about government, including the outdated oxymorons of "military intelligence" and "local government excellence." Old sayings seem to get to be old by being largely true, and "close enough for government work" is unfortunately one of the ones that persists. That is why the work Beth and her organization is doing is so critical. Her personal example of excellence is one to emulate.

Beth Kellar is President/CEO of the Center for State and Local Government Excellence in Washington, D.C. She has served ICMA in a variety of roles since 1976, including as Deputy Executive Director since 1990. Beth has a BA from Muskingum College and an MA from Ohio State University.

Story Ten

Being Bridges

As told by L'uba Vávrová

ICMA'S international exchange programs are well known within the whole local government professional's network worldwide. What might be less known is that the bridges created by this program between the US and Slovakia since the 1990s are still delivering benefits today, more than a decade later. These exchanges were supported by ICMA in the beginning, but were also supported by the US Embassy in Bratislava.

In my work with the Slovak Local Government Development Center, I can count names of 19 involved participants between the years 1998 and 2008. Some were women from the US who worked in city management and had strong financial backgrounds, and were willing to come to Slovakia to share their expertise. On the Slovak side, we helped the Slovak Association of Finance Managers, part of ICMA's USAID-funded project between 1996 and 1999. Both its President and Vice/President were women.

US partners – women – lessons shared in Slovakia

1. Cynthia Seelhammer, at that time the Town Manager of Queen Creek, AZ participated in an ICMA city

management exchange with Lubo Maciak from City of Levoca, Slovakia (www.levoca.sk) in 1998. Cynthia and her family spent two weeks with Mr. Maciak and the staff of the city hall in Levoca. She met with other Slovak city government colleagues as well, discussing mainly general management issues such as office structure and performance, project preparation and evaluation.

Mr. Maciak and his wife, Jana, then returned the visit about a year later, spending two weeks in Queen Creek. Because she had been to see Levoca, and had some understanding of the issues Levoca was facing, Cynthia and her Arizona colleagues were able to plan a curriculum for Mr. Maciak that focused on those local government best practices and service models that would be most interesting and useful to him. Cynthia has this to say about her time in Slovakia:

> "We were able to see Slovakia while it was still learning to be its own country, since it had become a Republic in 1993, just a few years before our visit. Local governments as we know them had not existed during the 50 years of communist rule, and cities were struggling to learn how to be effective local governments. Many cities had really suffered, having no funding and no local authority. City infrastructure and many old buildings had decayed and failed. Add to that the loss of jobs, when inefficient factories were closed, and the entire country was in flux.
>
> Levoca is a beautiful walled city established in the 13th century. When we were there, they had recently celebrated their 600th anniversary, something that seemed amazing to those of us from the American West. Levoca's medieval city wall, the central city square, the church and the beautiful buildings had

> survived all those centuries, but the overall impression was of decay. It was wonderful to think of how charming and beautiful the city might become with some public funding, private investment, and government oversight. But it was daunting to think of the work and expertise necessary to make that happen."

After the two exchanges, there were additional benefits that extended into the future in unexpected ways. I met Cynthia while she was in Slovakia, but our paths crossed again later at a number of ICMA conferences. Once email became widely used, we were able to communicate more often and share information on Facebook. When she worked as Deputy City Manager at the City of Phoenix in 2009, Cynthia was able to arrange for an unpaid internship in the City Water Services Department for a Slovak engineering student. And so the benefits of sharing expertise about local government continued to grow.

2. A special asset was Nachie Marquez, Communications Manager, Chandler, AZ who hosted two young colleagues as interns at her office when she worked in Tempe, AZ.
   A few years later in 2003, Nachie helped us with the project "Local Government Information and Communication." She came to Slovakia under the US Embassy-supported Speakers Program. Together, we did a very successful project for eleven Slovak cities. She presented a week-long seminar in local government communication and we later prepared two books based on the project itself. But mainly, the benefit to us was Nachie's personal and professional experience.
   Nachie said this about the experience teaching in Slovakia:

   > "We had people from eleven cities who went through that week of training. I remember being impressed that they all had such a desire for knowledge. They

> really wanted to know how cities communicate with their residents. They were particularly interested in our city Values Program. There was a real hunger for best practices. They gave me the feeling that they really cared and really wanted to do what was right. They wanted to move forward. They knew that change would take a long time, but they were determined to pursue it."

Recently, Nachie hosted one of our Slovak PhD students for two weeks. (An interesting result is that the student found a partner to come to Slovakia – a young student not from the US, but from China. She is working on her Master program at ASU, and was hosted by us here in Slovakia. Life sometimes comes with unexpected turns.)

3. Lee Ann Dumbauld, at that time Interim City Manager, City of Greenville, South Carolina, helped managers in Slovakia by sharing her expertise as finance officer and the impact of proper financial management on city manager's work. Lee was working with Ms. Hana Dienerova in the City of Trnava, Slovakia, (www.trnava.sk) and later, Lee hosted our young colleague as an intern at her office for several months. Lee is now City Manager of Lubbock, Texas.

Slovak partners – lessons learned in the US

1. Eva Balazova, President of the Slovak Association of Financial Managers, currently serves as a councilor in her City of Lucenec. She is also Interim Professor and Head of the Public Administration Department at the University, Nitra. Eva was the exchange partner of Mr. Terry Zerkle while he was working at the City of Tempe, AZ. Major lessons learned came from Terry's deep professional and personal experience, and she was able to job shadow. Eva has been

leading the Slovak Finance Managers' Association since 1996, is the teacher who has published about eight books (http://novohrad.sme.sk/c/6091344/najnovsiu-knihu-evy-balazovej-pokrstili-peniazmi.html.) She is also very busy as an elected city councilor at the City of Lucenec (and as great grandmom.)

2. Hana Dienerova, Vice - President of the Slovak Association of Finance Managers, currently City Manager of the City of Trnava (www.trnava.sk), was the exchange partner of Lee Ann Dumbauld. I believe that these strong ladies with great financial education and experience backgrounds influenced each other the most. Both had and were able to share best practices. They strongly and consciously lead their offices with clear vision. Both became City Managers, first Lee then Hana.

   Reasons to continue these exchanges:

   Personal experience is the best way to learn, especially if the experience is good. The examples I present were not only about the exchange of professional knowledge, practices, and materials …but also about understanding different cultures, different approaches, and professional performance.

   These women are all working to improve local self-government in their own home cities, but they made a big difference when they reached out to help us in Slovakia, and the positive repercussions are still being felt today.

   Perhaps with some women, building bridges comes naturally, because most women value networks and understand the importance of sharing information and passing on skills. Many of us have benefitted from this.

It was my pleasure to be involved.
Warmest wishes from Slovakia,
L'uba Vávrová

Appropriate Quote

"Perfection consists not in doing extraordinary things, but in doing ordinary things extraordinarily well."

Angelique Arnauld, Abbess of Port-Royal

Key Insight

The world is smaller than it once was. Being a global citizen is less difficult than it used to be. Much of this progress is due to pioneering women like those profiled in L'uba's story who gave of their time and energy when it was much more difficult to do so.

Virtually every manager I have talked to that has participated in an international exchange counts it as one of their most valuable professional learning experiences. If you are in a position to engage in one – do it!

L'uba Vávrová has 16 years of experience as a Senior Advisor. She has served as a Project Manager, Trainer, Coach and Trainer of Trainers. She has international experience as the COE International Advisor, as Lead Local Consultant under a project managed through the Office of Government in Slovakia with a focus on public administration reform. L'uba has local government project management experience in Slovakia with partners from CEE/ENI countries, USA, UK, France, Kazakhstan, Moldova and Serbia. She has served as Executive Director of Local Government Development Centre since 1999.

Story Eleven

One of Many Firsts

As told by Jane Bais DiSessa

THE first time I saw snowfall, I thought I was inside a huge snow globe that someone had softly shaken. As the snow accumulated on the ground, it transformed into a beautiful white blanket, covering everything it touched. Regardless of its beauty, after four months with little to no sun, the winter season can wear the spirit down. Michigan winters are often wet and brutal and can linger long after spring's official arrival. One evening, as I was driving home from work, my weary senses filled with frustration as I watched the large snowflakes quietly land on my car's windshield. To relieve my stress, I whispered, *"What am I doing here?"* I consoled myself by remembering that my work day had been productive, the City was safe, and that shortly I would be home with my loving family and sleeping soundly in my warm, comfy bed.

In order to stay alert while driving, I played loud music and allowed my thoughts to carry me to younger days in the hot Texas sun. This time I thought of my Tía (Aunt) Carmen's home and reminisced about the time my brother, sister and I had sat in her front porch, hoping that today she would allow us to play at a nearby park. I remembered that the park area was small, that it had few trees, and that its playground equipment was always in need of repair. In the evening, this same quiet park would transform into a haven for teenage gangs, which is why my Aunt had many misgivings about allowing us to play there. Sadly, it was also the only place where the neighborhood children could run and play. While no one did anything to stop the neighborhood gangs, I remembered hoping that they would at least leave the see-saw in one piece and that one swing would remain for us to play with. Finally, after much begging and pleading from three eager children, my Aunt gave in. To make sure she didn't have any time to change her mind the three of us zoomed out the door to quickly catch up with our friends. I thought of the sun's rays as they warmed my face while I ran and played. Best of all, I remember taking my turn on that one remaining swing, laughing and proclaiming out loud to my brother and sister that my feet had almost touched the cloud sitting on the hot, bright blue, Texas sky.

When I think about this childhood memory today, I can clearly see how others could view it differently. "Gangs" and "unsafe playgrounds" should have no place in a child's environment, but for a Mexican-American child growing up the way I did, they were part of everyday life. Other life challenges such as poverty, discrimination, and ignorance – were not foreign to me. As I grew older, I accepted them and worked hard to overcome them. For me, this childhood memory lingered in my mind as I went on to find my place in the world. Like others before me, I too had dreams of making the world a better place; not just for my family but for everyone. I wanted to make a difference… I wanted to end all hatred.

It was tough growing up in one of San Antonio, Texas's tough and poor Mexican-American neighborhoods, known to us all as "el (the) West-side." My family was strict and they held on to traditional Mexican family values and religious beliefs. We especially believed in those traditions that required women to learn to be homemakers; not future doctors or lawyers, and most certainly, not a City Manager.

Anyone walking through San Antonio's west side would be correct in thinking that opportunity did not live there, but hope and dreams were plentiful and I found inspiration in the stories my father would tell me in order to encourage me and my siblings to stay in school. He would recount the story of how he had missed his opportunity to attend college and would express his regret for failing to meet his families' hopes that someday, he would have become a lawyer. "A lawyer," he explained, "had the power to stop the world's injustices and could help anyone during times of trouble." For me, my father was my hero and he could do anything. When I asked him why he hadn't become this lawyer person, he stated that life had not been easy, and that he and my mother had decided to have three children instead. Because of his stories, I knew exactly what I wanted to be when I grew up. This was the first time I had ever heard of a person who could not only help others in need, but more importantly – change the world.

I wasn't sure how I was going to accomplish this tremendous feat. Since no one in my family had ever attended college, I had no one who could guide me through the maze of higher education. Harder still, I struggled with family traditions that expected me to learn to be a homemaker. My family was adamant that I first learn these important life skills, and worried that if I didn't, I would never succeed in life. No matter how hard I tried to learn how to sew, clean and cook (especially cooking), I could never meet my Aunt's expectation level. Unlike my sister, who had a special connection with cooking, I shrugged at the thought of cooking a dead chicken! My brother and sister would laugh at my oddly shaped tortillas and dreaded eating the meals I had made, especially since they were often burned or under cooked. "Good grief, I was headed for failure," Tía Carmen would often say.

Although my family was filled with strong women, I knew of no one who had broken with traditional family values. The majority of the women in my family married young and had many children. While I too looked forward to someday having my own family, I was determined to take a different path and to be among the first to challenge tradition, especially when it came to the role of a woman. My first revolt occurred at about the age of nine. I had been helping Tía Carmen with the dinner dishes, when I boldly declared to her that "men, not women, should do the household chores, and that my future husband would cater to me, and that he, not I, would be washing dishes and taking care of the children."

Not knowing that I had just insulted her way of life, my thoughtless remark helped me earn one of my first life lessons. "Well," Tía Carmen stated in a cold, matter-of-fact manner, "until then, you will do as I say and learn to wash dishes." My original task of simply helping her to dry the dishes was elevated to washing and drying each and every dish in her house by myself, pots and pans included!

This "attitude" of mine was also not readily accepted by other family members. I was sometimes humiliated and ridiculed for thinking that I was "better" than they. How dare I think I could change the world? Women were expected to stay home, do housework, and raise children. Why was that not good enough for me? What more could I possibly want? I must admit, there were difficult times in my life that made me think that "getting married and having children" was a way out, and that college was not for me. Those thoughts quickly subsided when I saw other female family members and friends struggle with their children and marriages. The traditional way of life for Mexican-American women seemed liked a vicious circle that had no end. I wanted no part of it, but college life seemed foreign and beyond my reach.

"Finish school, and you will do better than me… be better than me," my father would tell us. In his own way, my father understood the importance of a good education, and in order to help us get there, he moved our family to San Antonio's northwest side, where schools were considered better and whose academic curriculum was designed to help prepare their students for a college education. Life in San Antonio's northwest side was different; neighborhoods were more racially and economically integrated and for the first time, I went to a school with children from different social-economic backgrounds.

Although I did well in school, being from the west-side did not sit well with some of my teachers and classmates. The media's depiction of San Antonio's west-side set the stage to negatively stereo-type all

Mexican-Americans that lived there. I was often asked if I had been ever been a member of a gang, if I had tattoos (my Grandmother would disown me!), or if I had ever taken drugs. My shyness was misinterpreted by some teachers as a lack of self-confidence; even though my grades were good, some teachers felt I lacked academic interest. The simple truth was that in my family, children were taught to be silent, to never question authority, and to always be respectful to all adults. Of course, in my own inner-circle, I was far from shy. Although I rarely gave my parents any major cause for concern, I'm pretty sure they would say that I was a curious, strong-willed and independent child, who liked to "boss" her siblings around. It was difficult growing up in an already dysfunctional family that had one leg strongly held in place by the Mexican traditions of the past, and the other leg, fighting to be accepted in a modern world that saw Mexican Americans as second-class citizens.

College expenses had no place in my family's budget. Thanks to college loans and grants, mixed in with a lot of self-determination, hard work, and encouragement from a few family members, close friends and teachers, I went on to be the first member of my family to attend college. I chose St. Mary's University because of its law school and enrolled as a pre-law student, with the hope of someday attending its law school. I enjoyed my classes and was anxious to attend law school. After a few pre-law classes I learned that my father's description of lawyers was idealistic. I grew disillusioned with the legal field and began to look to other pursuits. Fortunately, as I was nearing the end of my senior year as an undergrad, a professor asked if I was still planning to apply for law school.

"What's the problem?" he asked. I replied that I wasn't sure if I wanted to attend law school, but that if I could go, I would have to move away from home in order to give it my complete attention. I explained that I was disappointed with my pre-law studies and that being a lawyer wasn't exactly what I had thought it was. More importantly, I explained to him that I was tired of struggling, and that I could not fathom the idea of going to school for another three to four

years, especially for a degree I no longer had an interest in. What a waste of time, I thought to myself.

In a serious tone of voice, my professor looked straight at me and asked: *"What do you want to do with your life?"*

Looking straight back at him, I told him about my dreams and that all I wanted to do was to work for an organization that would help to meet the needs of the people.

"Sounds like you want to work for local government," he stated.

"No," I quickly replied. *"I don't ever want to run for political office!"*

He then asked me if I had ever heard of a City Administrator or City Manager. The blank look on my face gave him my answer. He informed me that under a Council/Manager form of government, the City Administrators/City Managers were educated professionals who were appointed by elected officials in order to help them administer the day-to-day operations and that they would also help to develop and implement programs that would improve the quality of life for a community. This was the first time I had ever heard of a City Manager.

My professor went on to explain that St. Mary's University offered a graduate degree in Public Administration and he urged me to consider the program before making any major career changes. To help me with this decision, I was allowed to take a graduate class in Urban Affairs as an undergraduate student. For the first time, I met a professor who really cared about his students and I was one of them.

Needless to say, I went on to earn a Master's of Science degree in Public Administration from St. Mary's University in San Antonio, Texas. I am proud to say that I put myself through college. Although there were times when I wanted to give up, find a job and help my family pay the bills; I somehow found the strength to persevere.

An internship was required as part of my Graduate degree, and as one of over a hundred student applicants I was selected by the City of San Antonio as an Intern for their Planning and Economic Development Departments. During my internship I was allowed to write the section regarding citizen participation for the City's first Master Plan, and I learned how to administer federally governed grant programs such as the Community Development Block Grant (CDBG) and Comprehensive Employment and Training Act (CETA) programs.

After graduation, Interns, like regular employees, were permitted to apply for any job vacancies before the position was posted to the outside world. Fortunately, I was hired to work for the City's Department of Human Resource and Social Services. This was my first real job! Although I later went on to also work for the City's Department of Equal Employment Opportunity, serving as a Budget and Management Analyst for the City's Budget and Research Department provided me with my first work experiences that helped me to understand the fiscal and operational needs of a City.

As a Budget Analyst I learned the importance of comprehending both the internal and external issues affecting an organization so I could better prepare a fiscal plan. I also learned the importance of developing a financial forecast that would help me see the future in order to plan ahead and prepare for the potential ups and downs of an ever growing and constantly changing organization. However challenging it was to work within a complex operational system, an even tougher skill to learn was how to effectively organize, communicate, and manage a diverse work force. Of course, I also learned that it was equally important for a good Manager to understand the cultural and social-economic make-up of their customers.

In the mid-1980s, being a Budget and Management Analyst for the City of San Antonio meant giving up your summer vacation in order to help prepare the City's then $700 million-plus Annual budget and 10-Year Financial Forecast. It also meant you had potential, and the Budget Department had an excellent reputation for providing up and coming public administrators incredible work experiences. It was an exciting time, and I felt privileged to have been selected to become part of a Budget team that consisted of a diverse group of men and women with exceptional educational backgrounds. I was in awe of my co-workers and felt a little intimated alongside out-of-state people with masters' degrees from Harvard, Penn State, Rutgers, and the University of Kansas to name a few.

We were a well-educated, motley crew, but our cultural differences and competitive natures often clashed. Somehow through it all, we learned to work together and kept focused in the preparation of a balanced, cost-effective annual budget. Additionally, our strengths were best utilized by assigning us to work on major projects that could someday change both the City's economic path and structural landscape. I was given the opportunity to work on various major projects which included: the reorganization of the City's Convention Center Department, the selection of an architect for the first phase expansion of the City's convention center, the staffing study for the City's newly reconstructed historical Municipal Auditorium, and the staffing and operational study for the first phase expansion of the City's international airport.

However, the one work assignment that changed my view regarding the provision of public services was not considered a major City project. It came about when yet again, a homeless African American male was found slain in one of the many vacant houses, referred to as "crack houses," in the City's eastside area. In an effort to provide immediate aid to this distressed section of the community, a five-member Budget team was brought together to address the problem. Our assignment was to "clean-up" a one square block located inside the troubled area within one month.

To meet this aggressive deadline, the team was given direct and immediate access to all of the City's services and programs. Together we quickly developed a plan of action that included removing trash from the alleys and right-of-ways, replacing missing traffic signs, and removing graffiti. Before leaving the target area, we met with local residents to help them start a police neighborhood watch program. Additionally, we provided them with information and applications to the City's Community Development Block Grant (CDBG) low-interest home improvement loans. We completed our assignment on time, and certainly felt a sense of pride that we helped revive a poor, struggling neighborhood.

Unfortunately, within less than a week after we had cleaned the area, the alley ways were yet again filled with trash, the new traffic signs had either been stolen or vandalized, and the residents we were working with refused to participate in our programs. Their reason was clear: they did not trust us – and worried that if they signed any governmental agreement, their homes would be taken away.

In our final report, we wrote that our approach had been a "Band-Aid" to a much greater problem. We concluded that until we addressed the real problems – poverty, ignorance and illiteracy – the neighborhood could never change.

As crazy as this may seem, projects like these made me want to be a City Manager even more.

In my opinion, experience in dealing with other cultures and traditions can help a City Manager to better understand the needs of a community. For me, the ability to speak two languages (English and Spanish) has proven to be beneficial. My Great-Grandmother would be especially pleased to hear me say those words. I remember politely disagreeing with her and stating that we lived in America, not Mexico, and *"that learning to speak proper Spanish was a waste of time."*

In my culture, the elderly are revered and my Great-Grandmother was considered our family's matriarch. It is an understatement to write that I politely disagreed with my Great-Grandmother, because her decisions were always final. I was taught to obey and to question further was futile. But let me be clear, her decision did not mean that I should not be proud to be an American, nor did it mean that I should not also learn how to read, write and speak in English correctly. My Great-Grandmother understood the importance of assimilating into the American culture; however, this should not require a person to forgo speaking their native language. As a young child, I saw how bi-lingual people, especially those who spoke with an accent, were considered to be unintelligent, dull, and dim-witted. I couldn't understand why she wanted me to be viewed as such. *"Eres muy joven, algún día entenderás la importancia de hablar dos idiomas."* (Translation: You are very young; one day you will understand the importance of learning to speak two languages.)

I loved my Great-Grandmother dearly, and unlike other younger family members, I relished my time with her. She was smart, kind and most of all, funny. I learned so much from her, and even though she was going blind, my Great-Grandmother was the first person to teach me how to read, write and speak Spanish properly.

I had learned much from my work experience as a Budget and Management Analyst and after a few years I felt I was ready to take on my next challenge that would take me one step closer to becoming a City Manager. But as large as San Antonio was, they only had room for one City Manager and neither he, nor the Assistant City Managers were looking to move on any time soon. Of course, I wasn't that arrogant to think that I could have been chosen as a City Manager even if there had been a vacancy. I knew I needed more work experience, and to get that I would have to work for another community.

In the late 80's I was given the opportunity to work as the Assistant to the City Manager for the City of La Porte, Texas. Although I was only four hours away from home, Southeast Texas was another world when compared to Southwest Texas. In this part of the world, Texans spoke with a heavy southern accent, loved country music, and wearing blue jeans, cowboy hats and boots were the norm. Also, the petrochemical industry dominated the economy and summertime marked the beginning of hurricane season. I teamed with a City Manager who served as an early mentor, and my primary duties included overseeing projects dealing with economic development, public relations and hurricane preparedness. After experiencing three hurricanes and countless chemical emissions, I learned to prepare for the unexpected. Hurricanes are serious business and in this part of the world all residents are taught to always keep a hurricane preparedness kit, both at home and in the truck of their car.

As the City Manager's Assistant I had been assigned to attend a public hearing to address the proposed construction of a hazardous waste incinerator. Also attending this hearing was my future husband, who at the time worked as a Reporter for the Houston Chronicle. Never in a million years would I have guessed that I had just met my future husband and that this smart, tall, blond Michigander would someday convince me to leave my family and move to the state of Michigan. I laugh out loud, each time I reminisce about the first time I heard my future husband tell me that his favorite Mexican food was a "core-ree-zo" and egg taco. I wasn't sure what he was talking about, but after sounding out the word several times I figured out that he was trying to say the Spanish word "chorizo." Chorizo is a type of Mexican sausage and is often mixed with eggs for breakfast. To this day, my husband and I travel far and wide for his favorite Mexican breakfast.

Before moving to Michigan I attended an ICMA conference in Galveston, Texas and sought advice from the ICMA President, who just happened to be from Royal Oak, Michigan. I asked him questions about the communities I had applied to and after giving him a brief description of my work experience asked for his advice as to which community would suit me best. Looking back, I never thought that I would ever move away from all that was familiar to me. The thought of working as a City Manager was exciting, and I convinced myself by thinking that Texas would always be my home, that my family was just a plane ride away and that I could always visit home if I wanted to. I recall thinking out loud, besides the winter season, just how different would Michigan be? I was also anxious to know my new family and learn all about the wonders of "snow!" My husband and I moved to Michigan in 1990 and I began my executive career as the Manager for the Village of Holly.

During my first few days in office, I received the usual interviews from the local press. Several articles were written about the Texan who had moved to Michigan and I responded to the usual questions such as: Why had I chosen to move to Michigan? What were some of the challenges I was facing? And of course, without fail, what was it like being Holly's first female manager? While a few reporters causally asked me about my ethnic background, I was taken aback when one Reporter asked me how I felt to be working for a community with a large white population and I was even more surprised when the Reporter asked me how it felt to be Michigan's first Hispanic City

Manager. I remember responding that the racial make-up of a community made no difference to me, and that I was looking forward to working with the people in my community.

As for the second question, I explained to the Reporter that I was sure that I was not the first Hispanic Manager. I suggested that she contact the International City/County Managers Association (ICMA) to examine their records to further confirm her finding. A few days later, the Reporter again called my office and informed me she had spoken with ICMA, and had confirmed that although there was a Hispanic male who held the title of County Administrator in Michigan, I was indeed Michigan's first Hispanic female to hold the title of Village and/or City Manager.

The Reporter was very excited that she had been the first to come across this information and asked me if she could write a story about it. Although I was pleased to learn of my accomplishment, I was not prepared to address it. I knew that being *female* was going to be a challenge, but as naive as this may sound, I never thought my racial background would also be an issue. I thanked the Reporter for her interest and asked her to please not write the story. She was unhappy with my answer and asked if I was ashamed to let people know of my Hispanic background. I quickly replied that I was very proud to be an American of Mexican descent and that I had made no attempt to hide that obvious fact in earlier interviews. I assured her that my ethnic background would have no effect on my desire to do the best job possible, and that due to Michigan's racial riots in the 1960's, I explained that I wasn't sure how the story would be perceived by the people in my community and that I was concerned that this type of story could have negative consequences. *"Why should the color of my skin matter?"* I asked the Reporter. Reluctantly, she agreed. This is the first time I have ever written about it.

In order to keep abreast of all state and national issues affecting local government, I joined state and national manager's associations. Recognizing the fact that I worked for communities in which 90% or more of population was white, I looked for sessions that could help a minority manager work effectively in communities with limited diversity. After all, I thought to myself, there are sessions that help a manager learn to effectively work with communities that have large minority populations; surely there will be sessions that will address my situation. To my dismay, there were none. Whenever I presented my situation to a speaker, they seemed perplexed by my question and made me feel a bit foolish for asking. I no longer look for these types of sessions. Sometimes, if offered, I attend sessions that address the issue of race relations. If an opportunity arises, I raise my hand and talk about my experience and explain how I have been able to prevail and offer my time and assistance to anyone wishing to learn more.

Knowing what I know now, I believe that I would have dealt with race discrimination regardless of where I had lived – especially in Texas. I remember the first time I was reprimanded in elementary school. I had spoken in Spanish to a few Hispanic friends during recess. *"Teacher, teacher!"* they chanted. *"She is speaking in Spanish!"* After recess, my teacher called me to the front of the class. There, in front of the entire class my teacher reprimanded me for speaking in Spanish, she told me that it was wrong and rude. "*We live in the United States, and in the United States we speak English,*" she loudly stated. For punishment, I had to stretch out my hands and accept being hit with a ruler. I never told my family about this incident. Not because I thought they would be angry with the teacher, but because I thought they would be angry with me. Although I never believed in my teacher's words, I knew that I was supposed to follow the rules.

As a minority Manager in Michigan, I have dealt with racial discrimination. I have had residents come to my office to see what a "Mexican looks like." I have been asked by employers and colleagues "when did my family cross the river" to America. I have been told by disgruntled employees and residents to go back to "Mexico." And I have heard people say that I married an American in order to conceive a "white baby." To confront this type of hatred, I have learned to hold fast and respond to it in a professional and diplomatic manner. It's never easy, but it's always the right thing to do. Labor leader and civil rights activist Cesar Chavez said: "When we are really honest with ourselves we must admit that our lives are all that really belong to us. So, it is how we use our lives that determines what kind of people we are, it is my deepest belief that only by giving our lives do we find life." For me, being a City Manager, allows me to give and in a small way, help to make our world a better place.

Being a female City Manager in this male-dominated field has also brought its own set of unique challenges. Sadly, some employers still have a tough time believing that women are capable of dealing with issues such as union negotiations, supervision of employees, and implementing major construction projects. It was in the state of Michigan that I was first given the opportunity to become a City Manager in three of the four cities I have worked with. As a Michigan City Manager, I have worked on the construction of various major building and road projects, successfully negotiated numerous union contracts, utilized new technologies to improve sustainability, and implemented actions to help address a community's fiscal needs.

I was in the city of Lansing recently attending a work session, when I noticed that some people were wearing coats and gloves. I was a little confused, Michigan's spring came early this year, the sun was brightly shining, and the outdoor temperature was a little over forty degrees. To my surprise, I found the cool temperature soothing, and I wasn't wearing a coat. I guess this Texan is finally becoming part Michigander!

Given the tough times I've gone through, some people may think that working as a minority/female City Manager may not be worth it. They would be wrong. It is not easy to be a City Manager, but if you get the chance, you will embark on an incredible journey. To keep me going, I have a little sign in my office with a quote from Ralph Waldo Emerson that reads: "Do not follow where the path may lead. Go instead where there is no path and leave a trail."

Appropriate Quote

"The family unit plays a critical role in our society and in the training of the generation to come."

Sandra Day O'Connor, US Supreme Court Justice

Key Insight

Being a pioneer comes with many joys and wondrous moments. It also comes with hardships and pains. When the joys outweigh the pains the journey become worthwhile, especially when it honors those who influenced you early in your quest.

Jane Bais DiSessa is the 14th City Manager for the City of Berkley, Michigan. A native Texan, she received her Bachelor of Arts degree in Political Science and Master of Public Administration from St. Mary's University in San Antonio, Texas. Her career has taken her to Texas and Michigan where she has worked for six communities and has held the position of City Manager for three communities. Her experience is diverse and she has worked in all areas involved in the provision of public services. Jane has served as an ICMA Vice President, 2003-2006 and as President of the International Hispanic Network, 2009-2012.

Story Twelve

From Volunteer to CEO:
How a family tragedy set me on a course of public service

[Learn the Three Questions to Ask Yourself Before Making a Commitment.]

As told by Virginia Barney

IT was a typical snowy Saturday morning in February. Inside our warm, snug home, the kids' Valentine's Day decorations were still taped to the refrigerator door. My husband, Marshall, had gone to the office to catch up on some work. The kids and I were lounging in our pajamas. I was reading the paper. My five-year-old daughter, Joy, was watching cartoons and my two-year-old son, Brad was playing with his trucks. Every few minutes he would jump up, dash to another room, grab another toy and then race back. It was just an ordinary Saturday morning in Upper Arlington, a suburb of Columbus, Ohio.

Suddenly I heard a loud pop and Brad's scream. I jumped up and ran to the other room where I saw Brad racing toward me screaming and a wall of flames behind him. He had jammed something into the electrical socket that sparked and set the drapes on fire. I grabbed him, ran for the fire extinguisher on the basement stairs and screeched to a halt. With Brad in my arms and Joy now joining in the terror, there was no way I could put out the fire. *I didn't even know how to operate the fire extinguisher.* I ran to the kitchen phone; couldn't remember the number of the fire department (there was no 9-1-1 in 1980) and dialed my husband's office in a panic who (thankfully) called the fire department. I grabbed coats to wrap around the kids and ran outside and stood in the snow with the kids still wearing my pajamas and fuzzy slippers.

It seemed like forever, but I'm sure it was only minutes later when we heard the sirens growing louder and the fire trucks arrived. The firefighters rushed into the house and the medics ushered us into the emergency squad vehicle. One of the medics informed me that we needed to transport Brad to the hospital. I asked if I could go in the house to grab some clothes. He looked at me and said, "Lady, you aren't going back in there for several hours." At the same time, I heard another medic on the radio informing Children's Hospital that they were en route with a toddler with burns over 18% of his body. Reality set in and a deep sense of loss invaded my body and mind - loss of safety, loss of security, and loss of control.

Brad was admitted to the Firefighter's Burn Unit, a restricted unit due to the high risk of infection. Only immediate family were allowed to visit and then for only a few hours at a time. We had to scrub thoroughly before entering the unit for fear of spreading germs. Brad's hands and legs were bandaged. We would rock him, read to him, and sing to him. We tried to feed him. He was in pain and exhausted. When we had to leave the unit, he looked terrified and I felt utterly helpless.

In the house, fire damaged only one room, but smoke ruined the entire structure. Every rug, every drape, every wall, every piece of clothing smelled. Smoke invaded every piece of food including cereal that was still sealed from the store. It crept inside all the glasses turned upside down in closed cupboards.

Meanwhile, Joy, Marshall, and I moved into a hotel and my mother rushed to join us. She drove ten hours straight to be with us and arrived by nightfall. For days, she took care of all of us. We were exhausted, frazzled and numb from this ordeal.

Just as the smoke from the fire had invaded everything in our house, I realized that it had just as pervasively intruded upon my thoughts. I couldn't close my eyes without the vision of Brad running toward me screaming with the flames behind him. The first night I tried reading myself to sleep. Every time I nodded off, I jerked awake: terrified and reliving the day. Finally, I slipped out of the room and walked the halls of the hotel until morning. I was too frightened to sleep. After three sleepless nights, I went to the doctor for sleeping pills. The flashbacks slowly disappeared.

The knot in my stomach took longer to disappear. I knew I needed to keep up my strength for all that needed to be done, but I just couldn't force the food down. I lost ten pounds the first week and it continued from there. Eventually, logic stepped in and little by little, bite by bite, I regained my appetite.

When we weren't visiting with Brad in the hospital, we were getting the house back in order. Carpets were ripped out, walls were painted, food thrown out, dishes and clothes washed. The amount of work to do was overwhelming, but the response from our neighbors and friends was astonishing. People wanted to help and we needed them. Some brought food, some took loads of laundry home to wash and return, and some babysat Joy. One family even offered their house to us when they went on vacation. We wanted to be back in our house before Brad came home from the hospital.

After 14 days in the burn unit, we brought our little boy home and moved into our house. As Brad's burns healed, we continued to deal with the psychological effects of the fire. Every night, Brad had nightmares where he fought the fire again and again. Plus during the day, everyone had to get comfortable again being around backyard grills, fireplaces, birthday candles, sirens and doctors. We visited the fire station a lot and did family volunteering to raise money for the burn unit. Fire safety now became our family mission.

When I asked the Upper Arlington Fire Division to help us raise money for the Children's Hospital Firefighter Burn Unit, they agreed. In exchange, they asked me if I would volunteer to teach fire safety to children in the schools. In that moment of agreeing, little did I know my life of public service began.

I recruited two friends and together we researched educational materials, met with school principals, and scheduled presentations to every pre-school class through eighth grade class in the city. We wore red jackets with the city fire logo on them and carried photo identification. It was 1981 and we were the only comprehensive age-appropriate fire safety education program in the area. We were volunteers but we were experts. I ended up teaching firefighters from other fire departments how to start their own program. I even did a couple of workshops sharing a victim's perspective for hospital and fire emergency personnel through the State Fire Marshal's Office. That's how the Fire Safety Education Program in Upper Arlington began. I'm proud to say that it continues today with a paid staff.

That volunteer experience enabled me to meet my fears, share my knowledge, and feel like I was doing something important in my community. It felt good to be giving children and their parents the tools they would need to prevent a fire or, heaven forbid, what they should do if they were in a fire. With each class I taught, slowly my sense of safety and security returned. Knowledge gave me back my sense of control.

Five years later, I was asked to lead a Police and Fire Pension Levy. I said "Sure." It was a natural extension to my volunteer service. Two years later, when there was an opening on City Council, I was asked to apply for an appointment. Seventeen people applied and I was chosen to fill the unexpired term. I was subsequently elected to two four-year terms on Council including serving as Vice Mayor and then Mayor. In Upper Arlington, there is a city manager form of government. My leadership roles on council were to preside at the Council meetings and to perform ceremonial jobs. I was on the policy side of government.

To this day, I'm not sure I ever would have run for City Council if I hadn't been appointed first. It feels much more comfortable to be asked to do something rather than campaigning on a platform that I'm the best person for this job. It takes a lot of courage to stand forward, sharing your opinions, and asking for people's financial support and ultimately their vote. Politicians do it every day but it was not my style.

In public office, my business training gave me the skills to quickly understand the financial and operational side of running a city. My passion for children and interest in safety served me well on the programmatic side. I loved it. I was serving my community, working with great staff, and helping people.

However, I quickly learned that in some people's eyes I had turned from a wonderful community volunteer to a no-good politician overnight. The same people who were giving me accolades and awards, were now wondering what my motives might be. I was not prepared for that. People that had called me "Ginny" for years started to call me "Virginia" – the name used on the ballot and in the media. I call "Virginia" my stage name. (I'm now equally comfortable with either name.) After one particularly heated community discussion, I called up a friend who was on the other side of the issue from my vote. She happened to be the room mother in my son's fourth grade class. She was so angry with me that she said she couldn't talk to me and hung up. I remember climbing in the shower and crying, wondering what I had gotten myself into. I grew up quickly.

Many, many friends and residents did write me notes telling me how much they appreciated my community service, but the ones who didn't like what I was doing seemed to write letters to the editor for the whole world to see. That was tough, particularly for my family. I saved my letters of support and appreciation and threw away the letters that were not so kind. I knew I would need to reread my positive notes when times got rough and that I would remember the bad notes even without looking at them. I developed a thick skin but have tried to keep my heart soft.

In May of 1998, the Republican Party asked me to run for an

appointment to the Franklin County Clerk of Courts. In Ohio, the County Clerk supports the Common Pleas Court and the district Court of Appeals as well as running the Auto Title Offices for the County. It is an operation with more than 200 employees, with well in excess of $225 million dollars collected each year, and multiple offices.

The previous Clerk had just plead guilty for theft in office of about half a million dollars and was later sentenced to six years in prison. The office was in chaos, the employees all under suspicion, and the likely opponent in the Fall election was from a third generation political family with big name recognition. I'm sure other possible candidates were approached to throw their hat in the ring and they ran screaming in the other direction. For all intents and purposes, this looked like lose-lose scenario.

To me it looked like an opportunity to use my gifts, make a difference, and to help the employees find the right course for the office. I believe in good government and after interviews, was appointed as the first woman Clerk of Franklin County.

The first few days in the office of Clerk, I met with the County Prosecutor, representatives of the State Auditor's Office, and officers of the State Bureau of Criminal Investigation. They told me how the theft had been committed, how long it may have been occurring, who might have known about the crime, where the hidden cameras were in my office that caught the theft on tape. At the end of the week, I fired the top four people in leadership roles. If they didn't know about the crime, they should have known about it and we needed a whole new team to rebuild the public's trust in our Office.

I had an open door policy for any employee who had a story to tell, a complaint, or suggestion. I heard plenty: stories of sex acts on my desktop (I scrubbed my desk and chair after that conversation!); stories where raises were given for political campaign support; stories of racial discrimination; lack of financial controls; inconsistent personnel rules; and a lack of training opportunities. The Office was a mess.

Clearly, I needed some help. From my years of volunteering in the community, I knew volunteers sharing their talents with the Office could make a huge difference quickly. People were eager to help. From across political party lines, I formed a Blue Ribbon Task Force of experts. It included a CFO of a national bank and the managing partner of a large accounting firm to help with financial controls and money management, a VP of personnel for a national insurance company to work on personnel policies, CEO of a public relations firm to help inform the public how our Office works and many other volunteers who cared about good government. These task force members became our unpaid consultants and shared their gifts and knowledge freely.

The employees worked together to write a Code of Ethics for the office. All of us received ethics training and were trained on new financial policies. Everything was designed and implemented to give the public confidence that we protected the public's money and deserved their trust. Shortly after my appointment, I had to publicly campaign for the office I was now holding. I won my election handily! My hard work along with that of the employees and the volunteers paid off and it felt great

Two years later the Clerk's Office was running smoothly and the employees were well trained and proud. Written policies and procedures were in place to assure accuracy and consistency in operations. Our hiring practices enabled qualified people from all races and political parties to obtain jobs in our Office.

Elected office can be very seductive. People started planning my future for me. I could be the next County Commissioner, the next Member of Congress, the next State Treasurer. It's very dangerous to start believing your own press releases. It was amazing who they thought I could be next. In my heart, I wasn't so sure, but knew I would recognize the right opportunity when it appeared.

When I got a call to return to the City of Upper Arlington as its city manager or CEO, I listened carefully. I loved restoring the public's trust in the Clerk's Office meeting the challenge of organizing the Office and empowering the employees. Taking the non-partisan city manager position would disappoint all those folks who were planning my future but I was unhappy and uncomfortable in the bickering political party environment outside the office.

After considering all the advice from other people, I now needed to listen to my own voice. What was best for me? I asked myself three questions to help me make my decision. It is the same strategy I use today before I take on any new commitment even if it's a volunteer position.

1. Will it use my gifts? We all have talents and skills. If I'm working and using mine, I'm happy and productive.
2. Can I make a difference? Even if I'm using my talents, I might not be able to move the organization along. If I'm not the right fit for the organization, it's not the right fit for me.
3. Will it be fun? Sure there are difficult days in any job, but life should be enjoyable. If I dread going to work every day, I'm not doing my best and I'm not in the right place.

In considering the city manager position, the answer to all three questions was yes! The variety of talents in a city organization is energizing. Where else can I have engineers, CPA's, attorneys, fire and police chiefs, park and recreation experts, architects and more in the same room working on the same goal of a better community?

In my experience in private business, everyone guards their trade secrets and shares nothing. In public service, there are no secrets. Everyone shares their best practices as well as their problems freely so everyone can learn to serve better. It's a wonderful, giving environment where I thrive and have fun.

Working in a city enables me to meet with school kids and senior citizens daily. I have the opportunity to impact their lives every day. Through community committees and projects, I get to know what people care about and work together to help them enjoy the services and community they want. Upper Arlington is a city of about 34,000 residents. It's large enough to provide significant programs and projects and small enough to see them come to life. Public service is tremendously satisfying for me.

I have a weekly city manager column in our local newspaper, attempting to put a face on government as I share items of interest or importance to our residents. Over the years, people have come to recognize me about town. They stop and share a concern in the grocery store or thank me for a particular service they received. Mostly, I really enjoy talking with them. There are moments when a little anonymity would be helpful, like the time I was buying a bra and panties at Macy's and the man behind me in line chose to make my acquaintance at that very moment!

My job as a public servant is to help my elected leaders and our residents create a place where families can raise their children, where people can grow old and still stay connected, where people feel safe, where there are opportunities to play and enjoy nature in our parks, where we can shop and work. My job is to help people build a community.

When a house fire led me to my volunteer career as a fire safety educator, I had no idea I would hold elected office and eventually return to Upper Arlington as the CEO of the City. In my mind, there's no job more fulfilling. I leave my office every day feeling that I have touched someone's life. It's a responsibility I don't take lightly and a privilege I don't take for granted.

I am happy to report my son Brad is married, perfectly healthy and has a beautiful daughter, Lilly. He has forgotten the events surrounding our house fire. What he remembers is attending my fire safety classes.

Appropriate Quote

> "We may encounter many defeats, but we must not be defeated."
>
> Maya Angelou, Poet

Key Insight

The rewards in the public sector are as you find them. For many the satisfaction of improving the lives of others is enough to outweigh all other factors.

Virginia Barney lives with Marshall, her husband of 42 years in Upper Arlington, a suburb of Columbus, Ohio. They have two grown children, Brad and Joy, who are out of the house, but live close-by. Virginia served as the city manager of her city from 2000 until she retired the end of 2011. She sits on numerous community boards and continues to advocate for fire safety education. Virginia is currently a senior partner with the consulting firm, The Collective Genius.

Story Thirteen

A Local Government Love Story

As told by Evie Johnson

THIS is not a war story. If it was a war story, I would tell you that I was a 25 year old female standing five feet two inches tall wearing size seven high heels when I took my first job out of grad school as the City Administrator of Prairie City. I can't tell you that everything was easy in this job, or that people haven't judged me because I was young, small, blonde, or a woman. I've had to prove to others that I was qualified for this job over and over again—and that has made me a better leader, administrator and person.

This story—My story—is about love, acceptance, and growth.

I graduated from undergrad at the University of South Dakota with a Music Performance degree in 2008. The year everything crashed. I like to call it the year I became realistic. It was the year I realized that being a professional musician wasn't in the cards for me.

After graduation, I served beer for a summer and on a whim applied for grad school in public administration, thinking I'd start my own non-profit taking music into schools. It was a little more realistic, but not by much. While in my first year of the MPA program, several opportunities in local government kept piquing my interest. And finally, the summer of 2009, I took a summer position funded with stimulus money at the City of Vermillion. And this is where the love story starts.

My job in Vermillion was to communicate with residents about a new recycling program that passed by 52% to 48% in referendum vote. I like talking and problem solving, so I thought this would be a perfect fit for me. Little did I know that the City Manager in Vermillion would really let me run with the project. He let me work on the logistics of collection, route management, and the marketing of the program to residents. I won't bore you with the details, but I was getting really excited about the services that local government provided to residents!

I continued to work for the City of Vermillion through my second year of grad school doing communication for many different departments. That's when the City Manager came to me with what he called a "crazy idea." Develop a Citizens Academy. While a Citizens Academy wasn't a new idea, it was a new program in Vermillion. I had toured all the departments in Vermillion when I first started there, but until I had to write the curriculum for the program I really didn't realize how many facets there were in the City or how service oriented local government really was. I was in love and I knew this field was for me!

Graduation came rather quickly and I was fortunate to still be working for the City of Vermillion. I knew I couldn't work there forever, and continued looking for another job in the field. Sixty Six job applications later I was the City Administrator of Prairie City, Iowa. Yikes! I was sitting in the big chair—answering directly to the council. I had worked with the Council in Vermillion, but it's different working directly with and for a City Council.

I was so fortunate to work with a great council—a council that wanted to see me grow professionally and accepted me as a young woman. The staff was great too! They exercised patience with me, taught me about the City, and were flexible and adaptable to my needs. By the Council's and Staff's example, the community accepted me too!

After just finishing my first year as City Administrator, I am so thankful for the women who came ahead of me in leadership roles in local government, and I'm grateful for a council who thinks that a young woman can be a City Administrator. There have been some people who have doubted if I could do the job—and they may have doubted that because of my age, gender, or hair color—but ultimately, it is because of those who have come before me, mentored me, or trusted me that have allowed me to grow and be successful in local government management! I am in love with this field and hope to serve in local government for a long, long time!

Appropriate Quote

> "A loving person lives in a loving world. A hostile person lives in a hostile world. Everyone you meet is your mirror."
>
> Ken Keyes, Jr. Personal Growth Author

Key Insight

At some point we all started young and green. Like trees, in our young and green stage we are supple and grow fast. Putting down roots, growing stronger, taller and straighter is part of the journey.

Evie Johnson is the City Administrator for the City of Prairie City, IA. Prior to Prairie City, she was with the City of Vermillion, South Dakota. She is a member of the ICMA's Emerging Leaders Class of Fall of 2013. She is a graduate of the University of South Dakota with a Masters in Public Administration.

Story Fourteen

On Mentoring

As told by Jenny Hesseltine

I am one of those "spoiled Generation Y brats" who had it fairly easy entering the profession. That's not to say I didn't work hard to earn my degree and experience. But I did have great mentors whose training and discipline carried me through challenges; whose wisdom and discernment coached me to make right decisions, whose generosity and patience expressed a true commitment to the profession and developing the next generation of managers. This piece is meant to serve as an expression of my gratitude to these individuals…you know who you are.

Phones ringing, notes shuffling, visitors knocking and Outlook chime sounding, so kindly reminding of the meeting that *began* five minutes ago. The scene could easily describe corporate enterprise, non-profit organization or the busy life of a stay-at-home parent. This particular scene is within the office of a local government manager. A manager whose schedule always seems to overflow, who rarely takes a true lunch, who must prioritize the tasks of every day in order to focus effort appropriately.

Yet this manager maintains a healthy home life, meaningful relationships and even the coveted "me time," for this manager is dedicated to personal wellness. Biking his thirty-plus miles daily before work. Training with her kids to run the annual pumpkin run each October. Never missing a soccer game or a cross country meet. Spending time with parents, aging. Mentoring students—me. How?

One would find it understandable if the manager had such skills for personal life but wasn't wholly dedicated to the profession. To serving. To excellence. But this manager is. Again, how? How does one achieve such success? Serve daily the public pouring from body, mind and soul, yet still have a cup overflowing for home…and for me?

As a young local government professional, I understand I will strive long and hard, making mistake after mistake before I can claim to have even a fraction of understanding of how they achieved their excellence, let alone to ever hope I resemble them, even in part. In my desire to be like them, I vigorously took notes in my time learning from them—mentally, emotionally, in print. As I look and think back over those notes, I discover daily bits and pieces of what they truly taught me, more than likely without realizing it. What follows, *I think*, is *part* of how they do it.

In one of my favorite books on leadership, *The Servant*, author James Hunter defines power as "the ability to force or coerce someone to do your will, even if they would choose not to, because of your position or your might." On the contrary, authority is "the skill of getting people to willingly do your will because of your personal influence."

So, what is the real difference? Why does that difference matter? I think it's all about service. Service to team members and service to citizenry. The difference is attitudinal and, in my opinion, largely based on optimism.

Negativity is contagious, draining, defeating. It serves no purpose. Trickles down…and up…and in…and out. It's selfish. Toxic.

Tight budgets, lack of confidence in state and federal government and the general busyness of local government can make it easier to see the woes and challenges of the profession than its blessings and opportunities. When negativity is allowed to rule the thought process and govern the actions, the results can be calamitous: leaving us in an aftermath of defeat and humility. Feeling as though a power struggle has been lost, with followers of our leadership few and far between.

I'm still not sure how my mentors maintain positive attitudes seemingly all the time. They either have learned the importance of this great skill or they are extremely good at faking it, so as not to discourage the next generation of managers. I don't believe it's the latter. After 20-plus and 30-plus years in the profession, they still talk about local government passionately. Not a phone conversation closes with an attitude of anything but enthusiasm for the service they provide. I can't help but think their mantras, "no good deed goes unpunished," "you just have do the right thing," and the ever important, "what does the ICMA Code of Ethics say?" keep them poised for success in the realm of positive, realistic thinking.

Not only that, but gratitude seems to play a large role in their daily mindsets. Is it possible that being grateful for not only the good things in life, but also for the challenges and stresses the life of a public servant faces, breeds a joyful spirit? A positive outlook? Effective leadership? I think it is. I think my mentors have proven that, and for it and their contagious passion, I am grateful.

So I keep a list, a gratitude journal, so as not to lose sight of optimism. Most of the items on my list are not profound; they're simple. Yet, they are things that I could easily overlook in my day if I wasn't seeking them out. Things like:

...the way my two-year-old smiles at her daddy
...a complimentary phone call
...under 60 minute Council meeting!
...the tulips in radiant bloom outside my window
...that new idea that I hate
...the mentor's phone call to sing me "Happy Birthday"

Perhaps this optimism comes easily enough to these great managers that they don't have to so specifically look for it; I'm not sure I trust myself that much. So in my striving to follow their example,

I will continue to be intentional about gratitude and frequently and anxiously look back over my career…my life…to know if it made a difference. If it helped me to be more effective at home and at work, if it had a positive influence on the generation of managers to follow, whatever: it will be named. If, at that point, I can see that optimistic authority-breeding gratitude has impacted even one other person the way that my mentors have influenced my life, I believe I will feel joyfully fulfilled.

Appropriate Quote

> "There are lots of opportunities out there for women to work in these fields, they just need support, encouragement and mentoring to follow through."
>
> Sally Ride, Astronaut

Key Insight

One of the great things about public administration is the collegiality of the profession. Folks are very willing, almost desirous, of helping others be successful – especially in mentoring and making a difference. While there are exceptions (and they are so rare as to be infamous) virtually everyone you ask will make time to help make your career more successful!

Jenny Hesseltine holds a Master of Public Administration degree from the University of Kansas and has experience in large and small communities alike. She has worked in Douglas County, Kansas, for the City of Olathe, Kansas and currently serves as the Director of Administrative Services for the City of Pella, Iowa. Jenny has been fortunate to have great mentors in her career who have instilled within her a loyalty to the profession and a strict adherence to the ICMA Code of Ethics. Jenny enjoys developing relationships and thinking innovatively to improve the lives of the citizens she serves.

Story Fifteen

It's Not a Sprint, but a Marathon: Nine Lessons from the First Year

As Told by Charmelle Garrett

WHEN I started with the City of Victoria as Human Resources Director, I never thought I wanted to be a city manager. I was fortunate to have a City Manager, Denny Arnold, who saw something in me and gave me opportunities to learn about city management. He got me involved with "big picture" thinking, explained political land mines, and taught me to never get out in front of the Council. All were very valuable lessons.

But it was at the 2010 International City/County Management Association (ICMA) Annual Conference, held shortly after the Victoria City Council announced my new appointment, where a visit with Bob O'Neill, the Executive Director of ICMA, provided another very valuable lesson.

I'd had the privilege of getting to know Bob while participating as a member of the Leadership-ICMA 2010 class. During our conversation at that 2010 annual conference, we discussed many of the new ideas that I had. Of course, I had a plenty of ideas. Having worked for the City of Victoria for 21 years, my depth of knowledge was rather diverse (or so I thought.) Sixteen years were spent as the Human Resources Director and four as the Assistant City Manager. Local government in Victoria was not new to me. Bob gently reminded me that organizations can only handle so much change at one time. "Charmelle," he said, "you need to remember: it is a marathon, not a sprint."

As I write this short story, I have just completed one year as City Manager for Victoria. During this first year, we had a few challenges, lots of laughs, and days that made me want to run from the building as if I <u>was</u> training for marathon. With that said, most of the time it has been very rewarding. Here are nine lessons I've learned from the first year of my marathon.

Public service is an incredible field to be in on a day-to-day basis. Often I remind our employees that to serve in the public sector is a calling. However, what cannot be learned from mentors or textbooks is how fast one must think on one's feet at all times. You never know what type of questions might come from individual citizens or from city council members. *Marathon lesson number one: Stay on your toes.*

Recently I was asked what has been my biggest surprise as City Manager. Most would expect the numerous complaints that we receive to be at the top of the list. After all, one of the aspects of being a public servant is fielding questions in the grocery store, in church, or in a restaurant. This is truly a mobile office. I had another City Manager tell me that he couldn't even "pass the peace" in church without receiving a comment or two. That is simply a part of the job. I am thankful that private citizens are willing to share their opinion with me, however time consuming that may be. The complaints were not my biggest surprise. No, what has surprised me the most has been the amount of time that it takes to properly connect and respond. Any relationship worth having takes an investment in time and what I am trying to cultivate is a relationship with the people of Victoria. *Marathon lesson number two: Running takes endurance.*

Even though I had been with the City prior to my appointment, I knew that we would be faced with growth in Victoria that we have not seen since the 1950's. So I immediately start trying to figure out "how to see around corners" and predict what was next. *Marathon lesson number three: Visualize the course.*

I challenged department heads to review processes, determine what technology could help us be more efficient, and as Jim Collins would say, find out if they "have the right people on the bus." Governments have a reputation for being "fat" with staff. I can honestly say that is not the case in Victoria. My job within the next year will be to develop a strategy for where we will need to add more people and/or better tools to achieve the job. *Marathon lesson number four: Train, train, train.*

A few months after my promotion, our local Chamber of Commerce decided to cancel their contract with the City in which they managed the convention and visitors bureau (CVB.) As part of that contract, the CVB was to create, plan, and host a local festival. The contract cancellation occurred five months before the first festival. One month later, the CVB Director was no longer an employee of the chamber.

We were four months from the festival with a lot of coordinating and planning left. Shortly after this unexpected change of events, I looked around the room during a staff meeting at the twelve department heads and borrowed a quote from Gene Krantz. "Failure is not an option." Our department heads pulled off the impossible, and when appropriate, I got out of the way. Department heads are usually more successful when City Mangers get out the way! The festival was a success and our community is looking forward to the next one. *Marathon lesson number five: Keep putting one foot in front of the other.*

Shortly before becoming City Manager, we had started a downtown utility project to replace aging infrastructure which was approximately 75 to 100 years old. With the project came a golden opportunity to replace the sidewalks. While the utility project was underway, downtown events were curtailed. So we were excited to finish the project and once again have events in our beautiful downtown. One of the first events was "Lighting on the Square." We planned for the Mayor to speak. At the conclusion of his speech, we would flip the switch with great fanfare and the square would light up gloriously for the holiday season. As with any good statesmen, he had a very appropriate speech to set the tone of the event. In typical political fashion, it went a little long. During a dramatic pause for effect towards the end of his speech, the Parks Director flipped the switch, the lights came on, but the Mayor was not finished. We all got a good laugh out of this afterwards, but I know the Parks Director held his breath, as I did. The Mayor finished his speech with the square lights aglow. It's great to work with a Mayor who has a sense of humor. *Marathon lesson number six: When the race doesn't go as planned, adjust.*

I deal with the same issues all City Managers deal with so learning to live in the fishbowl here is no different than any other community. Some have more active community participants than others. I learned during my human resources days that you can't please everyone. Communicating is key and knowing when to shut-up is critical. An opportunity for the latter came early for me. When the prior City Manager announced his retirement, the Council could hire a recruiting firm and conduct a search, open it up to internal candidates, or interview the Assistant City Manager (me.) They decided to interview me and then make a decision. As I entered the conference room for my interview, the Mayor stood up and said, "Congratulations! You're the next City Manager." I quickly responded, "Don't you want to interview me?" This is when my inner voice said, "Shut-up and sit down." Past training paid off. I sat down and thanked them for the opportunity to serve. *Marathon lesson number seven: You have prepared for this, enjoy the race.*

When I knew the City Manager job was going to be open, I asked my husband if he was okay with the long hours, the negative press, and all the blogs. Through the years, I have attended seminars and read articles on work/life balance, but I'm not sure if this is possible. We agreed he would stop reading the blogs and I would try to devote weekends to him. As most of you would expect, that has not happened. Sometimes, we have to schedule time together. I am very fortunate to have the support of a great husband who is not only my biggest cheerleader, but a grounding force at times. While reading the local newspaper one morning, I was complaining about a letter to the editor. I was telling my husband that the letter writer did not have all the facts, and why would he comment on something he did not know about? Looking over his paper, my husband calmly stated, "Honey, you work in a business that a lot of people hate—government." Wow! Those were strong words but probably accurate. *Marathon lesson number eight: Marathons aren't for everyone: They take a special breed.*

As I start my second year as the City Manager, I will continue to work on the balancing of needs between the City Council and department heads, making professional recommendations to council knowing that there will always be political land mines, and having peace with not being able to make everyone happy. There are still days when I have to sprint, but I always remember those valuable words from Bob. This is a marathon. *Marathon lesson number nine: Lace up your running shoes!*

Appropriate Quote

> "I don't think there's any such thing as setting your goals too high. The higher you set your goals, the more you are going to work. If you don't reach them, then it's okay, just as long as you set it and then give 100% of yourself."
>
> Dan Jansen, Speed Skater

Key Insight

There is no anonymity in the city manager profession. In every community you are the only one, and therefore easy to spot – at the grocery store, at the gym or as Charmelle points out, even at church. The same is often true of, and even harder on, a spouse. After all, they have no control over the situation and experience any hurts just as painfully as you do. Although marathons aren't for everyone, if you sign up remember you often run as a couple.

Charmelle Garrett is City Manager of the City of Victoria, Texas. She has served as City Manager since March, 2011. Prior to City Manager, she served as Deputy City Manager for approximately five years and Assistant City Manager for a year and a half. She began her service to the City of Victoria in 1990 as Human Resources Director. Charmelle is a member of the International City / County Management Association (ICMA) and the Texas City Management Association (TCMA.) She is also a Credentialed Manager. She is a 1982 graduate of Louisiana Tech University.

Story Sixteen

Attributes of an Effective #2

As told by Karen Montgomery

ONE of the key strengths of a leader is learning how to be equally effective as a follower. This is often counter-intuitive because we don't see much written about how to be a good follower, whereas there are numerous books and articles that have been written about how to be a good leader. So while it seems that the attributes of being a good follower are often ignored when the attributes of a leader are identified, a good number two must do both very well.

Having served in both state and local governments, I have learned the value and importance of being a good follower. Much of what is required can be summarized in three ways: being loyal and trustworthy, being competent, and being communicative. I will explain the importance of each one below.

In local government, the loyalty factor is especially crucial since city managers cannot possibly keep their eyes on all the balls at one time. They have to rely on the trustworthiness of their direct reports to ensure that they know what's going on with the council members, the staff and the citizens on a wide variety of issues. The person who is "#2", whether a deputy, assistant city manager or department head, is in a position to have information that would be useful to the manager.

To be effective, it is critical that the #2 relay such information in a timely manner. Yet, it can be difficult to discern exactly what level of detail with which to provide the manager. It can also be tempting to withhold critical information in order to enhance one's own standing in the eyes of the council, staff or citizens. After all, as Sir Francis Bacon so aptly stated back in the 1500's about heresies in the church, "knowledge is power." To be an "effective #2" means not to hold onto that power, but rather giving it to its rightful owner – in this case the city manager. A willingness to be the messenger and deliver bad news is especially important and often means being willing to be vulnerable.

Competency is another important attribute of an effective #2. Serving the public is a noble calling and it is incumbent upon all those who answer "yes" to that call, to be the best they can be at what they are hired to do. What is required of us in order to be competent will vary depending on the job, but one thing that is common in the definition of competency is that it is more about interpersonal skills than technical skills the higher one goes in an organization. The irony of this concept is that most people are promoted to higher level positions based on their technical skills and therefore find that they are unprepared and perhaps unable, to exhibit the required interpersonal skills. Recognizing the need for this additional skill set, an effective #2 will seek ways in which to acquire these additional skills. This might be through reading books on the subject, attending seminars, obtaining some executive coaching, or all of the above. An important component to this professional development plan is a feedback loop to evaluate how one is progressing in this area.

A third very important attribute of an effective #2 is being communicative. Transparency is a hallmark of good government and it relies on people who know how to communicate. Someone in a key #2 position is similar to a spoke on a wheel, with many stake holders dependent on the information that person possesses. He or she must recognize the importance of answering questions that have not been asked by anticipating the needs of others in advance. This can seem overwhelming at times, but is also what makes being in the #2 role so meaningful.

In considering one's effectiveness as #2, put yourself in the city manager's shoes and ask yourself, "Am I the person that I would want in this position?" If the answer is yes, then you will know that you have mastered the skills necessary to be effective. But if the answer is no, don't lose heart. Simply commit yourself to obtaining the resources necessary to grow into the role. Although some of the trial and error lessons learned can be the most painful, they can also be the ones that are the most long-lasting; something about "pain being the best teacher."

I have spent much of my career as #2, and found it to be very rewarding. There is a great need in local government for those who commit to being good followers and are not competing for the #1 role. A city manager's office is surrounded by the egos, power and self-interests of those within and outside of the organization. My hope has been to offer the city managers with whom I have served a place where they could find something different, a place where they could trust that I "had their back." And should someday I find myself in the #1 position in an organization, that is exactly what I would look for in the #2 position.

Appropriate Quote

> "Making a decision usually means taking one of two roads. One is doing the right thing. To take the other road, you have to sit back and spin a story around the decision or action you are taking. If you find yourself thinking up an elaborate justification for what you are doing, you are not doing the right thing."
>
> Wayne (Soupy) Sales, American
> Philosopher / Comedian

Key Insight

Trust between the CEO and those close to her is a huge benefit when it exists and almost always a fatal flaw when it does not. Subverting your own ego to serve is a conscious act. If you have a second in command you cherish, be sure and let her know. If not, reread the first sentence of this insight.

Karen L. Montgomery is vice president for finance and administration at Texas Wesleyan University where she is responsible for the finance, budget, human resources, facilities and IT services. Prior to that, she served as an assistant city manager in Fort Worth, has served as chief financial officer and finance director for cities and counties, and has held executive level positions in state government. Ms. Montgomery is a certified public accountant, and holds a Master's degree in Public Administration from the University of Colorado at Denver, and a bachelor of business administration degree from the University of Oklahoma. She is an ICMA credentialed manager and was the winner of the 2010 NCTCOG Award for *Women in Public Management.*

Story Seventeen

The Value of Public Service

As told by Cheryl A. Hilvert

AS I look back on 31 years of local government service, I am both pleased, and humbled, by the importance of the work that we do, the people I have met, and all the many things I learned along the way. While the environment in which we work has never been easy, we can all take pride in the "difference" we are able to make in our communities and in people's lives. I can truly say that work in public service is a privilege and that I have "enjoyed the ride." . .and would bet that nearly all of my colleagues would agree!

We probably all come to our careers in public service in different ways. Many are driven by the opportunity to "make a difference." Others may be motivated by work that is varied and challenging. To some others, it may simply be a job—until they learn the true value and contribution that we make as public servants. For me, my interest and love of public service originated from a different source. . .my Dad!

As a child, when the other kids were out playing, I was the one that was taken to council meetings when important issues were facing our community or neighborhood. He made sure that I knew the name of our mayor and our school superintendent. He also made sure that I knew how important it was to be an active and involved citizen of my community and to understand that being educated about what was going on around me and that "giving" and not just "taking" was what I needed to do throughout my life.

In case you don't realize it by now, my Dad was a public servant. He was a math teacher, a football and basketball coach in an inner city school district for more than 33 years. He was also a WWII veteran—a B-17 pilot and prisoner of war. The work he did was never easy, but he loved his country, his community, and believed in the important work that is done by public servants. He was a role model to me and was also my hero. And, while he never told me what career to pursue, I suppose my destiny was always to work in public service.

Like many of my colleagues, my career was extremely rewarding and I have the great feeling that I made a difference for the communities, businesses and residents I served. Whether it is the assistance we provide in a natural disaster, implementing quality services and programs that make people want to live in the communities in which we serve, or simply helping the elderly woman in town who lives alone, there truly is a "higher moral purpose" to the work that we do. The opportunities for us to contribute in these ways are truly endless.

In addition to the services we help to provide, we are the builders of community and democracy. We stand by the charters that create our local governments. We support the elected officials—many of whom are part-time, and not career politicians – in their very difficult and demanding jobs. When confronted by naysayers, we stand behind the decisions, laws, and work of our organizations and stand up for what is right about government. At times, we confront citizens with their freedoms and challenge them to be contributing members of our communities. While this work is challenging, it is awesome to think of its power for our communities and organizations.

We also bring the best out in people. Whether it is inspiring people in a time of tragedy or simply encouraging people to do more than they think can, we have the opportunity as public servants to make a difference, not only to the quality of work in our cities, but to the people we encounter. It is refreshing to see the many talents and capabilities of the people who work in local government at all levels and to know that a big part of our jobs is to support an environment that permits everyone to contribute to the success of our organizations.

Similarly, it is encouraging to see when residents step up to be our partners in the work of local government and assist in building the types of community in which they want to live and work. This is the work of the public servant, regardless of position or location in the organization, regardless of pay grade or title. When we work together with a shared vision, with a purpose and commitment to the importance and value of public service, and a true commitment to working together to build community, we can accomplish anything!

This was the message my Dad taught me at an early age and that I continued to learn throughout my career in public service. I have tried throughout my life to help others see the value of public service, whether they serve in a paid position or are giving back to their community as an active and involved resident or business person.

Are you doing all you can to "pay forward" the many opportunities you have had and the gratification you have earned for a job well done? I challenge you to do just that and celebrate with me the true value of a career in public service. My Dad, and yours, would be proud!!

Your mom, too!

Appropriate Quote

> "Successful people form the habit of doing what failures don't like to do. They like the results they get by doing what they don't necessarily enjoy. "
>
> Earl Nightingale, Motivational Speaker

Key Insight

There are days when a City Manager might question their choice of professions. Much can go wrong and of course the CMO often takes blame it does not deserve. And yet! And yet, the value of public service cannot be overstated. Building community and delivering Democracy are high callings. Stop any of the folks with the 35 years plus service award ribbons at an ICMA conference and they will universally agree that it has been a grand road to travel.

Cheryl Hilvert is a Senior Consultant with ICMA. She has served as City Manager in Montgomery, Ohio and Fairfield, Ohio. She is on the Board for the Alliance for Innovation and is a past Regional Vice-President for ICMA. She has her BA and MPA from Eastern Kentucky University, and is a Credentialed Manager.

Story Eighteen

21st Century Women on the Move!

As told by Susan J. Daluddung

WHEN I moved to Peoria, Arizona to take on the position of Deputy City Manager for Development and Community Services, it could not have been a worse time. Over the first decade of the 21st Century, catalysts for change included explosive events such as the incredible shock of 9/11, the burst of the dot-com bubble, and then the sudden drop in the rapid trajectory of real estate value. What followed was the value of stock market dollars declined, capital investments shrunk, and home values imploded. City tax revenues plummeted, and bonding capacity constricted. The City hired me to manage a new frontier of growth when I made my move to Peoria in September of 2008. You all know the ending to that chapter, instead I arrived to an economic challenge this area had never before experienced, coupled with a downslide in growth never seen before in Arizona.

Lesson Learned #1. Yes, when you take on a position like city manager, or deputy city manager, it's important to understand that you will be moving. Let's put a finer point on that, in order to move up, you will need to move out and you will likely be faced with drastically changing situations. Women can and should take risks and prove our ability to rise to the challenge. First we need to stay flexible and realize the art of re-positioning is a key tool in mastering a move. You can probably count on the fact that what you will be doing on the job, is not what you expected to do when you were hired.

In my career I had already made three major moves spanning three states in order to seek growth in my positions within City governments. This included working for some great cities like Portland, Oregon and Ventura, California and experiencing professional city life in the California Bay Area. I have to say this move into city management was one good challenge. By facing declining situations and lack of resources, it was necessary to integrate all that I learned in the past about adapting to change, and to leave behind what I knew worked to discover new ways.

Lesson Learned #2. About the time you think you know everything; you discover that you actually don't. Even though you've handled situations like this before, it's likely not going to be anything like when you managed it the first time. This economic recession proved that true. In fact, it felt like driving my car down a familiar road in a blinding snowstorm with barely working headlights and a half tank of gas. I knew I'd been down this road before and I could make it through to the other side. Yet, in the profession and in the economy, none of us could really see where we were going or where the road would take us.

For city managers in Arizona, the most important thing was to keep a steady hand on the wheel while moving forward. I was hired to manage growth and development and project a bright future for an emerging desert city. Yet, the job at hand was to drastically cut back budgets, reduce the labor force, and help keep the City financially afloat. In fact, it required managing things down; people leaving Arizona with loss of homes and jobs for new opportunities elsewhere. As a city, we were driving slowly through the storm clouds of negative growth in all areas. We used a team approach and came up with new tools and solutions.

Lesson Learned # 3. Invent new tools if the old ones do not work. What tools does a city manager use to deal with ever-changing situations? We have lots of good basic tools including embracing leadership as part of management, developing our people skills, monitoring revenue and service performance and working more efficiently with fewer resources. Yes, this is an important bundle of tools to carry around with you, but even more important is the ability to be flexible and accept change. Women, in order to seek career growth, sometimes – in fact many times – have to leave behind what you know and choose new locations, new strategies and new solutions. You have to lead, not just manage.

So what new tools did we devise to block out the storm? We gave people incentives to leave their job and create a new life for themselves, collapsed departments, ran leaner staff levels, trained people to do new jobs they had never done before, created cross-functional teams to tackle assignments, and changed people's expectations. Also, we planned ahead to make our city organization more sustainable for the future. My job was to help the City be ready for a new economy through diversification and looking for growth industries. We kept our city clean and attractive to visitors and tourists, joined international marketing circles, and created a foreign trade zone. We did not raise taxes, cut public services, or increase fees, but we did learn how to do a whole lot more with remarkably less resources.

It's now 2012, four years later, and we survived and are cautiously optimistic about a new future here in Peoria, Arizona. We have a solid handle on sustainable development and a new economic strategy for the future, and our budget is modestly growing again. Those who were tough and strong (and maybe a little stubborn) hung on and worked through the years of sacrifice in order to be good public servants. But we did learn more about stretching and flexibility than we could ever imagine. We all learned to move ahead, change our business thinking, and create new ways of working with reduced resources while learning new technology. Did I mention I've been at this for thirty years?? I've realized in three decades that I've reinvented myself and my practices many times over. If I can do it, you most certainly can!

So my challenge to all of you women out there is to get moving and grab the great opportunities that are available. You only need to take a moment of risk to realize and seize a possible great opportunity.

Great plans and civilizations were born from a need to survive in difficult environments. Rising to that challenge requires creativity and those solutions create new adaptations.

Appropriate Quote

> "When I thought I couldn't go on, I forced myself to keep going. My success is based on persistence, not luck."
>
> Estee Lauder, Entrepreneur

Key Insight

At times just putting one allegorical foot in front of the other is all we can do. When we don't know the ending of the journey the path seems steeper and longer. By sharing our challenges and trials with others we can lighten the load and hasten the sunshine.

Susan J. Daluddung is the Deputy City Manager for Peoria, Arizona. She has served as the Director of Community Development for Hayward, CA, and Ventura, CA, as the Director of Development Services for Springfield, OR and as the Chief Planner for Portland, OR. She has her PhD and MUP from Portland State University School of Urban Affairs, and her BS from Minnesota State University and is an AICP Certified Planner.

Story Nineteen

When Opportunity Knocks Someone Must Be Listening

As told by Terry Brechtel

WHILE I was City Manager in San Antonio in 2003, the biggest economic development opportunity since AT&T's decision to move their headquarters to San Antonio discreetly floated through my doors in a cloud of secrecy. The story of how San Antonio successfully landed Toyota's 6th Motor Manufacturing Plant on the City's Southside is one of those leadership opportunities filled with lessons for a lifetime and speaks volumes about when the challenge arises - what type of leader will you be?

In the era of post 9/11, while Wall Street was reacting to questions of national security, our economic development team at home was capitalizing on our geographic location in the state, our young and abundant workforce and the opportunity to deploy these resources in higher than average wage jobs.

Through many years in public service I have refined the principal ingredients that make up my leadership style and they were all about to be put to the test.

First of all, because of the size, quality and competitive nature of the opportunity, the environment demanded secrecy. The project code name - "Starbright"- as it came to be known, quickly gained political support from the Governor to the Mayor and County Judge and it was not until Toyota's public announcement that San Antonio was the preferred location, that the finite details of the deal were hammered out. That does not help when you are trying to operate government in an open and transparent environment.

As luck would have it, the Mayor had been working on a balanced growth initiative that included annexing 50 square miles on the City's deep Southside and in the heart of where Toyota was looking to locate. Although it did not start out that way, this annexation became the linchpin to being able to deliver Toyota's most important requirement.

Understanding the requirements to make the deal work became an essential part of our success all while navigating through a third party and competing across the country. Someone had to be actively listening.

The deal killer: Toyota had to have a 3 miles buffer that would restrict residential development around the Toyota plant thus, the city needed to annex to control land use.

And for a City that has a long history of valuing diversity and culture, this was a new experience, we were not only navigating the Japanese culture but just as important we were quickly learning the "Toyota Way"! Understanding this new environment was critical to negotiate in the business climate.

And finally, the key ingredient was our secret weapon: Mrs. Shirane, a relative of Dr. Toyota, brought credibility to our team. The City was now ready to capitalize on a 20 year relationship with Mrs. Shirane, our former Mayor Henry Cisneros was on our team and our sister city of Kumomoto. These relationships brought integrity and trust to the San Antonio name.

Thus Team Toyota was born! It was an **all-inclusive** team that included leadership from every level of government (State, County, City, Utility agencies) and the chambers of commerce (Greater, Hispanic, South.) Never before had our city come together with all levels of government and partners solidly working together to make this opportunity a reality.

The package to attract a company like Toyota can stretch the resources of any single community. As for my part, it quickly became apparent that every agency had to step up to make the deal work. My recommendation to the Council was that the City purchase the land and pay for workforce training while the County and the utility companies participate in infrastructure improvements. The City and County also agreed to grant tax abatements. Lastly, the Governor's office stepped up their contribution from the economic development fund in order to reach the level of incentives needed to be competitive with other cities.

Toyota selected San Antonio to locate their 6th Motor Manufacturing Plant in the US. That was 2003. Since then a lot has happened, but Toyota has kept their promise to San Antonio. Our community is a partner with Toyota and our relationship with Japan is strong. Toyota is now part of the culture of San Antonio and the plant plays a significant part in the manufacturing sector of our economy. The strong bond that was established over 20 years ago continues as part of our history. As a leader for that day and time in history I am proud to have been part of the team that brought Toyota to San Antonio.

Key insight: The only real training for leadership is leadership. There is no substitute for experience, but there are steps you can take in your career that prepare you for leadership roles so when your time comes you can make a difference by what type of leader you will be. Never underestimate the importance of long term investments in relationships and their impact in creating a better future for your city.

Appropriate Quote

> The secret of success in life is to be ready for your opportunity when it comes."
>
> Benjamin Disraeli, Statesman

Key Insight

Once in a great while all of the pieces fall into place – that time when preparation meets opportunity occurs, and good things result. As local government professionals the credit for all the good things goes to others, but the satisfaction of knowing we were ready to open the door makes it all worthwhile.

Terry Brechtel serves as Executive Director of the Alamo Regional Mobility Authority (ARMA) in San Antonio, Texas, responsible for development of over $2 Billion of transportation improvements through toll and non-toll financing. Ms. Brechtel was the first woman named City Manager of the City of San Antonio, Texas in 2001, and held that post until 2004. Ms. Brechtel has held various positions in Finance and Budget throughout her career.

She currently serves on the Board of Directors of the International Bridge Tunnel & Turnpike Association; serves as Co-Chair of the Women and Girls Development Fund of the San Antonio Area Foundation and is Treasurer of the Artist Foundation of San Antonio.

Story Twenty

Sometimes it's Just Hard to Make the Clerk Happy

As told by Dr. Barbara S. Blumenfield

EVERYONE always remembers their first CAO position. For me, it's memorable because I always subscribed to the 'other' interpretation of the *ICMA* acronym – I Can Manage Anything. Confident in my ability, nothing could damper the enthusiasm that enveloped me when I walked into that municipal building for the first time, ready to take on the world. And then, reality quickly set in.

'Reality' for me occurred after spending more than a dozen years working in the public sector for elected officials who represented large local governments. Believing in '*ICMA*' (*I Can Manage Anything),* I had no doubt that working with local officials at any level would be a continuation of what I had already experienced. After all, I had worked in several of the largest local governments in the state – "What could I possible encounter that I hadn't already dealt with?" I naively asked myself.

So when the position of town administrator for the largest town in the state opened up, I decided it was a great opportunity and applied, as did 110 other candidates.

I always believed that once the best candidate was selected, that everyone would be willing to work together in a positive manner for the best interests of the community, including the clerk....right? Not so much!

Let me explain.

At the time of my application, the clerk had been in her position for many years. She didn't report to anyone, set her own schedule and wasn't required to work with the administrator. Still, I had hoped that she might welcome me as the new administrator, since there were so few female administrators in the profession, much less in Wisconsin, right? Wrong again.

The clerk, having spent six months as the 'interim' administrator, had decided, unbeknownst to me at the time, that she not only didn't want a new administrator, but that she really didn't want a woman in that position. Figure that one out.....

And, because the local elected officials were frugal (i.e., did not want to spend money to hire a recruiter) and the administrator position had been vacant for almost six months, the board thought that having the clerk coordinate the selection process for them would be acceptable. Little did they know that she would ultimately try to impact the selection process.

The first part of the process went smoothly enough as the field of candidates was narrowed from 110 candidates to 10 by the board. The board then requested that the clerk arrange interviews for the finalists, which she did, with her own little twist.

The clerk selected a weekend date for the interviews that was acceptable to the board, but what they didn't know was that the letter to the 10 semi-finalists included a caveat that indicated that no exceptions would be made to the final interview date-period. Bottom line was that if the candidates couldn't make that date and only that date, no interview. Period. What I didn't know, was that the clerk somchow *knew* I would be out of town on that date, conducting official business for my then employer, which prompted her to include the 'no exception' language.

But remember, I subscribed to the *ICMA* mantra-I Can Manage Anything! So even though the letter stated that only the clerk should be contacted regarding interviews, I called the board chair and asked if my interview could be arranged for a different date. Thankfully, the board members were quite accommodating, made an exception and changed the date, much to the clerk's displeasure. Ultimately, I was selected as the new administrator, despite the clerk's unsuccessful subtle attempt to usurp the authority of the board and possibly affect the outcome of the selection process.

Unfortunately, that was just her first attempt to undermine my position, not her last!

The Clerk's next attempt to usurp my authority occurred before I even began work. She announced to just about everyone that she would not be vacating the office space assigned to the administrator, which she had commandeered as 'the interim'. Now mind you, we're not talking about the corner office in a high rise building here; we're talking about an almost windowless office that would make most people claustrophobic.

The clerk had graciously decided that I could move into her old office, which she deemed just as acceptable. Need I tell you that even if the administrator's assigned office space had been in a trailer, there was no way the clerk was staying there, rather than returning to her designated office. My thought was that if I couldn't get the clerk to cooperate before I began as the administrator, it would be almost impossible to have a successful working relationship after I got there. Ultimately (and prior to my start date) the clerk determined that it would be in her best interests to relocate (having been made aware of my position by 'others.') Again, the clerk was not happy.

In fact, for the first several months of my tenure, the clerk continued to challenge my authority on a variety of issues – from supervision of clerical personnel to being excluded from closed sessions of the board that dealt with personnel issues. In several instances, the clerk contacted board members, other employees, residents, and, on occasion, anyone who would listen, to bemoan the diminished role of the town clerk due to the role of the administrator.

Eventually, the clerk adjusted to the new balance of power, but it was not a smooth transition – for her. For me, it was an excellent learning experience for so many reasons and solidified my commitment to professional public administration. Ultimately, we developed an acceptable working relationship, even after she became a member of the board!

In retrospect, even though it might sometimes be hard to make the clerk happy, I still adhere to *ICMA*!

Appropriate Quote

> "Some of us learn from other people's mistakes and the rest of us have to be other people."
>
> Zig Ziglar, Author

Key Insight

There are two schools of thought on personality and role conflicts. I Can Manage Anything CEOs invest incredible time, energy and enthusiasm to bring folks into the fold. Sometimes it even works...

Dr. Barb Blumenfield ("WOO" to her ICMA Board Colleagues) worked in the public sector for 25 years for a number of communities in the greater Milwaukee (WI) area as a City Administrator; Town Administrator; HR Director; Director of Administrative Services; Liaison for a County Executive/Board and Senior Legislative Analyst. She also served as a Regional VP for CIGNA Health Care, as well as a consultant for both public and private clients; taught graduate courses at three local universities and served as a Regional VP on the ICMA Executive Board. Although retired, she still teaches for ICMA as part of the ELDP and serves as the chair of the Board of Zoning Appeals in her hometown.

Story Twenty One

An Honorable Calling

As told by Dr. Penelope Culbreth-Graft

AS a little girl, I sat at the dinner table with my sister and three brothers, hearing my parents debate who had more power—the County Sheriff or the Chief of Police. My father worked as a police officer and my mother as a deputy sheriff. My desire to serve the public began in a home environment where local government service was as common as meat and potatoes.

My father gave his life for public service, suffering a brain aneurysm while transporting a prisoner. He died at 48. What I remember most about his sense of duty was how fully he gave himself to his community, without fear for his own life. While his death was not at the hand of another, his department deemed it job-related. At his funeral, I heard amazing stories of how he went above duty and helped turn around drug abusers and youth traveling down the wrong path.

Thanks to my father's help in obtaining my first job at the age of 15, I worked as a Library Page, repairing books. That launched my local government career, taking me to eleven cities and one Indian Nation. My path included police cadet, secretary, purchasing agent, administrative analyst, assistant city manager, tribal government manager, and city manager.

I kept my family name until I married and divorced within a short time. The divorce had nothing to do with my work but my ex-spouse's infidelity caused me to ponder why I had abandoned my family name. I reclaimed my maiden name. Reconnecting with my father's memory led me to promise never again to abandon his name.

My first city manager position was with a two-square mile coastal community in California. My six-year old son and I felt at home with a City Council made up primarily of grandfatherly types. It was in this town that I met the man of my dreams. Within 60 days of meeting him, I became the wife of William G. Graft.

One of my council members, bothered by my last-minute wedding announcement and short engagement expressed concern that I should not marry. His reason?

"We can't have *Graft* in city hall. We'll be the laughing stock of the county."

I assured him it would be okay, as I intended to keep my maiden name and hyphenate with Graft. His objection dissolved. My Council embraced my new husband. If only the IRS would have embraced him. . . .

After filing our first joint tax return, William entertained a visit from the IRS. The IRS accused him of taking the identity of a dead man—William G. Culbreth—my deceased father. It did not take long for the explanation to exonerate him. The IRS recanted the accusation, apologizing that rarely did they see the breadwinner of a family being the woman much less keeping any part of her maiden name, and marrying a man with the same first name and middle initial as her father.

Two cities later, I took the number two position with the City of San Diego. The newspaper announced, "Graft comes to City Hall." My mother-in-law wrote a scathing letter to the editor, decrying the attack on her son's honorable family name.

"He's from a proud heritage of Grafts—a strong German name." I was still new to the family and had never counseled her on the dangers of responding to the press from a defensive position. The press never spoke of it again.

Four years later, a Southern California Indian Tribe invited me to serve as its Tribal Government Manager. "We want you to create for us a democratic form of government from scratch," the Tribal Council said. It took just a couple of weeks of introducing me as Dr. Penelope Culbreth-Graft before the Tribal Chairman asked me, "Why do you hyphenate with your maiden name when your married name is so beautiful?"

"What do you mean? That would leave me with Graft . . . in government," I said.

"Graft is a wonderful blending of two trees of life to make a stronger, more resilient growth."

From that day forward, we agreed the Tribe would call me Penny Graft, exchanging ten letters for the tongue-twisting 23 letters.

Some 32 years after I began my public service career, my only child has taken up the mantle of public service. Working for his second city, Michael bears his father's name but his mother's love for serving communities. When in junior high, he told me he was glad he had a different name because his science teacher read a news article to the class that quoted his mother on the impact of El Nino on the town. "It would have been so embarrassing if they knew I was your son." Now, he tells me, "How could I want to be anything other than a city manager when that is what we know and love to do?"I am grateful for my parents' public service and am proud of my son's career choice. What I have learned over the years is that a name is only a name and what they call you is not as important what you are called to do.

The call to public service by any name is called '*honorable.*'

Appropriate Quote

> "If you want more, you have to require more from yourself."
>
> Dr. Phil, Motivational Author and
> Talk Show Host

Key Insight

It is always a joy to see a second or third generation coming into local government. The message of honor and service resonates just a bit more when the challenges and frustrations are known in advance and the path is chosen anyway.

Dr. Penelope Culbreth-Graft is a retired, credentialed City Manager. She served in public agencies for over 32 years in 11 cities and one Indian Reservation. Her positions included City Manager and Assistant City Manager in cities ranging in population from 12,000 to 1.2 million in California, Arizona, and Colorado. Dr. Culbreth-Graft taught for five universities over 18 years in the Masters' programs in Public Administration and Criminal Justice. She has a Doctorate in Public Administration from the University of La Verne; a Master's of Public Administration from the California State University Consortium; and, two Bachelor's degrees from California Polytechnic University, Pomona.

Story Twenty Two

It All Goes Back to the Playground

As told by Kim Dobbs

IT all goes back to the playground…

While we may have learned everything we needed to know in Kindergarten, the finer skills for a career in city management were honed on the playground.

In the last few years, I have unwittingly drawn the attention of a highly opinionated, self-appointed, self-proclaimed and vocal "watch-dog." Initially, I thought to myself, "Hey, this is not a problem; I have nothing to hide. Everything is in order. She will see that she has been mistaken and will apologize for her ridiculous accusations." More than two years and 61 public information requests later, I am still waiting for an apology. Boy was I naïve.

Frustrated in her attempts to find or expose anything amiss, the citizen escalated her efforts and became rather creative with her interpretation of events and information. Never mind that what she routinely said and continues to say in public meetings and writes in an internet blog and mass email messages to media, community leaders and all of the city staff is inaccurate or false, she still gets the opportunity to express herself.

Much to my mortification, in response to her persistence, her accusations were referred to the Texas Rangers for review in the summer of 2010. As expected, subsequent to their review of the 251 pages of information the citizen provided, the Texas Rangers' conclusion was that, "No evidence of a violation of criminal law was found. No investigation will be initiated..."

That's when the citizen accused the local District Attorney, the Texas Rangers, the Mayor and the Texas Attorney General of being a part of the conspiracy that might possibly extend to the White House.

In addition to her ongoing public criticism, the citizen subsequently broadened her accusations to include other city staff and City Council members. In public service, we learn very early on that the high road is always the preferred route; we simply cannot, will not and do not engage in this type of dialogue. It would be unprofessional and impolite, right? We hold our head up, keep a steady gaze, sit quietly, hope and pray that the public will recognize nonsense for what it is.

One evening at home, my ruminating on this experience led to me to announce to my husband that, "I AM a Weeble!"

Understandably, he did not quite follow how I went from expressing my frustration at the unfairness of the situation to referencing the egg-shaped Hasbro toy from the seventies.

[You remember what a Weeble is, right? Sing along with me in your head... "Weebles wobble but they don't fall down"...]

Simply put, you cannot knock a Weeble down. Wikipedia says, "Tipping an egg-shaped Weeble causes a weight located at the bottom-center to be lifted off the ground. Once released, gravitational force (called torque) bring [sic] the Weeble back into an upright position, though inertia causes the toy to wobble briefly before coming to a standstill."

By design, the Weeble eternally rocks back to the upright position. Whenever someone tries to push you down or cast aside your ideas, model the Weeble. *Be determined and centered, never give up, never lose sight of your goal; remain steadfast and you'll finish upright.*

This citizen's assaults, which by the way strongly resemble some of the meanest playground bullies' antics that I ever knew, reminded me of playing Dodge-ball during recess. Jump to the right, jump to the left, lean over…all sorts of contortions in hopes of avoiding a crushing blow from the ball being hurled at you.

Dodge-ball victory belonged to the child who remained unscathed. Here the general parallels to city management are several: *Agility is good. Being slow is bad. Being indecisive can result in a blow to the face. Having good aim is a real bonus. Strength can be conquered by intelligence. You don't have to cream somebody to win. Being a good sport makes people want to play with you again at recess the next day.*

Thinking about dodging balls brought to mind comforting words from a friend during the height of one of the citizen watchdog's more vicious attacks. She said, "Strong women build a firm foundation with the bricks that others have thrown at them." This mental picture was encouraging and further affirmed my belief that being a Weeble in public service is a very good thing indeed.

Note: before offering my friend's remark here, I researched it and learned that she may have taken a bit of liberty with a quote attributed to American television journalist, David Brinkley, who said "A successful man is one who can lay a firm foundation with the bricks others have thrown at him." Wise words.

Another playground experience that prepared me for a career in city management was Red Rover. In Red Rover, two teams of children lined up at opposing sides of the field and held hands/locked arms. Each group conferred and took turns yelling an invitation to ask the child who they perceived to be the least threat to run over.

The invitee would leave their line and run for all they were worth at what they perceived to be the weakest link in the opposing line hoping to break through. Being one of the smaller children in my class, very early in the game I frequently heard the chant, "Red Rover, Red Rover, let Kimmie come over!"

I learned that to overcome size and strength and to find success at Red Rover, I had to be smart and choose my angles wisely. I also learned that it took at least two people to "hold the line." This is true in public service. *You are only as strong as your line and the bonds you form with your team. Choose your team wisely. Plan before you act. And always run at it with everything you've got.*

Two other playground favorites that helped to prepare me for a career in city management were the Hula-hoop and the Footsie. You had to be quick in line to get these coveted toys at recess check out.

The Hula-hoop by Wham-O was entertaining and brilliant in its simplicity. Like the Weeble, the laws of physics made the Hula-hoop fun. A Hula-hoop was a large hoop that you put around your waist and gave a good whirl. Then with skill, agility, concentration and stamina you kept the hoop spinning around your waist by moving your hips and body.

In addition to determination, the Hula-hoop bred a healthy respect for the power of momentum and balance. How many times did you have to pick that Hula-hoop up from your ankles and try again and again to get a good session going? And how many times did inattention cause the hoop to waver or go off balance and fall? *Balance, concentration and determination are all required if you want to Hula-hoop with the big kids. Just like city management.*

The other playground toy was the lesser known Footsie. Some might recognize a re-tooled version of the Footsie called "Skip-It." A personal favorite, my Footsie was red and had a ring that you placed around one ankle. Attached to the ring was a rope or chord that had a weighted ball or bell at the other end. Similar to the Hula-hoop, you had to give a good swing to get the Footsie going. The ball would pull the chord taut and as it would swing around, you had to jump over it with the foot that was not attached to the ring.

The multi-tasking and juggling skills we learned with the Footsie are invaluable today as we balance the many demands on our time and resources. It only took one miscalculated hop to ruin a great Footsie run. *The ability to multi-task and juggle resources equals success. If the left side doesn't know what the right side is doing, you will likely get tripped up.*

Although individually played, the Footsie and Hula-hoop were very social games. Rarely did a child Footsie or Hula-hoop alone.

Clusters of like-minded children gathered in specific areas of the playground to visit and challenge each other while they played, enjoying one another's successes and consoling one another when needed.

One final playground game that provided wisdom and insight into what was to come in a career in city management was the game of "Gossip" also known as "Telephone Operator." In Gossip, the children sat cross-legged on the ground in a circle. The leader whispered a statement consisting of a couple of sentences, into her neighbor's ear. That child whispered the leader's message in her other neighbor's ear and so on until the message made its way all around the circle. The final child who received the whispered statement proclaimed aloud to the group the message as she heard it.

Predictably, everyone squealed with delight when the leader announced what her initial statement was and the two statements were compared. Rarely were they remotely alike; the sillier the distortion the better. Take your pick as to where in local government this phenomenon occurs.

In a zoning case, a gentleman wanted to build an art/woodworking studio on a vacant property that would require a zoning change. The gentleman was an artist who carved beautiful doors, furniture for sanctuaries, stair-case finishes, etc.

The required notices were published and mailed to neighboring property owners. On the night of the public hearing, the room was filled with neighbors and members of a church located in the vicinity. They were outraged that the City would consider allowing a saw-mill to be located in our city. A saw-mill! (Outcome: denied.)

Another resident applied for a conditional use permit to build an over-sized barn of stone and hewn-timbers, including a green house, to complement the existing home and guest house and to store supplies for property maintenance. By the night of the public hearing, the rumor mill had transformed the proposed structure into a huge metal party-barn for parties and receptions and the neighbors did not like it one bit. (Outcome: approved after much clarification.)

A colleague tells a story about a comment he made to his wife while their family was driving around town one day. He showed her a vacant corner and explained that a well-respected Indian development firm was planning for a strip shopping center there. Imagine his surprise when several days later, he heard his young son in the backseat confide to a friend that there was going to be an Indian strip club coming soon.

In the game of Gossip as in our profession, a clear concise and simple statement has the greatest chance of successful transmission. Chances of success increase if the audience is considered in the delivery. A clear message is important in everything we do.

Another useful "Gossip" lesson is to plan for what happens to the message once it leaves your lips, web-page, press release or internal memo. *Part of the challenge is in the message and the other in the delivery. And then don't be surprised if your words are re-gifted to you in a totally different package. Be prepared.*

Unfortunately, or fortunately, the playground was not just a place of fun and games. The playground was also where we learned the intellectual and social skills to handle friendly disagreements as well as deal with bullies.

We normally employed these skills peaceably without adult intervention. It's no coincidence that the teacher was rarely anywhere nearby when a bully chose their moment to strike.

An article written for children on KidsHealth.org suggests the following tips for dealing with bullies: "avoid the bully; stand tall and be brave; feel good about you; get a buddy/be a buddy; ignore the bully; stand up for yourself; don't bully back; don't show your feelings and tell an adult."

Although good advice for a child, sadly not all of these tips translate into our professional arena. In most instances, children seem to grow out of bullying. They develop the self-esteem or confidence that they need to interact appropriately and rationally with others. They learn to treat others as they wish to be treated.

But, it's been my recent personal experience that some do not.

What my resident critic helped me to recognize however, is that the playground did equip me with a survival mentality. Without realizing it, through play and socialization, we gained the experience needed to address the challenges associated with the continuous harangue sometimes encountered in public service.

On the playground, playing with the Weeble, Hula-hoop and Footsie, participating in games such as Dodge-ball, Red Rover and Gossip and dealing with skirmishes and bullies on our own terms imbued us with valuable skills. The skills learned at play should not be underestimated. Reflect on your own hours spent on the playground. You may have never enjoyed the wobbling of a Weeble; your toys and games may have provided experiences different than mine. But I imagine the parallels are apparent – several principles that we employ daily in our public service professions were first revealed on the playground.

Playground lessons summarized:
Weeble – Dogged determination
Dodge-ball – Skillful adaptation
Red Rover – Intelligent commitment
Hula Hoop- Balanced momentum
Footsie – Coordinated communication
Gossip – Concise message, consistent delivery
Bullies – Dignified bravery

Appropriate Quote

> "Risk! Risk anything! Care no more for the opinions of others, for those voices. Do the hardest thing on earth for you. Act for yourself. Face the truth."
>
> Katherine Mansfield, Author

Key Insight

The games on the playground of the professional local government administrator are played for keeps. Rarely are there do-overs and being thrown out can mean just what it says. Most folks play nice.

Occasionally one does not and when (not if) that time comes it helps to know your own strengths and the rules of that particular game.

Kim Dobbs has served as the Assistant City Manager for Heath for over thirteen years. As part of the executive team, she works with the City Manager, Council, appointed boards and commissions and staff to serve the immediate needs and plan for the future benefit of the citizens of Heath. Kim has worked in two other Texas cities, serving as an Administrative Analyst in Waco and as an Independent Research Consultant in Tyler. Additionally, she worked for seven years for the Texas Workers' Compensation Commission, ultimately serving in senior management positions in field offices in Tyler and in Dallas. Kim is a member of the Texas City Management Association (TCMA), the International City/County Management Association (ICMA) and the Urban Management Assistants of Texas. She is a past Chairman of the Texas Municipal League's Small Cities Advisory Council, of which she has been a member for thirteen years.

Story Twenty Three

The Glass Ceiling

As told by Jennifer Fadden

THE Glass Ceiling. This term is used in popular culture to describe the unbreakable barrier in a woman's career because of the perception that we cannot devote the time and energy away from family to have a successful career and that we are not capable of being executives because we are more emotional and less decisive than our male counterparts. In my experience as a city manager, these views are not insurmountable hurdles. Rather they are unique strengths that have proven to be assets in my career.

In 1994, as a junior in college, I was as familiar with the term "the glass ceiling" as I was with the terms "ad valorem tax" and "eminent domain." However, at that same time, with the experience of seeing my father use ethics, service and passion to guide him as a city councilman, and the fact that my mother had a career of her own, I chose city management as my career. I wanted to be part of something greater than any individual accomplishment and the fact that I would be pushing up against the proverbial glass ceiling never even crossed my mind.

Early in my career, I was fortunate to work for a strong female leader who illustrated for me that gender had nothing to do with one's success or ability to make a lasting mark on a community.

Congresswoman Kay Granger was mayor of Fort Worth, Texas when I went to work in her office. Although not terribly strategic on my part at the time, working on the policy-making side of the business gave me an understanding and appreciation for how, as many in the industry call it, the sausage gets made. Working for a strong female leader also illustrated for me that possibilities were endless. A number of female staff that worked for Mayor Granger have gone on to great career and personal success. Mayor Granger also encouraged me to stay in local government, where I could pursue and hopefully achieve my goal of becoming a city manager.

Many years later, as my career trajectory was headed in a 45 degree angle, I finally came in contact with the glass ceiling. I heard things like, "You're so young; You're a woman; You're a mother." These things were said to me in the context of becoming a city manager – almost as if it were impossible to be all of those things AND a city manager. I thought to myself, "The same concerns wouldn't have been voiced if I were a man!"

Although it bothered me, I remembered the work my father did as a city council member – how the most important victories were often the hardest to attain. During his most difficult times in office, he leaned heavily on our family, teaching me that gender is not a demerit and family is not an anchor.

I have come to realize that having people I love and trust in my corner, who not only help me at times think through decisions, but who also support me no matter what, is priceless in this job. Instead of being an energy drain, my family is a source of inspiration that I use at work on a daily basis. Living in the city where I work, I get to see my children enjoying the fruits of our labor. They play on the playgrounds we provide and they spend much of their summer at the library engaged in meaningful programs designed to entertain and enrich their lives. It is through family that I am able to experience city services as a customer and realize the tremendous impact those services have on our citizens on a daily basis.

We all know human beings are emotional creatures. Males in executive positions have historically left their emotions at the door in the workplace. However, that may not be the best for the overall success of an organization. A 2010 McKinsey & Company study of all industry sectors worldwide found that companies with more women in leadership positions had better financial returns compared to companies with no women in leadership positions. Gender diversity in leadership brings behaviors that might not otherwise occur in organizations, including collaborative decision making and the nurturing of the organizational environment.

But helping to promote a collaborative, nurturing environment does have a potential downside: as women, we tend to become personally attached to our organizations, and therefore we tie professional successes and failures to our personal identity. A common piece of advice I hear is, "You cannot take these things personally," and "They don't really know you as a person."

Seasoned managers have long told me that people in this profession must have thick skin to do what we do, but it is only after several years of actually sitting in the manager's chair that I have come to really understand that. In this profession, you typically never hear when things are going right. But it feels like you are hearing it from everywhere when things go wrong. You have to take criticism in stride and work hard to focus on positives—in whatever form or fashion they come in.

As in any profession, it seems that women still must work twice as hard if they want to break through the glass ceiling. I believe that those elements that the world has told us are the reasons why we aren't as successful as our male counterparts – family commitments and leading with our hearts – are not excuses for second place. They can and should be our sources for strength and inspiration. Like the Athenian Oath states,

"...we will fight for the ideals and sacred things of the city both alone and with many; ...in all these ways we will transmit this city, not only not less, but greater and more beautiful than it was transmitted to us."

The Athenian Oath was not written for men only. It was written for those people who were so inspired to fight for those ideals that are best for their cities and communities, no matter what their gender.

Appropriate Quote

> "Go confidently in the direction of your dreams. Live the life you have imagined."
>
> Henry David Thoreau, Author, Philosopher

Key Insight

Public service is a high calling and it calls to those who dream of ideals and character. Either alone or in concert with others, working to overcome barriers or raise ceilings makes a difference. Sometimes the difference is for us, and at times it is for those we transmit the city to.

Jennifer Fadden has more than 15 years' experience in local government leadership. She joined Colleyville, Texas as City Manager in March 2009. She holds a Bachelors of Arts degree in Political Science and a Master's of Public Administration from the University of North Texas. Jennifer is active in her community as a member of Leadership North Texas, the Colleyville Chamber of Commerce Board of Directors, the Colleyville Lions Club, the Northeast Leadership Forum and the Girl Scouts of Texas Oklahoma Plains Board Development Committee.

Story Twenty Four

A Meaningful Memento

As told by Karen Daly

NATURAL disasters. It's one of the few circumstances where city managers can make the news and positively demonstrate some of the skills that make our profession so essential to successful communities. Now I have the pleasure of serving in the Gulf Coast region of Texas. An area that is prone to natural disasters – most commonly in the form of hurricanes. I also bring an unusual perspective to disasters – I am a big fan! I believe it brings out the best in problem-solving and responsiveness of each and every city employee. It allows us to show how our skills make a difference in our city.

I have had the opportunity to work a hurricane that produced 140,000 cubic yards of debris; an ice storm that paralyzed the city without power for 3 days; and, the aftermath of Hurricane Katrina that required the hosting of over 200 evacuees. I actually look fondly back on each of these incidents because I remain so proud of how the employees responded and our ability to respond quickly to unanticipated and unprecedented needs of our residents and visitors.

This story is about the Hurricane Katrina aftermath. After days of watching rescues and the shelter conditions after Hurricane Katrina on television, we received word that our county was being asked to host some of the evacuees from New Orleans. The County Judge convened a group to put together a plan of response. As City Manager of the County seat, I was asked to attend the meeting that was held on the Saturday morning of Labor Day weekend. Not having been provided much information at all, we planned in a vacuum. We didn't know how they would arrive, how many would arrive, or what condition they would be in. We were simply asked if we would take Katrina refugees and shelter them and of course, we said "yes."

The initial intake was established at our local YMCA. When word went out about the location, we were completely unprepared for the community response. Instead of deploying our on-duty police officers to look out for an incoming bus of dislocated persons, we had to immediately set up traffic control at the YMCA to better manage the flood of cars with donations. While communities were flooded in Louisiana, our community of Greenville, Texas was flooded with donations! Fortunately, the Greenville YMCA had three racquetball courts. Within 7 hours of opening the intake facility, the three racquetball courts were filled up over 5 feet high. Imagine the looks on the faces of the volunteers who were sent in to sort through the donations!

I became the intake facility coordinator before noon and within four hours we were ready for what we thought might be a busload of evacuees. And there we waited – for the next six hours. During that waiting period, we perfected our intake process: we reprinted our intake forms, set up a medical screening area and we created a "spa" atmosphere in the bathroom and shower areas. We even had designated "beauty divas" who secured every donated soft robe, slipper, towel and nice smelling soap to give our new arrivals a relaxing experience and a warm welcome. If there was something missing, we had collected a list of people who could be called and any type of request could be made.

Our intake operation lasted about 36 hours and we welcomed two busloads of evacuees during that time. We were able to convert the intake facility back to a functional YMCA within a week. Remember? there were over 10,000 square feet of donations to sort out. How lucky our community was to have a Rubbermaid manufacturing plant. Rubbermaid donated over 500 totes that enabled the volunteers to sort, and for our new residents, to take all of their new belongings with them.

We then turned our attention and support to the temporary shelter that was established at the County fairgrounds. Within three days of operation, it was clear that the County didn't have enough personnel to adequately oversee the shelter that was being managed by the Salvation Army. Once again, the County Judge asked me to become a shift commander at the shelter.

Trying to hold down my "day job" as a city manager, meant that I either took the early morning or evening shift. Both shifts had their pros and cons. The morning was quiet and all I had to do was rouse up all of the school-aged children and make sure they were dressed and ready when the school bus came to pick them up. While it was fun waving goodbye to them and telling them to have a good day at school, it was absolutely miserable trying to get them to wake up. The kids' sleep patterns were disrupted by the noise and number of people in the shelter and they were not getting enough quality sleep. I finally negotiated a later bus pickup time with the school district so I could ensure we got them all to school every day. By the fourth day as morning shift commander, it was getting better with the school bus but I should have knocked on wood.

That following weekend as I arrived at the shelter on Sunday morning, I was told by the Salvation Army employee that two of our "residents" had come in after curfew and disrupted the sleep of everyone in their building. So I located the residents, told them they had broken the rules and that they were no longer allowed to stay at our shelter. I asked them to pack their belongings and tell me where they wanted to go. They said, "San Antonio" and so I called the bus station, bought them tickets, called one of my stand-by volunteers (who also happened to be a City Councilmember) and asked if he would drive them to the bus station. Fortunately, he brought his Suburban because the number of Rubbermaid totes that they had amassed in less than a week was very impressive!

After that ejection, I was the shift manager who was feared (which was OK by me since I was far younger than most of the evacuees!) At this point, I switched to the evening shift and shared responsibilities with the Fire Chief. Now when I worked the evening shift, there were numerous requests to sort through – mostly for batteries and cigarettes. Some of the evacuees had found jobs in the community and would not get back to the shelter until after dinner had been served. We quickly found we needed some "a la carte" items to ensure everyone was fed at night. The washing machines were maxed out at night and so we had to create rules for washing clothes to ensure everyone had an opportunity to do laundry. There was never a dull moment with 200 residents and almost as many volunteers each evening.

My favorite night for working at the shelter was Wednesday. In Texas, Wednesday night is church night and we had two pastors who would come and hold service at the baseball field at the fairgrounds. Aaaah, the peace and calm that stayed throughout the night after the church service had me following the pastors to their cars and asking them to come and hold a service every night!

Eventually, we decided we needed to close the shelter and compel some of the evacuees to make decisions about what they were going to do. Everyone successfully made living arrangements or was able to locate family and reunite. As we closed the shelter, I was struck by the magnitude of the generosity of our community. It continues to make me so proud of my profession and the positive impact we are able to have on people's lives. I have one memento left from my Katrina experience. It is a Styrofoam statue of a woman and a flower. It was given to me by one of the more senior evacuees as she was leaving the shelter to reunite with the rest of her family in Houston. She came with no belongings but used the $25 Wal-Mart Card given to her by the Red Cross to buy me a thank-you gift. That gesture stands in my memory as signifying the importance of why we serve and that statue will always be proudly displayed in my office!

Appropriate Quote

"It is the sweet, simple things of life which are the real ones after all."

Laura Ingalls Wilder, Author

Key Insight

Local government professionals do not win trips to Hawaii or get success bonuses. Occasionally there is a plaque or even an ICMA Award. Mostly the mementoes that matter are those that are the most personal and never make the news. They are the ones we treasure in our hearts. They are real.

Karen Daly is Assistant City Manager in Sugar Land, Texas. She has 27 years' experience in city management and served as Greenville's city manager for four years. Daly began her career with the North Central Texas COG then worked at the cities of Arlington and Longview, Texas. She is an active member of ICMA and TCMA. She is President of The Arc of Fort Bend County and belongs to the Sugar Land Exchange Club. Daly holds master's degrees in Urban Affairs and Social Work Administration from the University of Texas-Arlington. Daly and husband, Steve, have two daughters. To keep her sanity, she plays soccer.

Story Twenty Five

The Evolution of a Mom-a-ger

As told by Jamie Laughter

IT all started with my disdain for shoulder pads. Being a child of the eighties, I witnessed the social disaster that was shoulder pads when my mother abandoned her nursing uniform to pursue real estate. I watched her morph into the era's prominent stereotype on the television set of what a working woman should look like. Her wardrobe was quickly taken over with a wide array of blazers, each with its own set of foam shoulder pads that transformed her feminine hour glass figure to that of the local high school quarterback ready for the big Friday night game. I hated the shoulder pads and everything they represented, but I have to say that the message did sink in to my impressionable brain - it's a man's world and if you want to succeed you have to be one or look and act like one.

Fast forward eighteen years later when I applied for my first job in municipal management. A town had incorporated just three years earlier in the county I grew up in and they were hiring for their second manager. At this stage I had been working in government for six years and had completed my Masters in Public Administration four hours away in Raleigh, North Carolina.

Public service was an ethic rooted deeply in my upbringing and family heritage. Choosing it as a career appealed to me at the most basic of philosophic levels. It had always appealed to me to be a part of bettering the community in the public interest.

I was excited at the glimmer of opportunity to move back with my husband and young daughter to serve a community near home. During my second interview things seemed to be going very well until one councilman pulled out a note pad. He turned red as he began to ask me about my husband and child and informed me that "if you take this job, you will ruin your marriage and your child will not know your name."

I was not naive that this type of attitude exists in the workplace, but I have always been surprised when I found myself witnessing it. By this point in my career, I had been blessed with several great bosses that were supportive, fair and interested in my professional development. I also had experiences that were not so rosy. I briefly had a boss who was more interested in complimenting my lip color or my figure than whether I was good at my job. His habit of asking me to come sit in his office so he'd have something pretty to look at had me networking my way out of there the first week I started.

Knowing that there are still those out there who think very little of women's capabilities is one thing, but going head to head with one still requires tact and grace to preserve one's own dignity. I carefully maneuvered through the councilman's attempts to scare me away from the job and received the offer that same week. Clearly I had the support of at least most of the board and the other four did not seem to share his opinion. In fact, my new mayor pro tem was a strong female role model that had served and retired from a local manufacturing facility having achieved a management level job in her career there.

While I knew the one councilman was wrong to categorize me by my gender, I have to say I worried that the public might agree with him. I was a young mother stepping into a big new role professionally; I felt uneasy about whether I would be forced to embrace one role at the sacrifice of the other. That small worry was not helped when I moved and quickly heard rumors about myself through the ever reliable small town grapevine. Apparently, the Town had hired "some young, unqualified single mother" and there were concerns that with an all-female staff there would be "catfights in town hall." My age, gender, being a young mother and even my marriage seemed to hang over my head as if I could not stand alone with the resume I had worked hard to build while juggling school and work. Even so, my first days in the town were a warm reception and I knew it was my responsibility to dive in and prove myself.

I felt that I had to be careful to keep work life and home life distinct and it made me uneasy at times where they seemed to bleed together. I worried that perception would undermine my professional gains and undermine my ability to be effective in implementing policy. One of the first tests for me was the first snow that same year. While all roads weren't terrible the school system and my daughter's daycare were closed. I had a meeting with a developer scheduled and had no options for her to be watched by someone else so she was going to have to come in with me. Bella was almost two and was still adjusting from the move. My staff offered to watch Bella while I went into the meeting, but shortly after we started you could hear her whimpers from the conference room. I was distracted by her while trying to answer the developer's questions and feeling like a rotten mom ignoring her. I finally just stood up, walked out of the room and returned with her on my hip. She laid her head on my shoulder quietly and I walked over to the developer's plans and started giving them the clear answers they needed and her presence didn't seem to bother them. It occurred to me that day that by doing what was right as a mom and as a professional without a wall in between, I was actually doing both jobs better.

A couple of years later I would find myself in a situation that almost forced me to completely blur the distinction between career woman and mom. The Friday I went into labor with my second daughter, Mady, was the last day of work for my administrative assistant. She had been offered a job that would be a promotion for her with a nearby town. While I was sad to lose her, I was proud that she was advancing in her career. My small staff had just gotten smaller. On top of that, I was supposed to be out for at least 6 full weeks myself.

Needless to say, 48 hours after Mady came into the world, she was with me in the office making copies of job applications and moving the process along to get someone hired.

One of my staff walked in the office asking how my weekend had been from behind the screen at the copier. She turned the corner at the copier only to stop and stare at me with infant sleeping in one arm and the other shuffling job applications. I realize that it may sound extreme, but I can honestly say the memory is one that still makes me smile because it illustrated my life at this point so well. I found myself in a situation where there seemed to be little choice in what to do. I had a responsibility to nurture Mady's new little life. I also felt the responsibility to my staff not to leave them with two positions down for longer than it would take to get someone hired. Both roles were important parts of me.

Working a few hours a day over the coming weeks with Mady in tow went very well. I felt the tension between my responsibilities as mother and manager begin to release as I settled into a routine that allowed me to balance both. I also began to see that the same qualities that make me feel like a good mom were playing out to make me feel like a good boss. I wouldn't put aside Mady's needs to meet those at work; but I also wasn't willing to walk away and not worry about letting down my staff either. And, really, as I look back the connection between being a mom and being a manager has always been there. One of the reasons I chose public service is because I want to be a part in making our communities places to live and thrive. That drive is based in my belief in the future and the world I want my children to grow up in. I also chose my career because I wanted to have a job as a means to have a family someday and provide for my children.

Even in day to day practice the two worlds naturally collide. I find myself some days worrying over whether I am making sure my children receive the right education for their future. At work I find myself pondering if I am insuring the correct training for my staff so that they can do their jobs in the most efficient way possible and progress along their career paths. At times I find myself feeling like I can't win in negotiating a disagreement between my daughters. There are days I feel just as helpless navigating discord between my staff. The essentials are truly the same and I don't think that they are rooted in maternal instincts alone. As I look back over my own managers of both genders, the ones that I admire most – and that I was most satisfied working for – where the ones that also happened to be, or would have been, great parents. People know when you care, and people sense when you only care about yourself.

I could never say that I make the correct decision every time and in management you have to set a course and move forward almost constantly, but I can say that with each decision I do care about the impacts and outcomes for everyone involved. Just as I want the best for Bella and Mady, I want the best for my staff and those in my community. I realize that the results of my decisions will not always be fair, nor will they always be easy. I will at least try, with my mindset truly rooted in what is best for all, to take in the big picture before making those decisions.

For me, success is achieved when I see my children, or my office, functioning so well I'm not necessary in the moment. It is the reward of having coordinated the groundwork to get to that point that makes me feel accomplished. It is not to say that boundaries between work and personal life are not required. Indeed, there is potential catastrophe from bringing the stressors of home to work, just as there are consequences to bringing home work stressors. I think what I have found within myself is the permission to be comfortable being the same woman in both roles and acknowledging that those elements are part of who I am in all areas of my life. I'm a person and I can't be compartmentalized.

You can't function without constantly learning in municipal management because change is always happening. You have to adapt at the same fast paced rate. As I find myself approaching the midpoint in my career, I find that the lessons so far have less to do with the important and necessary practicalities of technology or policy and more to do with learning to embrace the principles that brought me to public service in the first place. I care about people — the ones in my home and the ones that aren't. It has occurred to me that the shoulder pad wearing career pioneers before me fought for social and corporate change with the same principle of changing the future in mind. Their work has opened the door for women like me to have the opportunity to approach municipal management without overwhelming stigma, so that our unique talents and principles could drive our work success. And ultimately, it isn't about wearing shoulder pads and trying to be something or someone we are not. It isn't about choosing to be a mother or a manager, it is about choosing to be authentic to who we are as a person and embracing those qualities that make us successful.

Appropriate Quote

> "You gain strength, courage and confidence by every experience in which you really stop to look fear in the face. You are able to say to yourself, "I lived through this. I can take the next thing that comes along." You must do the thing you think you cannot do."
>
> Eleanor Roosevelt, American First Lady

Key Insight

Being a local government professional is one of the true 24/7 jobs around. Especially in a small community there often simply is no one else to do the job or fill in. That means it truly becomes a family affair. Kids get dragged to weekend events in the park, spouses to dinners and mixers and the whole family to community celebrations. The Bible says to "Train up a child in the way they should go, and when they are old they will not depart from it." Perhaps that applies to public service, especially when they start at 48 hours old.

Jaime Laughter has been in government service for twelve years with six years as the Town Manager for the Town of Mills River in North Carolina. She has a Master's in Public Administration, a Bachelor of Science in Political Science and a Minor in Geology from North Carolina State University. Her accomplishments include being the N.C. Women's Transportation Seminar Member of the Year in 2003, receiving her AICP Certification in 2006, and being elected Board President, 2010-2012 for the Children and Family Resource Center. She is a North Carolina native and continues to reside there with her daughters, Zorabella and Madeline.

Story Twenty-Six

The Need for Professional Bonding

As told by Nadine Levin

Prologue

IT'S 1976, and I'm on the move. I'm roaming among the other attendees at my first city managers' state meeting, new to both the profession and my position in the city manager's office in a midsized Midwestern city. I'm excited—and a little anxious—anticipating the conference sessions and small group discussions. But right now, in secret, I am mostly longing to meet other young women in the profession. I need professional bonding experiences.

Walking into the opening session, I'm struck by the vast number of males. Scanning the room, I realize there is a near total absence of females—of any age. For the rest of the meeting I remain puzzled and disappointed at the dearth of female attendees. The technical sessions are good, and the war stories from city managers are notable, and I am grateful for the opportunity to learn, but my main personal take away is an undefined, empty feeling.

Women In the City Management Profession Through the Mid-1980's

Source data substantiate that very few females were working in the city management profession prior to the mid to late 1980's. The reasons for this are uncertain to a degree, as the data are open to interpretation and speculation. But my own personal experiences and a collection of anecdotes from others have allowed me to identify a number of causes.

For example, there was intolerance to the possibility of female employees, even professionals who are aggressively moving along their intended career paths, would abandon their workplace jobs to raise children. Or there was the fear that women would in a variety of ways create a distraction from the real work of managing a city, or even worse that some elected officials would not take women managers seriously. It had even been remarked that women did not know how to lead or that they were too polite to do what it took to get the work done.

None of these reasons were ever articulated directly to me. However, some were subtly conveyed. In my early career I felt conspicuously out of place, certain that I needed to work twice as hard both to prove myself.

The few women in the city management profession felt that they needed to be standard bearers for those who followed, and I thought how glorious it would be if they provided a support network. But it was more difficult then, before the internet and its derivative forms of social networking. My aching feeling of professional isolation was nearly palpable.

Don't get me wrong, the other gender in the profession was not an enemy. I know from personal experience that well-intended male mentors did abound. The problem was…these mentors were not women. They could not truly appreciate the personal context that women brought to their professional lives. Strong mentoring requires an appreciation of that personal context to properly reflect on core issues and effectively guide the mentee.

Ultimately, ICMA recognized a need and worked to create opportunities for women to develop in the city management profession. Later, the programs were widened to serve all young professionals entering the profession. With the composition of city councils changing to include more women, and with the changing political and socioeconomic landscape, more women became involved. Many of them actively sought opportunities to be mentored by the "early" women professionals. Informal and formal structures were created to facilitate the mentoring.

Growth Of the Number Women In the Profession Since the 1990's

Women are well represented in the city management profession today. This significant growth began in the early 1990's and continues today. By the mid to late 1990's, women were becoming city managers and executive team members in some of the largest council-manager governments in the country. As the saying goes "you have come a long way baby." Does that mean women no longer need mentoring without the "glass ceiling"? In short, "No!"

Women are now mentoring and being mentored widely. In fact, I am asked by both men and women who are either new to the profession or looking to make strategic changes in their careers to mentor them. Indeed, there are a number of us who are saying "yes" to these requests. Early into my mentoring experience, the questions asked by young women were largely about work / life balance, seeking secrets to happily growing both their personal life and their high-demand careers. Now I hear this question from young men as well. This is likely a sign of our widened societal view of family roles. It also speaks to the fact that cities are realizing the value in enabling all their employees to make good life-work balance decisions.

Several of my mentoring relationships have been in ongoing

for several years now. Technology permits "close" connections, even with reduced in-person time due to schedules and geography. I have watched women grow and make personal and professional choices that were "correct" for their situations. They, their communities and the profession are benefitting. And one of the most personally satisfying experiences is that they now are mentoring others.

Epilogue

I attended the annual meeting of my state's city managers' meeting a year ago—thirty-five years after the first one—and quite frankly I can't recall noticing the gender balance of the attendees. But there were many women. I recognize that women of my generation were able to forge professional paths without same-gender mentoring. Thankfully, that is no longer the case.

Today, each of us, regardless of our own mentoring history or lack thereof, should experience the sense of fulfillment, and fulfill the sense of duty, by serving as a mentor.

Appropriate Quote

> "The future belongs to those who believe in the beauty of their dreams."
>
> Eleanor Roosevelt, American First Lady

Key Insight

Mentoring has become a way of life in local government. Formal programs exist in many states. Many managers do it routinely as part of their "give back" to the profession. We never get too seasoned to need or lend an ear.

Nadine Levin is currently in her encore career doing consulting, interim city management, university teaching and mentoring. Prior to entering the encore years Nadine was the Assistant City Manager (and acting City Manager) for the City of Mountain View, California for 20 years. She served in 4 other cities in a variety of management roles and in the private sector managing the local government consulting practice in northern California for Ernst and Young. Nadine earned a MPA from Wayne State University and has done continuing education in mediation, facilitation and strategic leadership.

Story Twenty Seven

Exactly Where I am Supposed to Be

As told By Kay Love

MY story is a simple one. My path to public service was not planned or intentional, yet I know that I wound up exactly where I am supposed to be.

Growing up I wanted to be a chemist most likely because I got this really cool chemistry set and microscope for Christmas one year. Soon after, I almost blew up our garage with one of my experiments and my parents "strongly encouraged" me to find another passion! Subsequently, I discovered math and accounting and always thought that I would wind up as a private sector accountant. That dream fizzled with each consecutive college accounting class. Once I realized that I would likely be relegated to sitting behind a desk with limited interaction with others besides fellow bean counters, I knew I had to make a change or die from boredom. I switched my major to Business Administration and took finance courses as electives.

In the meantime, I got married and needed a full time job. I started working for a public school system in Alabama as a payroll clerk and went to college at night. I worked my way up to Financial Director by the time I finished my undergraduate degree. I left the school system after seven years and went to work for Columbus Technical Institute as the Director of Business Operations and Finance. After four years, I got the opportunity to go to work for the Columbus Georgia Consolidated Government as a financial analyst. This was a much bigger organization and I thought it would be a great opportunity to stay in the finance arena while I figured out what I wanted to be when I grow up.

I enrolled in a local MBA program to continue my education. I knew that I would need an advanced degree to remain competitive in the job market over the course of my career…no matter what that might be. People continually asked me why I was pursuing an MBA instead of an MPA since I was working in local government and the MPA would be the logical choice. My only thought at the time was that the MBA would allow me to keep my options open in the private sector if the public sector gig didn't work out. Ironically, since college I have never worked in the private sector. I was hooked on public service before I even realized it and I can't imagine a more honorable or rewarding career.

I completed my MBA and stayed in Columbus for eleven plus years. During my tenure I progressed through the finance department to the rank of Finance Director. This was an experience of a lifetime. It was true "on the job training" so by the time I became the director I had a good understanding of what each function in the department was and how it fit in overall. This ranged from accounting, budgeting, strategic planning, purchasing, treasury, revenue collections, and business licensing. My boss, the then finance director, continually gave me "other duties as assigned" and at the time I hated it. I later came to realize and appreciate that he was simply preparing me to take his place when the time came.

I left Columbus for an opportunity in Roswell, GA as the Deputy City Administrator. My finance background is one of the main reasons I landed the job since they were looking for someone with financial management experience to complement the planning experience of the City Administrator. I served as Deputy City Administrator for three years. In 2007 I was appointed City Administrator by Mayor and Council when the previous City Administrator left to move back closer to family.

The MBA has not gone to waste. One of the many things that I learned as a graduate student is that decisions should be based on a factual business case and I have tried to emulate that approach in local government, sometimes more successfully than others. One of my most memorable learning experiences was the first time when politics won out over my perfectly sensible business case. That's when I discovered that the best political decisions are not always the best financial decisions and vice versa. Elected officials are only as good as the information that we provide to them. In the end, they have to make decisions that they believe are best for the community and it is my job to see that those decisions are carried out.

When I was first appointed City Administrator a reporter asked me how it felt to be the first female City Administrator in Roswell. The question caught me off guard because the first thing that comes to my mind is not that I am a female. My first thought is that I am a public servant who has the distinct privilege of serving in a proud and engaged community. I just happen to be a female. My career decisions (other than what to wear) have not been based on being female. I do not subscribe to the cliché of "being a woman in a man's world." I believe that public service is everyone's world.

I have been extremely fortunate to have role models and mentors in my life who unselfishly gave of themselves and helped create defining moments for me. They include people who were ahead of their time and not afraid to pursue their passions. Some of them were pioneers in fields that were either non-traditional or where they were not easily accepted. Ironically, only one of them has been a woman, my mother.

My parents had the biggest impact of all on my life. I was raised in a traditional middle class southern family where the values of religion, pride, hard work and honesty were instilled in me and my older brother. They continually encouraged and supported me by telling me that I could do anything that I "set my mind to" and I believed it. Never once did I hear that being a female made it harder or different for me. This was especially true when my Dad made me learn to change a tire and the oil in the car before I could drive it!

In my career, I have been taken under the wings of some of the best public sector leaders around. They pushed me, guided me, nurtured me, taught me and believed in me. I am eternally grateful to Clarence Bowen, Jr. and Dr. Carmen Cavezza who patiently and generously shared their knowledge and taught me by example.

Some of the lessons that I have learned along the way include:

- Bad news does not get better with age
- Never believe the first answer…trust and verify
- Ask questions and don't reinvent the wheel
- You only get one chance to make a first impression
- You can't take the politics out of politics
- People don't care how much you know until they know how much you care
- At the end of the day, the only thing you have is your word
- Don't forget those who helped you out along the way
- Give back
- Say thank you
- Never underestimate the value of the information that you provide to decision makers
- Laughter is a great stress reliever
- Give credit where credit is due
- Never stop learning
- Listen, listen, and listen some more
- Never ask your staff to do things that you yourself are not willing to do
- Read what you write before hitting the "send" key
- You can't take it back once you say it
- After the vote, salute and march
- Give "stretch" experiences to staff to help them develop

- If people aren't talking about you, then you aren't really doing anything worthwhile
- Leadership has nothing to do with your job title

Many things have happened in my journey over the past twenty five years both personally and professionally that have enriched my life and brought me to this point. I have the highest regard for my colleagues who work in the public sector. I believe our greatest responsibility is to recruit the next generation of public sector leaders. It saddens me when I read articles and see the statistics about the dwindling numbers of people interested in entering public service. There is a critical need and our challenge is to create innovative ways to attract and retain tomorrow's leaders. I look forward to being a part of it!

Appropriate Quote

> "People are like stained-glass windows. They sparkle and shine when the sun is out, but when the darkness sets in, their true beauty is revealed only if there is light from within."
>
> Elisabeth Kubler-Ross, M.D.,
> Swiss American Psychiatrist

Key Insight

The next generation of city managers will face interesting dynamics. Fortunately they are educated, experienced and enthusiastic. Their path may be different, but they do indeed have a path.

Kay Love is the City Administrator for the City of Roswell, GA. Before joining the City of Roswell in 2003 as Deputy City Administrator, she worked for 10 years in local government financial management for the Columbus Consolidated Government and ten years in public education financial management. Kay was appointed City Administrator in 2007. She holds MBA and B.B.A degrees from Columbus State University. She is a member of the International City Managers

Association (ICMA), Georgia City-County Management Association (GCCMA), Government Finance Officers Association (GFOA), and is a past president of the Georgia Government Finance Officers Association (GGFOA.) She is a member of the Roswell Rotary Club and serves on the Board of STAR House Foundation.

Story Twenty Eight

The Hair Salon

As told by Margie Rose

I had been City Manager for about three (3) years and thought that I had experienced everything that could go wrong in local government. This was the case, because I had been in local government about 13 years prior to becoming City Manager. For some strange reason, I felt that there wasn't anything that could not be easily handled. Well, that was until an issue arose within the Building Department.

The issue started out as a standard building issue. A couple had gone to the Building Department to pull a permit to convert a building, in a commercial district, from a single family home to a hair salon. The home had been grandfathered in during the commercial rezoning. However, once it was no longer a home, it had to comply with the most current zoning. The conversion to a hair salon did not pose a concern under the current zoning district. The issue was, making sure that the building complied with the Building and Fire code for a hair salon.

The codes required that the couple spend more money than they had allocated to address the Building and Fire code issues. When the Building Inspector informed the couple of the concerns and the need to comply, the couple became outraged and got into a heated debate with the inspector. The inspector tried, during that discussion and subsequent meetings to explain that there were safety issues they had to comply with. While the couple was still upset, the husband decided that he wanted to engage a relative in the conversation since the relative was a member of the City Council.

The relative was always careful about getting engaged in issues that were not of a policy nature. Therefore, the relative, as I had expected, contacted me and asked me to check to determine the nature of the problem.

At this point, I thought that it was still a very simple Building Department issue. I followed up with the director of the Building Department and asked him to investigate to determine what the problem was and to resolve it. Because City Managers have so many issues going on at any given time, I made the assumption that this issue, like many others, would be investigated, resolved and we would move on to the next issue.

After turning it over to the Director of Building, I informed the Council member (relative of the couple) the status of what was going on and that the issue would be resolved. At that point, I felt that everything was fine; at least this is what I thought. A few days later, the Mayor and another Council member were discussing issues with me and one of them indicated that there was a big problem with the hair salon issue. They asked if I knew about it. I verified that it was the same issue that the Building Director was working on.

I was informed by the Mayor and the Council member that they were told by the Council member who is related to the couple that there had been loud exchanges between the Building Inspector and the couple, especially the husband. The concern seemed to have been centered around the fact that a Building Permit was issued to begin work but the major concerns, which were safety related, had to be addressed before a final inspection and certificate of occupancy permit could be granted.

I decided that I needed to see what the status of the issue was, recognizing that it had only been a few days after having given it to the Director of Building. When I spoke with the Director, it was true that the issue had gotten out of control. The Director decided to arrange a meeting with the couple, and the Building Inspector, to try to get to the bottom of the issues.

When the meeting occurred, I decided to attend. One of the Council members, unrelated to the couple, had been invited by the couple to attend, which I did not know until we all arrived at the meeting. The Building Director explained the situation and allowed the Building Inspector to share his concerns. The wife of the couple made a few comments followed by a heated exchanged between the Building Inspector and the husband. It was during that heated debate that it became clear that nothing would be resolved during the meeting.

I went home that evening realizing that this issue was not just a basic building issue anymore. The creditability of the Building Department was beginning to be questioned by the couple. The concerns were also being spread among Council and it was clear, that they did not want to get involved, other than to bring closure to the issue.

During the night I pondered on how to resolve this issue to make sure that the safety of the building and the citizens of the community were not compromised. The next morning, I met with the Building Director, to share with him my concerns and to determine if he had any suggested solutions to the issue. The Director felt that the inspector was only doing his job and that a final occupancy permit should not be issued unless the couple addressed the safety concerns. I expected the Building Director to support the inspector as I supported the inspector also.

The issue, at that point, was bigger because the couple no longer had confidence in what the inspector had to say, based on the exchanges they had during discussions related to the issue. By this time, the other inspectors in the department had also agreed with the inspector dealing with the issue.

After meeting with the Building Director, I decided to make contact with one of my colleagues in a neighboring community to see if I could use one of their inspectors to inspect the property and provide their professional opinion. My colleague from the neighboring community agreed and we were able to get a second opinion.

Before the inspector from the neighboring community inspected the property I informed the couple that we would be getting another opinion.

Our inspector did not know the inspector from the neighboring community. Also, the outside inspector did not know how political the issue had gotten. The inspector knew the pertinent details of the issue. The report from the outside inspector revealed the same concerns as our inspector, especially as it related to safety. The couple eventually accepted what was needed and complied with the requirements of the inspection.

Appropriate Quote

> "Have the courage to say no. Have the courage to face the truth. Do the right thing because it is right. These are the magic keys to living your life with integrity"
>
> W. Clement Stone, Author and Speaker

Key Insight

City Administrators are often confronted with issues that challenge their ethics. It is always important to do the right thing even when it is unpopular.

Margie Rose is Assistant City Manager in Corpus Christi, Texas. She has served in that capacity since April, 2002. Prior to Corpus Christi, Margie held various positions with Wayne County, Michigan. She was City Manager of Inkster, Michigan for five years. She is a member of the International City / County Management Association (ICMA) as well as the Texas City Management Association (TCMA.) She is a Credentialed Manager.

Story Twenty Nine

Much Has Changed in 37 Years – "The Path May Now Be Well Traveled, But We Need To Keep Moving Upward"

As told by Jan Perkins

IN Spring 1975, when Helen Reddy was singing "I Am Woman," several of us in the MPA Program at the University of Kansas were planning our first conference on and for women in public administration. There were few women on the city management track in those days. ICMA had recently appointed a Task Force on Women in the Profession, headed by Judy Mohr Keane, graduate of the KU MPA program. An article in *PM* called "Mrs.-Ms. Manager" was soon to be published (July 1975.) The number of women in local government management at an ICMA conference back then was so small we could easily all fit into a small room.

The 1975 conference program brings back memories. We did not have a woman city manager to invite as a speaker. Rather, we had women executives in other fields (mainly lawyers) and elected officials to provide inspiration. Our keynote speaker was Sissy Farenthold, the Democratic candidate for governor of Texas in 1974, attorney, activist, and member of the Texas Advisory Commission to the U.S. Commission on Civil Rights. Other speakers were Margaret Jordan, District Attorney in Johnson County Kansas, and Debra Millenson, Trial Lawyer for the EEOC. We had a surprise visitor, Jimmy Carter, who was on the campaign trail and happened to be in Kansas at the time. He talked to us about his mother, Lillian Gordy Carter, and the inspiration she was to him, and some anecdotes about her time in the Peace Corps, which she joined at age 68.

Much has changed in 37 years. Our women's luncheon at the ICMA Conference now takes up a whole ballroom. Women serve as city managers of some of our largest cities: Debra Figone in San Jose, CA, Sheryl Sculley in San Antonio, Texas, and Betsy Fretwell in Las Vegas, NV. Women head some of our county organizations, too, such as Susan Muranishi in Alameda County, CA and Katy Simon in Washoe County, NV. One woman has served as ICMA President – Peggy Merriss, city manager of Decatur, Georgia, and Bonnie Svercek will be the first woman Assistant to serve. Women lead some of our state associations.

We still have a long way to go. We have more women at the management analyst and assistant city/county manager level, and we must continue to encourage women to aim for the top job. Our cities and counties deserve and need bright, energetic and bold women providing leadership for the wellbeing of our communities. This decade and the next should result in even more women providing outstanding leadership for our cities and counties.

Appropriate Quote

> "If you want the rainbow, you've got to put up with the rain."
>
> Dolly Parton, Entertainer

Key Insight

Things that we take for granted today often started as a bold initiative at some point in the past. We owe these trail blazers much gratitude. They had the courage to take risks then so that we can enjoy a safer reality today.

Jan Perkins is a Senior Advisor for ICMA as well as Senior Partner with Management Partners, Inc.. She is former city manager of Fremont, CA and Morgan Hill, CA; Assistant City Manager of Santa Ana, CA; Deputy City Manager of Grand Rapids, MI; and Assistant City Administrator/Community Development Director of Adrian, MI. Jan has her MPA from the University of Kansas and a Certificate for Executives in State and Local Government from Harvard University. She is an ICMA Credentialed Manager and serves as a board member of ICMA's Women Leading Government.

Story Thirty

Rolling Hills

As told by Miriam Porter

AS with the rolling hills of southern Iowa where I was born, there was as much behind me as in front of me of the vacillating path. My career in local government was not my first stop on the path, nor was it my last, but I spent 14 dynamic years in local government management.

My first career stop was in nursing. Not a logical career step from nursing to local government management, you might think. Not unless you look at all of life's experiences as being important, particularly those which involve working closely with people. An understanding of human needs and the human spirit lays a good foundation for the multi-faceted job of a city manager.

My work in local government management took me around the suburban area of the Minneapolis-St. Paul metropolitan area. The three communities in which I worked were dynamic and growth-oriented. Each presented the trials and rewards of working in local government in the 1980's through the 1990's. During this time I also married and had my first child. I'm not sure that you can really have it all; career, family, and personal fulfillment. But I've tried. Sometimes I've felt self-actualized (top tier of Maslow's hierarchy), other times, just tired and frustrated (bottom tier of same hierarchy.)

At one point, when I was feeling very diluted, stretched too far, and wondering what else there could be, I decided to go back to school for a Doctorate, where I could reinvest in myself. It was something I had always planned to do. I remember in my nursing days, I was once asked by a co-worker how I liked my work. I told her that I liked it for now, but someday I'd like to teach at a university. And so it came to be. During my doctoral studies, I had my second child. An infant and the writing of a dissertation presented a whole new set of challenges. I wouldn't recommend it, but I did find it doable. And I ended up with two amazing rewards, my 2nd son and my doctorate.

I began teaching at the Urban and Regional Studies Institute, the oldest of its kind, at Minnesota State University, Mankato, MN, in the mid '90's. This allowed me to take my local government management knowledge and experiences to new audiences. It has also allowed me to create and contribute new knowledge and research to a very important field, one that affects our quality of life every day.

But let me digress and introduce myself. While I am not typically self-disclosing, I'd like for you to know how I came to be.

Miriam H. Porter

Miriam Helen Porter was the name given to me at birth. I was named after two of my mother's sisters. My last name is Welsh, which represents my father's ancestry. That is the name that has stayed with me throughout my life. After I married, a colleague asked me what my husband thought about me not changing my last name to his. I told him "it didn't bother him in the least. If such things bothered him I wouldn't have married him."

I was born in Atlantic, IA, the 7th of 11 children. The concept of "public interest" became well known to me at an early age, as well as the concept of "community responsibility." I once asked my mother how many children she would have had if her faith condoned birth control. Without a blink, she looked at me and said, "You wouldn't be here." Enough said.

I was known as a shy child and, while I grew to be quite sociable, I have remained private with most personal feelings and experiences. But you can know, I have not been immune to life's harsh blows nor excluded from its great joys

Some of the harsh blows came to me as a child. While in kindergarten, I contracted polio. The Salk vaccine had been known to give polio to people to whom it was administered. When I was diagnosed I was sent to a "polio ward" at St. Joseph Hospital in Omaha, NE. I was there for 3 months. It was the kind of experience that would take a shy 5 year-old girl and spit her out fighting. The emotional and physical toll of that time would take a full book to fully recount, but then I have moved a long way from that now. In most respects I won the battle. While it has continued to challenge my life, I have rarely let it limit me.

Several months later another illness was to strike my family. My younger sister died of pneumonia. Life again had changed dramatically, and so too had the people around me. There was no grief counseling then; one was left to cope however they could. I often think of these times as the "dark ages."

These were some of the experiences that contributed to who I am, but they haven't defined me. There was so much more to come and opportunities for which to reach.

Gaining Altitude and Attitude

The following years through middle school and high school became much more manageable. We did have to leave the land in which my ancestors settled, and its good and bad memories. My father, an inspector for the US Department of Agriculture, was transferred at various times. After four moves and school changes, we moved to Minnesota. This was the place I have stayed, the place where I have pursued my education and careers. This is a place that prides itself for making people hardy, capable of withstanding the extremes of heat and cold. That ability may have translated itself into the ability to withstand political extremes as well.

I was educated in parochial schools through 8th grade. I moved on from there with some solid values and left behind some concepts that I just couldn't apply to my own life. However there were answers to questions to be derived, like "Did the teachers really put chili powder on the erasers to keep kids from chewing on them?" Well, I did develop a love of spicy food. High school was my first experience since Kindergarten in a public school.

My parents provided for the needs of our large family. If we wanted more than our parents could afford, we had to make our own money to buy it. I had a paper route and baby-sat until I was old enough to take a job as a nursing assistant in a health care center. One of my more costly ventures was a horse. My brother really wanted a horse and I was intrigued with the idea. So we set out to earn the money. Our parents said we could get one if we bought it with our own money and paid for its boarding. I don't think they believed we really would, but we did. But the expenses did not stop. He ate like a horse.

I particularly enjoyed music and played the trumpet, and I also became a cheerleader. Much later, I was to marry a musician and much later than that, I was to have a son who is a gifted musician. Also my family enjoyed camping excursions and seeing sights around the country. That gave me my appetite for travel. But I was always drawn to politics and public policy debate: and the Times, They Were A-changing.

Times Were A-Changing

The concept of public involvement has evolved in me over my lifetime. I remember the discussions among the men and their smoke at my grandparents' house as a small child. I didn't understand exactly what they were talking about, but I could sense from the impassioned discussion and declarations that it was important. Talk about the events of the day at my parent's dinner table was often the main course. I saw the impact of action, for example, the achievements of my aunt, Cora Porter Hendricks, who designed the handicapped symbol seen throughout the world marking accessible locations. She successfully lobbied for cut curbs and public facility redesign to accommodate handicapped people in California. California became the first state to embrace legislation for the handicapped which became a model for the rest of the country.

I grew up in a period of time where we changed how we saw ourselves, particularly we as women. The earlier family facades and roles were being changed. More choices came before us. There have been a number of situations where I have been in the position to be the first; First of the daughters to not marry at 19 years of age, as did 4 of my older sisters. This was also the age when my mother married. In my Master's program, one of the longest running in the country, I was the first woman graduate to obtain the title of City Administrator. I was the first woman to rise to the rank of assistant manager in a previous organization for which I worked. I was the first woman to receive a doctorate in the Public Administration program at Hamline University in St. Paul, MN. Finally, I am the first woman elected to a full-term as Chair of the Urban and Regional Studies Institute. There is no question in my mind that there is more scrutiny of the "First," regardless if it is a man or a woman. There are rewards with these achievements, but there is also an elevated pressure to perform. That has been an element of my work.

My Work

After high school graduation, I went into a nursing program. I had worked part-time as a nursing assistant in high school. It was something I was certain I could do, and it seemed like a logical step. After training, I went to work for the Mayo-affiliated hospital in Rochester, where I had exposure to people from around the world. I took care of a variety of people, from the inventor of the milk carton to an admiral in the British Navy. I was awestruck by the strength and fragility of the human condition. But after work, I sought out community connections. I volunteered as a Big Sister, helped organize a food co-op, and was active in political issues. I liked the connectedness that I felt in these activities.

So after a few years in Rochester, I was ready to go back to school, this time with a clearer direction and a better understanding of my deeper interests in the public arena.

My college days were a time of openness to new ideas and ways. While I took my education seriously, I rarely missed an opportunity to have fun. I also had ample opportunities to become involved in community projects. I helped to establish a shelter for battered women, worked on political campaigns, and worked on social and environmental issues. Since I had to be self-supporting, I needed yet to work as a nurse to support myself and my education.

After an engaging and fulfilling university experience, I emerged with a Master's Degree in Urban and Regional Studies with a concentration in local government management. My first position was an internship in a medium sized suburb of Minneapolis. My first assignment was to do an operational study of the engineering department. Of course I had never done anything like that before. But it became the first of many things I had never done before. My education was really just beginning, and whoever said that learning is life-long was absolutely right. My next position was as management analyst in another mid-sized suburb of Minneapolis. My positions there were "progressively more responsible." In my last position of assistant city manager, I supervised three city departments, as well as doing project management for the City Manager.

It was a time when sensitivity about gender roles in the workplace was starting to take shape. The City Manager at that time did show sensitivity to that fact, and did not ask the secretary or administrative assistant to do the quintessential job of buying donuts for his meeting. Rather he asked me. I didn't realize that was something the previous assistant, who was male (!), had done without question. I, on the other hand, took it as an affront to my professionalism. But I went out and bought the blasted donuts. I then delivered them to the meeting being conducted by the city manager with other metro area managers in attendance, including my previous boss. I plopped the donuts down and greeted my former boss, stating "It pays to get a Master's Degree." I then turned to the manager I worked for and said, "Keep the change", as I tossed out coins. After I exited, the story was that the City Manager was given a very difficult time, albeit undeserved, by his colleagues for my treatment. Later he came to my office to suggest, "Not every manager would let you get away with that", to which I answered, "Touché." I was still learning, although not quite ready to admit it. Later, when I began to work as a City Administrator, it was apparent that, as a team, we all needed to take turns delivering the goods, gender roles and organizational roles aside.

I was very fortunate to work for two excellent city managers, with distinctively different management styles, prior to taking on my city. When I became City Administrator of another Minneapolis suburb, I had taken the traditional career track to the position and had had a plethora of experiences to support me in this quest. However working directly for an elected body, no longer having a buffer zone, had its unique challenges. It was particularly difficult to build consensus among diverse personalities and competing positions on issues. In spite of some difficulties, local government management has some unique rewards in being at the forefront of facilitating a community to build its vision. Also, matters that directly impact the quality of people's lives are addressed. I reveled in the myriad of issues that came my way. But at times the demands took their toll. My first son was 2 and 1/2 years old when I took the position. There were days that I wouldn't see him at all because I needed to leave before he was up and I didn't get home until he had already gone to bed.

That was a high price for a mother to pay. I like to think, though, that the focused time I tried to provide to my family when I could made up for the times I couldn't be there. It's something that has always been unsettling to me, though.

The 14 years I spent working in local government management spanned a new era in cities. The issues of the 1980's and 1990's were complex. Federal and State funding for local government was diminishing. The mantra was "Do More For Less." Reinventing government, quality management, and program-based budgeting were the rage. In

Minnesota we had an added challenge of implementing what was initially known as "Comparable Worth," which is now referred to as "Pay Equity." I was appointed to the Statewide Steering Committee to implement the legislation not just in my community, but throughout the State of Minnesota. It was, and remains, a trailblazing piece of legislation that redefined the value of work. Also during that era, the fishbowl of public work was enlarged to include Cable TV broadcasting, civil discourse became more of theory than practice, and consolidation and collaboration among jurisdictions became a necessity. "Never a boring day", I tell my students today who hope to enter the field in the future.

When I was asked if I might like to teach for a year, I was delighted. I could share what I knew about a field that excited me with others equally excited. I had not planned on leaving the field permanently, but that year has now turned into 14 years of "professing." I feel that I have the best of all worlds. I stay closely connected to one of the most dynamic professional fields that exist. I conduct research which contributes to that profession. My dissertation was titled: "City Managers in the Role of Civic Educators." Most importantly, I can have impact on the future of our cities as I work with the next generation of city managers. My first students are now successful practitioners in the field, and my current students have all the potential for it.

At this point in my academic career I have had the tremendous privilege of presenting my research in 4 countries on 3 continents. I have also taught for a year at a university in Ghana, introducing courses in local government management. Living in Ghana for a year afforded me the opportunity of walking into a page of National Geographic and then seeing this vastly different world come alive. The sounds, colors, smells, rhythms, and people, particularly, became very real to me. The friends, neighbors and colleagues I had there continue to be integral in my life. With this experience another area of research and publication emerged, "Global Solutions: Experiences from a Vastly Different World."

My husband, Ralph (CPA and musician), and my two sons, William (computer guru), and Andrew (a budding musician), have helped create our home as a place we enjoy together, where we renew our spirits and spring forward to give our best to the world, hopefully with the idea of helping to recreate it as a better place. I would wish that to be our legacy.

But I won't spend any more time looking back now. There is a lot more to do. As my great-grandfather who settled here from England two generations ago might say, "Carry on!"

Appropriate Quote

> "If one advances confidently in the direction of his dreams, and endeavors to live the life which he has imagined, he will meet with success unexpected in common hours."
>
> Henry David Thoreau, Author

Key Insight

"Other duties as assigned," is as true in the manager's office as it is elsewhere in the organization. Whether it is buying donuts for the meeting (and giving back the change) or helping bring pay equity to an entire state, local government professionals simply do what it takes to Keep Democracy Strong.

Dr. Miriam Porter is the Department Chair / Professor of Urban & Regional Studies Institute at Minnesota State University, Mankato, Minnesota. She has served in this capacity for 17 years. She also serves as the Internship Coordinator and Graduate Program Director. Dr. Porter was a Visiting Scholar at Kwane Nkrumah University of Science and Technology, Kusmasi for a year. She is a 2000 graduate from Hemline University with a Doctorate in Public Policy.

Story Thirty One

Looking for Your Lifeboat

As told by Charlene Stevens

WHEN I was just starting my career, I had the opportunity to relocate across the country to Southeastern Pennsylvania with my soon to be spouse. After six months of unsuccessfully looking for a job, an opportunity as an Assistant Manager in a suburban Philadelphia township opened up. There were a number of warning signs that this might not be a good move, such as they lacked a manager, the Board of Supervisors took great pride in being sued by developers and so on. But, after six months, I needed an income and I needed to get started somewhere in the region, so I took the job.

The Governing Body pursued an aggressive anti-development agenda, while simultaneously working to antagonize neighboring jurisdictions, as well as involving themselves in the day to day city affairs. Staff turnover was high and morale was low. The meetings of the governing body often lasted past midnight and I would find myself making a 45 minute commute home at 1 a.m. Stopped at a traffic light during one of these wee hour commutes, it started to occur to me that this was perhaps not a good organization in which to be employed and that was even after they had hired a new Township Manager for whom I really enjoyed working! She too must have been an optimist who thought "I can make this better."

The light bulb moment for me came two years later, when I was shuffling through some photographs and I saw a picture of myself when I had first started the job. I literally thought "I have got to get a new job!" I was at overweight and over stressed and I looked and felt much older than I was. According to some friends and my now spouse, I was not a barrel of laughs either.

An opportunity came to make a lateral move to a nearby community. It was a smaller community, the pay was almost equal and not everyone thought it would be a good move. But, I was unhappy and the organization was not improving. Plus, the manager in the next community was well regarded, so I made the move.

I remember when the first meeting of the governing body ended at the reasonable hour of 8:30 p.m. I went to the grocery store – it seemed too early to go home. I stayed in that community for seven years and had wonderful opportunities for growth and development and still consider the manager a mentor and friend and the Board Chairman still serves as a reference for me. I also got back to the gym, lost the weight and stress and rebalanced my life.

The lessons for me were: First, you really can hang in there and make the most of a difficult situation. I lasted two years in a very dysfunctional organization, but I still managed to act professionally, accomplish some goals such as developing a budget and a personnel manual, make lasting relationships and leave on my own terms.

Secondly, when you need a life boat, don't be too choosy about the color…you can repaint it later, when you are safely ashore. Not too long after I had left the organization, the manager was fired and ultimately replaced by one of the elected officials.

Finally, take control of your own career….don't be afraid of lateral moves or any move that you believe will be better for you. If a job is not a good fit, it's time to move on, rather than expect the organization to change for you. I made a lateral move that I still believe was one of the best moves of my career and ultimately led me to where I am today.

Appropriate Quote

> "I have no regrets. I wouldn't have lived my life the way I did if I was going to worry about what people were going to say."
>
> Ingrid Bergman, Actress

Key Insight

The future is hard to predict in local government. Great city councils get unelected or term limited. Great bosses get hired away. The present, however, is easier to see. Dysfunctional councils do not suddenly have an epiphany. Judge your pain tolerance correctly. Look at your picture from a couple of years ago while you are in front of a mirror, and pay attention to the scales. Lateral does not mean less.

Charlene Stevens has worked in local government since 1996, beginning as a Neighborhood Assistant for the City of Wichita, Kansas. Prior to that, she worked in the non-profit sector. She has broad experience from urban to rural and city to county government. She has worked in five different local governments in three different regions, currently serving as City Administrator for Willmar, Minnesota. Charlene has held leadership positions at both the state and national levels, serving as Vice President for ICMA from 2003-2006. Charlene and her husband, Dave Paulsen, are the parents of three young boys whose antics provide welcome relief from the day to day challenges of local government management.

Story Thirty Two

Give a Lady a Chance

As told by Cynthia Wagner

MY first "real job" in local government was as the management/budget analyst for the City of Bowling Green, Kentucky. This was a newly created position which moved oversight and responsibility for budget development and management from the finance department to the City Manager's office.

I was fresh out of my internship following graduate school and had an entire year and a half of budget experience under my belt having worked in suburban Boston. I was all of 25 and a woman in the south.

Upon the recommendation of several mentors and with the support of the City Manager, I scheduled meetings with all the department directors during my first couple of weeks of work. I wanted to get to know them, what their operational responsibilities were and what they saw as the major issues in their department.

When I showed up at the office of the Chief of Police, I was a bit shocked when I walked into a room full of uniformed men and woman (yes, there was one woman in the room.) I realized the meeting I'd envisioned as a one-on-one meeting with the Chief had been scheduled to coincide with his weekly meeting with his command staff. He then proceeded to let me know in no-uncertain terms that

I was a young, inexperienced woman coming into a job that had a lot of organizational expectations. He and the members of his staff then peppered me with a number of scenarios and how I would react, what position I would take in making recommendations to the City Manager, etc. I muddled my way through the meeting the best I could and was just happy to escape the building still breathing. "What had I gotten myself into?" I thought.

Later that afternoon, I was back in my office, almost recovered from the morning's drama. In walks one of the Police Captains who had earlier in the day peppered me with questions. He closed the door behind him as he came in. He started our conversation by telling me how excited he was when the position of management/budget analyst had been created, that the opportunity for departments to have better access to the city manager's office through the budget process was much needed at this time and a lot of staff were very excited about the prospect. Then he noted that he learned they had hired some "young whipper snapper" who was still wet behind the ears….and a WOMAN to boot. His confidence in and excitement about this new position had been completely lost.

I sat there for a moment, my ego bruised and my confidence not yet back from the morning's experience. What was I to do? What could I say that would do anything to instill confidence of this person I had just met? Then I told him that I truly appreciated him coming to speak to me in person regarding his concerns. I was certain that there were any number of people in the organization who had similar concerns, but who would not express them to me in person. I told him that I understood his concerns, and that I knew he didn't know me, but I asked that he give me some time to prove myself, my abilities and my desire to work with him and others in the organization to provide the best level of services to the citizens of the community. I told him I knew that I was asking a lot, but that he would have to give me that chance.

Over the next several months I worked with the Captain on a number of projects relating to police department staffing levels, purchase of equipment and vehicles and on organization-wide issues. We also spent countless hours together as I served as project manager on construction of a new police station. We didn't always see eye to eye. But I think I always tried to listen to his viewpoint, understand his concerns and work to find solutions which provided the best possible outcomes to serve the residents of the community. We built a solid working relationship built on trust and mutual respect.

Just short of a year after I began working in Bowling Green, the Captain announced his retirement. In his last week of work, he walked into my office, closing the door behind him. I kind of sighed, "Oh Bruce, what's up…?" He just smiled and told me that he wanted to let me know that he HAD listened to what I had said in that first meeting with him, that he HAD gotten to know me, that he HAD given me a chance and that although he hadn't always gotten his way, he was proud and honored to have worked with me for almost a year. He said he had appreciated the opportunity to work with me and hoped that I considered him a friend.

I know we all have stories of similar experiences in our early career. I reflect on my initial interaction with Bruce often and am grateful to have this example of how we must continually work to establish and maintain our credibility with co-workers, supervisors, employees, elected officials and the public and that in many cases, the best foundation for that credibility is relationship building.

Post Script: Where is that retired Police Captain now, you ask? He was recently elected as Mayor of Bowling Green!

Appropriate Quote

> "We are not what we know, but what we are willing to learn."
>
> Mary Catherine Bateson,
> Writer and Cultural Anthropologist

Key Insight

Age is not always an indicator of wisdom or of ability. University communities (like Lawrence) ferment fearless learning. Students will always be on the cutting edge of something. Similarly, rank is not always an indicator of maturity. It is always nice when it turns out to be.

Cynthia Wagner is Assistant City Manager in Lawrence, Kansas. Over the course of her 20 year career in local government, Cynthia has worked in the cities of Liberty, Missouri; Overland Park, Kansas; Bowling Green, Kentucky; Lexington, Massachusetts and Winfield, Kansas. A Kansas native, she studied at the University of Kansas, obtaining a BA in Political Science and an MPA. Cynthia and her husband Scott have four children: Adam, Abby, Ava and Emma.

Story Thirty Three

What is Your Legacy?

As told by Linda Witko

DURING the 40 years that I have worked in local government I have been privileged to work for two of the finest City Managers in the profession. My first boss served as my mentor and my role model from the time that I met him as a college sophomore and interviewed him for a class project. Frank Koehler was the City Manager of Scottsbluff, Nebraska, and he so obviously loved what he did that I could not help but be drawn to the idea of working in city government.

Frank took a special interest in me and sent me copies of ICMA publications as well as provided encouragement and recommendations on class choices. He pointed out that there were not many women in City Management positions. I think the statistics at that time indicated that only 2% of the members of ICMA were women. Still I persevered and Frank hired me to work as a summer intern in Scottsbluff, and then provided an introduction that resulted in another internship with the League of Nebraska Municipalities during my senior year at the University of Nebraska.

I had two job offers after graduation – one with the Nebraska Department of Economic Development as a Policy Analyst, and then Frank offered me a low paying job as an Administrative Assistant which I jumped at. What a wonderful opportunity it was – I worked in every department and learned the operations of city government from the bottom up. I was promoted to Assistant City Manager and then during a series of budget reductions I took on the additional responsibilities of HR Director after the Department Head retired. I wrote grants and conducted fund raising to support new programs and services that could not be funded from the local property tax.

One special project involved organizing a citizen's support group to conduct a campaign to pass a special option sales tax to build a community zoo. For a City of 15,000 people this was truly a stretch for everyone involved but somehow with five years of long hours and over 200 volunteers the project was completed. The dedication weekend included a presentation by the Governor and over 25,000 visitors who came to see what had been built. I felt that I had found my legacy to the community because of the contributions which I made to that project.

In 1991, I left the City of Scottsbluff and moved to Casper, Wyoming to take on the job of Assistant City Manager. I found myself working in an environment that provided new challenges, and an opportunity to achieve another career milestone, as I completed the requirements for an MPA from the University of Wyoming. Thomas Forslund was the Casper City Manager. At the press conference to introduce me to the media, one reporter asked Tom if I would be groomed to take his job one day. He laughed and said that they should give me a chance to figure out what my job was all about.

During the 20 years that I worked for Tom I learned a lot of lessons about how to be a better local government professional, but the most important lesson I learned was about leaving a legacy. One Monday after I had made a visit to Nebraska where I still had many relatives and friends, I told Tom how disappointed I was in what the community had done with the zoo. They had let all of the hard work done to build the zoo and secure a national certification from the American Association of Zoological Parks and Aquariums fall by the wayside. They had fired the zoo director and put the zoo under the Parks Department. They dismantled the marketing program and cut the budget to the point where many animals had to be moved to another facility. They allowed the exhibits to deteriorate and community support to disappear. I was so upset because I thought the zoo was my legacy – my lasting gift to the community. What Tom said was that I should never look back at a specific project or individual accomplishment as my legacy. Instead the real legacy that professional managers bring is to know that you have given your best effort to the organization and the community every day to make it a better place. This is a reflection on the fact that public service is an ideal, and for those of us that are committed to this profession, it is the gift that we bring to the places and people that we serve.

Appropriate Quote

> "You must learn day by day, year by year, to broaden your horizon. The more things you love, the more you are interested in, the more you enjoy, the more you are indignant about, the more you have left when anything happens."
>
> Ethel Barrymore, Actress

Key Insight

Managers "ride for the brand." In the American West – out where Linda lives – this meant that you did your best to accomplish what the ranch owner wanted done as if it was your ranch. If you found a mother cow with an unbranded calf, you branded the calf with the brand of the mother. If you found an unbranded calf without a mother nearby (a "maverick") you branded it with the brand of the ranch you rode for. If at any time you felt you could not support the actions of the owner, you "drew your time," saddled your personal mount and went looking for a new brand. After you left you always had the satisfaction of knowing that while you were there you rode for the brand.

Linda Witko has 42 years of experience working in local government including an internship with the League of Nebraska Municipalities, 20 years as the Assistant City Manager and Personnel Director for the City of Scottsbluff, Nebraska and 21 years as the Assistant City Manager for the City of Casper, Wyoming. Linda has served as the Department Head for the Information Technology Division since 2001 and has provided the leadership and direction for the City's Energy Efficiency and Technology Development programs. She served as the Acting City Manager for 4 months in 2011 when Casper's long-term City Manager resigned to take a position in State Government. Linda is a member of the International City Management Association and has served as President of both the Nebraska City Mangers' Association and the Great Open Spaces City Management Association.

Story Thirty Four

On Being The First Woman In a Man's World

As told by Joyce Wilson

WOMEN are emerging in leadership roles in local government in record numbers. Still, they represent a minority of city managers around the nation and world. Despite significant inroads, women as CEO's still confront a different reality than their male counterparts. The El Paso city manager opportunity came along at a unique point in my life and career. I had recently relocated back to my home community, Arlington, VA, and had a great position as COO/Deputy County Manager for the Arlington County government. My aging mother was still in the family home, so I was able to be close to her after an extensive absence, while also being closer to my daughter and oldest grandson. I saw this period as a time for family and balance with career. I also saw Arlington as my transition from city management to other opportunities.

When El Paso began recruiting for its first city manager, I initially thought about applying but then decided not to. Having come in second in a couple of previous recruitments, I really did not want to go through the motions when I believed that it was a long-shot given the geographic location and size of the city. The executive search firm sent me several notices and I had a verbal conversation but still did not apply. Finally at the last minute after one final overture, I decided to submit my resume for consideration. Ironically the process moved very quickly and in less than 30 days I was interviewing along with seven other candidates, all male I might add. I wrote the position off when I realized I was the only female in a group of eight. To say the least, I was stunned when after the first round several council members wanted to vote to negotiate with me after only one interview. After a brief second round, I was offered and accepted the position, telling myself that I was moving on blind faith that this was meant to be for me.

Needless to say, the first couple of months were rough. It was clear that the elected body and organization were not prepared for this change. I had no staff, no budget resources, and several council members who obviously did not want to yield any power to an appointed official. Each week I'd start off optimistic and quickly succumb to hopelessness. By week's end I would be more encouraged. City staff were very dedicated and committed but most of them had never operated in an environment outside of El Paso and had little knowledge of best practices or what a city manager form of government was supposed to be like. Regardless, we chugged along for the first nine months and made some minor progress. Council held a planning retreat – the first in anyone's recollection. We set out some short term goals to get us through the first year and upcoming election. I succeeded in getting some legislative changes that delegated more to the City Manager, and earnestly embarked upon a path of change.

Throughout these first several months, a group of professional El Paso women leaders opened their arms to me and embraced me in a way I had not experienced in any of my other city management positions. We would meet and socialize frequently. They gave me the lay of the land and history among the 'movers and shakers' and were wonderful and nurturing. This bond continues today after nearly eight years.

The big moment came the following spring at the first council election, post charter election establishing the city manager form of government. The incumbent mayor and council were basically ousted. A new mayor and six new council members with two returning incumbents took office in spring 2005. Six of the eight council members were under 35 years of age; three were in their late 20's. They gave me a green light to make all the changes necessary to reform El Paso city government. This period (2005 thru 2011) became known as the progressive period in El Paso's history and the City Council was dubbed the 'young progressives.' The City Council overhauled land use policy, dramatically invested in infrastructure at unparalleled levels, brought forward more city charter changes to further strengthen the new form of government, developed a 21st century transit vision, and pushed for downtown revitalization at unprecedented levels.

While there were challenges along the way, the sense of focus and commitment among the elected leadership was intellectually stimulating at a level I had not experienced anywhere else in my career.

The executive leadership coalesced around a very ambitious agenda. We assembled an awesome group of talented professionals and began grooming an extremely bright generation of new leaders. Our annual achievements have been too numerous to list here. El Paso has been recognized nationally in all areas of public management – safety, transportation, land use, technology, and communications. Everyone involved is genuinely excited and outcome focused, even as winds of change started blowing in 2010. Three of the 2005 council members either termed out of office or left for other pursuits. Council adopted a domestic partners health benefit that prompted community objections and a resultant referendum. The Mayor and two council members are facing recall as this chapter is being written.

Despite these uncertainties, the City continues to move forward with a bold agenda including a reform of the city's and regional economic development programs and a bond election targeting quality of life and major signature project investments for the fall 2012.

Regardless of the outcome of any recall election in 2012, there will be a major transition of the elected body in May 2013 as a new mayor and two new council members will be sworn in – given that the incumbents are term limited and unable to run again. The 2013 and 2015 elections will see the transition of all 2005 elected officials and the beginning of the next generation of elected leaders. It also hopefully will see the complete institutionalization of the city manager form of government and development of the next generation of city managers for El Paso.

I often wonder if my being female impacted my success differently than a male manager might have fared. I believe that I had a type of 'mother effect' on the young city council – meaning that they were intimidated to some degree by my seniority and their youth so it created a different type of relationship and atmosphere – one of mentoring for lack of a better term. I also am convinced that women do lead differently and that this nuance was important to allow for the conflicts to be smoothed over as we went through this transition. Collaboration was extremely critical to creating the types of change opportunities that were needed to make the new form of government successful here.

The past seven years have been the most significant in my nearly 30 year career in local government. It has been a challenge like no other but among the most meaningful work I've ever done. My devotion to this community is like none other I've ever experienced. It has been a labor of love on a grand scale. I look forward to successfully concluding my city management career here in El Paso and turning the helm over to one of the many talented professionals I have hired and cultivated over the past seven years. I feel confident El Paso is in a good place and on the path to one of the great cities of the 21st century. I'm honored to have been a part of that journey.

Appropriate Quote

> How good it is for us to recognize and celebrate our heroes and she-roes!
>
> Maya Angelou, Poet

Key Learning

Some positions are such that everyone holds their collective breath hoping for a home run. We would settle for a single, applaud for a double and holler for a triple. Every now and then there is a grand slam. Joyce hit one in El Paso.

Joyce Wilson was appointed El Paso's first City Manager in August 2004. Prior to El Paso, she was the Deputy County Manager for Arlington, Virginia where she functioned as the Chief Operating Officer. Before Arlington County, she was City Administrator of Yuma, Arizona. Wilson was also Assistant City Manager/Chief of Staff for the City of Richmond, Virginia. She has received numerous awards including: the 2006 Administrator of the Year from Texas City Management Association. Wilson is a graduate of Virginia Commonwealth University and holds a Master of Public Administration degree from the John F. Kennedy School of Government at Harvard University.

Story Thirty Five

Use Every Tool

As told by Kristi Aday

Mentoring

I have always had a mentor. Some are active, some informal. Some are short term, some are long lasting. And some of them don't know that they are. Since beginning my career with the City of Dallas, Mary Suhm has been my mentor. She hired me as her Management Assistant when I was SO green - I knew next to nothing. But I learned as I watched her work, sat in the back of her meetings, studied her career, read what she wrote. She gave me a successful model to emulate. There are times today that I channel my "inner Mary Suhm," or ask myself "what would Mary do." She doesn't know it, but she still has an impact on my career today.

My most long-term active mentor is a male. I worked for him in two organizations. Much of my success is due to the opportunities and experiences he has afforded me and because he let me actively learn from him and work without fear. He continues to be a sounding board and wealth of advice today, although we no longer work together.

It was when I found myself in an organization where I didn't have an active mentor and in an environment that did not value camaraderie amongst its executives that I realized how vital mentorship is to success. I always tell young professionals - find a mentor. Whether it's a formal relationship in which you interact regularly and get direction or advice, or informal in which you model another's action (or even better, both) seek it out. It is so helpful to have the guidance or even the ability to develop your own "what would Mary Suhm do?"

Tools

I often say that the most successful women use every single tool in their arsenal. There are limits, of course, but one of our advantages, I believe, has always been our ability to assess and adapt. I started with the City of Dallas, Texas as a budget analyst. As was the practice, the new analysts were given the smaller departments in order to get their proverbial feet wet and learn the ropes. Since turnover was relatively high, it wasn't long before a newbie became a senior analyst with larger, more complicated budgets to oversee. One of those was the Water Utilities Department. It was particularly difficult because of its Budget Manager, a surly guy who had been with the City seemingly since its incorporation. When I was assigned Utilities, my fellow analysts snickered and said, "Just wait 'till you meet him."

The Budget Manager had been around long enough to see more than his share of new master's degree graduates who had book smarts, boundless energy, and a fair amount of naïveté. What they didn't have, and often discounted, was his years of real experience, survival skills, and organizational and hierarchical sophistication. He knew all the tricks in the book, and knew how to play the game.

The analyst who was losing the Utility Department offered to take me up to meet the Budget Manager and sit in our first meeting to review the budget and issues. I declined, choosing to go up and meet him on my own. I spent my first meeting just getting to know him. We had something in common - we were both from West Texas. So I used my best thick Texas accent to talk and tell stories. I must have spent an hour just shooting the breeze with him that first meeting.

I did this regularly - I would go by to visit and turn on my West Texas drawl (and I admit it - my West Texas charm) and before long we were fast friends. I never had difficulty with the Manager and he even complimented me to my boss. My fellow analysts couldn't understand how we got along so well. But it was a good lesson in using a tool that I might otherwise have tried to sublimate in the name of professionalism, and connect with someone who taught me lessons to add to my arsenal.

What Not To Do In An Interview

There are a ton of books, articles and people who will give you advice on how to interview. But I'm pretty sure no one has covered this nugget.

In one of my communities, I participated in interview panels for Fire Department promotions. The process was particularly arduous (at least I thought so) as the candidates were required to make a brief presentation on their experience and qualifications, participate in a formal panel interview, conduct a role-play exercise, an in-box exercise, and the obligatory technical field competency testing. Candidates were given creative freedom in their presentation in order to allow the panel to get to know them. They were encouraged to talk not only about their public safety experience, but demonstrate their personality and personal achievements to express why they believed themselves to be the best candidate. I saw great presentations such as a candidate's family history in the fire service, to one's work towards achieving an Eagle Scout badge, to some more humorous presentations on unconventional avenues candidates have taken in joining the fire service.

One particular candidate took the opportunity to use humor a little too far. Actually, a lot too far. He was called into the interview room and entered wearing a magician's cape over his dress uniform, carrying a magic wand, and a thankfully clothed blow-up doll who he called his assistant. He began his presentation, and I was literally dumfounded (which is unusual for me!) I wish I could remember his angle - the story he had concocted - but I was too engrossed in the thought that this man actually thought it would be appropriate to use a blow up doll in an interview. I was the only woman on the panel and he knew I would be there (not that my absence would have made it OK!) He got no reaction from any member of the panel - no one laughed, snickered, and his colleagues couldn't even look at him. Eventually, I saw the realization come over his face at what he had done as he turned red, took off the cape, put the doll away, and then read his resume to us.

The next day I received a handwritten apology from the candidate. I'm told he was directed to apologize to the panel after a long, hard "discussion" with his Lieutenant.

Appropriate Quote

> "Somewhere out in this audience may even be someone who will one day follow in my footsteps and preside over the White House as the President's spouse. I wish him well!"
>
> Barbara Bush, American First Lady

Key Learning

Language can be a barrier, or it can bring people together. A good West Texas drawl is always a fine attribute.

Kristi Aday has been a city management professional for almost 20 years, beginning her career in Dallas, Texas following graduation from the Texas Tech University MPA program. In The Woodlands, Texas, she served various positions including Director of Community Services, Interim Deputy Fire Chief and as the project manager for the Future Governance initiative. Since relocating to Florida, she has worked as the Director of Growth Management in Altamonte Springs Florida, and served as the Deputy City Manager in Sanford, Florida.

Story Thirty Six

Tammy's Top Ten Tips for Leadership Success

As told by Tammy Letourneau

LITTLE did I know when I was visiting my Mom at work at a City Employee's Federal Credit Union when I was a toddler that I would grow up to become a city manager but that is exactly what happened. I was 18 years old when I got a job as a part-time clerk in the Public Works Department in the community I lived in while I was going to college full-time. At that time, I wanted to become a Certified Public Accountant until I started working in local government and I discovered that I loved building communities and leading organizations to accomplish great things. That is really where the love affair with local government started and it has never stopped and that was over 24 years ago.

I have worked in five cities starting as a part-time clerk and working my way up to city manager. I became a city manager for the first time at 31 years old. Being a young female working my way up the ranks in local government I have learned a great deal over the years. These are principals I have always lived by which have helped me achieve my dreams.

1. ***Be Courageous*** - It takes courage to be a leader in any organization, especially local government. Being a young female

city manager I have often been the only woman in the room or at the negotiating table. I have never let that fact change who I am or how I approach situations. I have looked at those situations as opportunities. You will find many situations that you are in which it takes courage to do the right thing, even though it is difficult. Stay the course and make that courageous leap. You will be glad that you did.

2. ***Never Give Up on Your Dreams*** - Eleanor Roosevelt said, "The future belongs to those who believe in the beauty of their dreams." Fortunately I had many people in my life who supported by career choice. However, there were also people who tried to discourage me along the way. I always knew in my heart that I had a calling to be a city manager and I never gave up on my dream. That does not mean that my 24 year career has been easy. It has been a great career, but there have been tough times along the way. If you love what you do it will make it easier to get through the tough times.
3. ***Have Integrity*** - Integrity is the cornerstone of our reputation. A career in local government is a very public life. There are often things said and written about you that may not be true. If you are a person of the utmost integrity those people who take the time to get to know you will know that your character is one of honesty and they will disregard those untrue statements. At the end of the day the only thing we have left is our integrity and credibility. Make sure that yours is of the highest caliber.
4. ***Be Professional*** - Professionalism is a critical element to success. This means everything from how we interact with others to how we dress determines our level of professionalism. I have met with employees who want to move up to the management level, but they do not demonstrate that they have the skills to be in that environment. If moving up the ladder is your goal make sure that you conduct

yourself in a manner in which those around you know that you care about the community, organization, and the people in it. It is important to remember that dressing professionally is key to conveying your message. A person who dresses in jeans and wrinkled clothes is making a statement that they don't care about themselves or their work. Although it may be untrue it is the message that is being sent. However, a person who is in a business environment who is well groomed and wears nice business attire will be taken seriously. Like it or not people make judgments about us in the first 30 seconds they meet us. Make sure you are making a great impression every day. Remember perception is reality.

5. ***Be Humble*** - Be humble in everything that you do. No one wants to work with, for or next to an arrogant individual who likes to share how wonderful he or she is all the time. Being confident in your abilities and graciously accepting compliments will be characteristics that people will admire.
6. ***Be a Good Listener*** - My husband has a saying, "We have two ears and one mouth because we are supposed to listen twice as much as we talk." Being a good listener is a critical skill for any leader, but this is especially true for local government leaders. You need to be able to listen first to residents, business owners, elected officials and employees in order to understand what the issues are in order to solve the problem.
7. ***Kill Them with Kindness*** - My Grandpa used to give me this advice all the time when I talked about dealing with difficult people. It is a principal I live by and it has served me well. No matter how difficult the situation, at the end of the day the only thing we can control is our own actions. Be kind to everyone you come in contact with. It is a much happier way to live.
8. ***Deliver More than You Promise*** - Be the one who goes

above and beyond the call of duty in all that you do. Turn in your project sooner than expected. If you are asked to complete 10 tasks by Tuesday then complete 12 by Monday. This will take hard work and determination, but I promise you it will pay off. You will have a great reputation in the organization. This will open doors for you in the future.

9. ***Be Accountable for Your Actions*** - We all make mistakes, we are human. Hopefully we do not make the same mistakes twice. The goal is to learn from our mistakes and move on. However, when you do make a mistake take responsibility for it and accept the consequences. Whatever you do – don't blame someone else for your mistakes or try to hide from it. You will get caught and it will be difficult to restore your reputation in the future.
10. ***Take Time for Yourself*** - Good leaders take time for themselves to rest and recharge their batteries. I do not find it virtuous when people tell me that they have not taken a vacation in 10 years. Everyone needs to take time to stop and clear his or her mind and have some fun. If you don't you will burn out. I know it is much easier to say than it is to do, but it is critical if you want to go the distance.

Leading a life where you are fulfilled personally and professionally is wonderful. Make it your priority today to practice these principals. You will be amazed at the results and the opportunities that come your way.

Appropriate Quote

> "A bird doesn't sing because it has an answer, it sings because it has a song."
>
> Maya Angelou, Poet

Key Insight

Every career demands commitment, sacrifice and caring. A local government career, especially. Hopefully you serve in such a way that you are happy with the exchange.

Tammy Letourneau has over 24 years of local government experience. She is the former city manager of two California cities - Yorba Linda and Sierra Madre. Prior to becoming a city manager she also served the California communities of Claremont, Arcadia, and Monrovia. Since joining Management Partners she has assisted numerous local government clients in California and Nevada with organizational reviews and strategic planning. She is an adjunct professor at California State Polytechnic University Pomona. Tamara is the past chair and a founding member of Women Leading Government and she is a current member of the Cal ICMA Ethics Committee.

Story Thirty Seven

Babies on Board

As told by Cynthia Seelhammer

WHEN I was Town Manager of the new Town of Queen Creek, AZ, in the late 1990s, it was a challenge to recruit and keep staff. The Town was growing, but because it was small and located on the very edge of metropolitan growth, we were competing for staff with other, higher paying organizations. It was a boom time everywhere and hard to compete for good employees.

Since we could not compete in salaries, I decided to focus on making the workplace so good that the lesser salary would not deter people from working for a small town. We focused on flexible schedules, employee training and team-building, and I allowed our one-and-only code enforcement officer to bring his dog to the office. That proved very popular since the dog was extremely smart and well-behaved. We later won an award for that since having a big friendly dog along seemed to help reduce tensions when the officer called on property owners needing code enforcement attention.

When one of the young women on staff had a baby, she really struggled to find childcare since there was none available nearby. So I allowed the new mom to bring her infant to work while he was very small. I figured that as long as the baby was not disrupting the workplace, it was a big benefit to the mom to have him with her, and having a baby around was in keeping with the City Council emphasis on building an especially family-friendly community. The staff seemed very happy to have a baby around, almost sharing him. I would often find the Finance Director with the infant on her lap as she typed, or the receptionist rocking him to sleep on her shoulder while she answered phones.

Little did I know that I would eventually do the same thing with my own baby.

I married when I was 40 and the likelihood of children seemed very low. But when I was 43, my son Damon was born. I arranged for a retired City Manager to fill in for me after our baby was born.

After being off on maternity leave for 12 weeks – the fastest 12 weeks of my life – I returned to work with my infant son in a sling across my chest. I "wore" him everywhere, at meetings, attending workshops, going to the Council Retreat, and lunching with the contract fire fighters to talk about service levels. This made nursing much easier, of course, but it had an extraordinary humanizing effect, reducing tension in nearly all interactions.

One instance really demonstrated the humanizing effect. I was called up to the front office by my staff because an angry citizen was demanding to talk to the boss. I knew enough about the situation to understand that the man was a property owner outside of town who operated some sort of trucking business from his residentially zoned property. He was very angry about what he saw as a threat to his business, and was looking for someone to blame, even though the matter was entirely outside the town's jurisdiction.

I came out of my office and walked down the hall, wearing my son in a sling as usual. He was awake and his fuzzy little head peaked out to view the people around us.

The angry man was very, very tall and broad, and obviously very upset. He seemed to fill the entire hallway and was clearly primed to yell and swear – until he saw the baby looking at him. His entire demeanor changed, as he seemed to physically melt, relaxing from his threatening stance.

Maybe he had children or grandchildren of his own. Or maybe we reminded him of images of the Madonna and Child. Whatever the reason, his anger diminished and we spoke in a reasonable way, without rancor.

I had never really considered the challenges facing families with a new baby before I had my own son. Since I was an older-than-usual mom, and the boss of the city staff, I had many more options for childcare than most new mothers. But I chose to take my son to work. It was magical for me to have him nearby, sometimes sleeping on a blanket near my desk or lying on his back, kicking and watching the shadows from the tree outside the window. One day a staff member was talking to me and we noticed the baby was rocking and trying to roll over. Soon the doorway filled with staff people and we cheered as my son rolled over on his own for the first time.

My son was with me most of the workday for the first months, and then I began taking him home to his father in the afternoons. Things changed when he reached about nine months and began to have his own opinions and questions, often expressed quite loudly. That was when we arranged for a sitter to come to our house to watch our son. But I still continued to bring him with me to social events and festivals on evenings and weekend, keeping him with me whenever I could.

From the experience of having an infant in the workplace, and later my own baby son, I learned that there is a benefit to reminding people of the smallest of our citizens, and thinking about the effect our work and decisions will have on children and families. People react differently to each other when their defenses are lowered and they see each other's humanity. We are reminded of our own families and how in many ways, we are much more similar to each other than it first seems.

Appropriate Quote

"Love comes when manipulation stops; when you think more about the other person than about his or her reactions to you. When you dare to reveal yourself fully. When you dare to be vulnerable."

Dr. Joyce Brothers, Psychologist

Key Insight

Whether you call it creating a Family Friendly, Flexible or Humanistic work environment, being flexible and innovative in the workplace is always a strength – especially when it is in fulfillment of Council's Vision!

Cynthia Seelhammer is a semi-retired City Manager who helped to start two new town governments in Arizona (Queen Creek and Tusayan.) Cynthia's first job out of college was as a newspaper reporter where she learned to make complicated information understandable so readers could make decisions about what was best for their community. She completed her MPA while working for the City of Mesa, and later worked in both California and Minnesota. She retired as Deputy City Manager in Phoenix in 2010. She won the Outstanding City Manager award from the Arizona City/County Management Association in 2012.

Story Thirty Eight

Milk Glass

As told by Diane Stoddard

WE get to deal with irate people in local government from time to time. There are many books written on how to handle these sorts of situations. I would like to offer a rather non-routine strategy that I have found helpful in my local government career: milk glass! People who have seen my office often comment on my decor saying "Wow, you have a lot of glass" or "What is that stuff" and many say things like "Oh, my grandmother had a vase just like that." I have an extensive collection of milk glass - a white opaque glass manufactured throughout the last century for everything from floral arrangements to candy dishes. The unifying color of the collection, juxtaposed against the distinctly different shapes and sizes of the vases and dishes create a striking display. I am convinced that people are calmed by the glass collection and perhaps it has the effect of humanizing me and makes my office feel less bureaucratic.

I got the idea from one of my first bosses, Gary Greer, who was an avid baseball fan. His office was full of baseballs, bats and gloves. There were many good conversations sparked by his memorabilia in his office. It was a great ice-breaker. I have had numerous, similar experiences with my milk glass. Milk glass is so popular, many people can relate to it and most have at least seen it previously. It has been quite a good conversation starter leading people in my office to tell stories of their grandmother, or favorite aunt, who had similar pieces. Also, I have had many employees and citizens give me pieces over the years, correlating me with the glass.

Milk glass has created great connections. There have also been some humorous times with the milk glass. My favorite involved a group of visiting Japanese tourists from our sister city in Japan. They were completely enthralled at seeing the glass and vigorously pointed and chatted about it. Finally, their translator asked me what famous artist made the glass! Smiling to myself, I explained that the glass was quite common and generally very inexpensive. The type of milk glass that I have acquired is the kind that is often amongst those last items that don't sell at a garage sale!

This past summer, I was visiting with a friend who was a newly appointed city administrator and a new entrant to the profession. While visiting in my office, he noted the milk glass and asked me about it. I told him about my collection and then explained how it was a great conversation starter. He just caught me a month ago, six months into his new position. He told me, "It works!" I didn't know what he was talking about at first and then he explained that he had used the milk glass collection trick with his collection of Navy hats. He said that it had diffused several difficult conversations and gave people something to relate to.

It might not be found in any textbooks, but I have found my milk glass to be a great conversation starter and a something that makes employees and citizens alike more comfortable in my office.

Appropriate Quote

> "Ideas are a dime a dozen. People who implement them are priceless."
>
> Mary Kay Ash, Entrepreneur

Key Learning

Most local government professionals spend more time in their offices (or at work) than they do in their own homes; well, at least their awake time. Consequently it makes sense that the office itself reflect the personality and personal interests of its occupant. When this reflection can also serve as a deflection of anger or ill will, it becomes even more valuable – even when the reflection itself isn't. Like Milk Glass.

Diane Stoddard is Assistant City Manager for the City of Lawrence, Kansas. She has served the cities of Manhattan, Ottawa and Lenexa, Kansas during her 20 year career in local government. Diane holds a B.A. in Political Science and an MPA, both from the University of Kansas. Diane enjoys spending time with her family and friends and she and her husband, Brian, keep busy enjoying activities of their two sons, Nathan and Adam.

Story Thirty Nine

The Chief

As told by Susan Thorpe

AS a new city manager, you usually get lots of advice from long-term managers; most frequently it involves the dangers of "messing with a police chief." Even though I resolved to never allow myself to be placed in that position, while a newly-minted city manager in my first city, I found myself in just exactly that spot.

Our community was well known for a huge annual celebration that all the city departments pitched in to execute. We created a special fund for the event, which was used exclusively for raising revenues from sponsorships and paying the operating expenses of city operations, the labor and the supplies used to conduct the event. All the department heads worked together, divided up duties, purchased supplies and turned in receipts, which were reimbursed by the special fund. This process had been in place for several years before I arrived. My first year as city manager, the event seemed to unfold seamlessly and I was very pleased. Then, just a few days later, the assistant police chief and the chief's executive assistant asked to meet with me confidentially.

They were both clearly shaken and said that, although they were afraid to come forward, they both knew they had to do 'the right thing.' They had discovered what they believed were falsified receipts turned in by the police chief for reimbursement from the special event fund. The amounts in question would add up to a few thousand dollars—not something you would dream anyone would risk their career for. I reassured the assistant chief and executive assistant that I would protect their anonymity in the investigation. A swift, quiet investigation ensued, involving my finance director and our contract city attorney (a rather elderly gentleman.)

Armed with the information that pointed to the chief's guilt, I had to decide what route to take – fire him and pursue criminal charges to the fullest extent of the law, or allow him to resign. I decided, in consultation with the attorney, to force his resignation and allow him to leave with dignity. Thinking back on the incident, I still wonder whether I should have taken the other approach.

The entire process, from the staff coming forward to completing the investigation, took only a few days. It all went by in a blur! With the documentation completed, I asked the chief to meet with the city attorney and me at the attorney's office off-site. I wanted to protect the chief's reputation even though I knew he would have to resign or be fired.

Confronted with indisputable evidence, the chief offered several different explanations, first denying the charges, then saying the money was for a former employee with cancer, and then finally realizing the jig was up and admitting that he had deliberately falsified the receipts.

The chief had driven his unmarked car to the meeting. The assistant chief warned me that the chief kept his personal firearm in the glove box. I asked the chief to get his personal items out of the car, turn over the keys to his office and car, and he would be given a ride to his home. As we walked to the car – the chief, elderly attorney and me – I opened the passenger door and asked him to slowly remove the gun and give it to the attorney. Afterward, I had visions of what might have happened if I hadn't known the gun was there!

After 5:00 pm, the chief, assistant chief and I met in the chief's office to clear out his personal effects. The next day the attorney and I held an executive session to inform the council of the general circumstances of the chief's resignation.

The entire affair went as smoothly and quietly as any city manager could have hoped for. Luckily the chief had not built a strong power base in the community, and luckily I knew about the gun in the glove box, or this story might have ended very differently!

Appropriate Quote

> "The person who pays an ounce of principle for a pound of popularity gets badly cheated."
>
> Ronald Reagan, 40th U.S. President

Key Insight

A loss of life in local government, even in the public safety arena, is thankfully rare. A highly trained, well equipped workforce helps keep this true. The loss of a firefighter, or a police officer or a utility worker is truly mourned, and this is as it should be.

Also rare, but regrettably more common and perhaps more painful is the loss of a professional due to an ethical lapse. These losses impact not just the local government but also the family and friends and acquaintances of the transgressor, in a way more profound than the loss of life in a dangerous profession.

One of the most difficult things a local government professional will ever do is look in the eyes of a spouse or child and tell them their wife or mother or husband or father will not be coming home. There is no training or preparing for it. It is hard and it hurts.

What hurts worse is having someone in a position of significant trust violate that trust. There is no funeral, no mechanism to grieve, rather there is only loss.

Susan Thorpe has over 27 years of municipal management experience and has served as a City Manager and Assistant City Manager for cities in Arizona, Texas and California. Susan has been Deputy City

Manager in Peoria, Arizona since January 2006. She currently oversees Public Works & Utilities, Finance, Management & Budget, Human Resources, Information Technology and City Clerk. Susan has a B.A. in Political Science and a Master of Public Administration from the University of North Texas. She is an ICMA Credentialed Manager.

Story Forty

Chicks in Charge

As told by Susan Thorpe

THE first person to welcome me to my new position as deputy city manager in Peoria, Arizona was Jerene Watson. Jerene is a dynamic, friendly woman who knows how to connect people. She initiated a monthly lunch meeting for women assistant city managers and managers from West Valley cities, and I was excited to be included and to get to know my counterparts in an informal, welcoming setting. When Jerene moved for an assistant city manager position in the Tucson area, I continued the tradition. One of our members started calling our group the "Chicks in Charge" – maybe a corny name, but it stuck! Once a month we gather at a local restaurant (each paying our own way) to share ideas and problems, ask questions, seek advice, keep each other updated on issues within our cities and in the region, build relationships and get to know one another.

My friend Jerene has started something similar in her new position in Flagstaff, Arizona. She has broadened the scope of the women's executive networking group to incorporate women from the private and non-profit sectors. Another great idea!

In the Dallas-Fort Worth area in the late 1990s, Kay Godbey, former city manager of Euless, established a lunch meeting for women managers in the Metroplex. It began with a quarterly meeting of women city managers and assistant city managers. Because we saw the value of this networking and sharing opportunity beyond the management ranks, we added a periodic meeting with an expanded group that included younger women in emerging leader and management assistant type roles. I hope they have continued that valuable practice.

I would encourage anyone reading this book to establish some type of women's networking opportunity for local government managers and emerging leaders in your area. It requires very little effort – a centrally located restaurant and someone to send out an appointment to the group – and the benefits are well worth it!

Appropriate Quote

> "Courage is the price that life exacts for granting peace. The soul that knows it not, knows no release from little things; knows not the livid loneliness of fear."
>
> Amelia Earhart, Aviator

Key Insight

No person is an island and those folks who reach out to others as bridge builders make an indelible impression. Almost all of us can immediately call to mind the face and name of that person in our history who connected us to our group. Be a connector!

Susan Thorpe has over 27 years of municipal management experience and has served as a City Manager and Assistant City Manager for cities in Arizona, Texas and California. Susan has been Deputy City Manager in Peoria, Arizona since January 2006. She currently oversees Public Works & Utilities, Finance, Management & Budget, Human Resources, Information Technology and City Clerk. Susan has a B.A. in Political Science and a Master of Public Administration from the University of North Texas. She is an ICMA Credentialed Manager.

Story Forty One

Thoughts While Moving

As told by Mindy Moran

I met Mike Conduff at an ICMA reception while I was transitioning from a Town Manager job I had held for eighteen years to a new position as a County Administrator. I knew of his book ***Democracy at the Doorstep***, and I knew ICMA was seeking stories from women in local government for a second edition. Since I was already juggling the demands of wrapping my Town work, packing, putting my house on the market, buying a new house, hiring contractors to work on the new house, preparing to take on a new job, and relocating my family, I felt like my plate was pretty full! With a twinge of regret, I did not respond to the ICMA request to share a story. But then I found myself chatting with the extremely personable Mike Conduff at the reception. I am still not sure how he worked his motivational magic on me, but I found myself agreeing to write something for this next edition.

I had time to think while I packed, and I thought about the Town job I was getting ready to leave and the County job I was getting ready to start, and I thought about the first Town where I worked for three of the 21 years I've served as a manager. What I concluded is that the absolutely most important aspect of my professional experience is the relationships I have formed with my colleagues, elected officials, staff, consultants and citizens. While this might sound like a "Captain

Obvious" conclusion, I think it is easy to lose sight of the value of these relationships when you are up to your eyeballs in projects, problems, and politics. Your ability to form functional relationships will determine your degree of success in navigating the projects, problems, and politics.

The County job I am getting ready to start is in the same region of my state as the Town where I started my career, and I will be working with some of the same people once again. I'm excited about becoming reacquainted after an 18 year absence, but it is definitely bittersweet, because accepting this opportunity means I have to leave people and a Town I have grown to love.

My thoughts also focused on the fact that while I have been very involved in the town I have managed, it is not in fact "my Town." I think it is important for professional managers to be invested in their communities while never losing sight of the fact that we are the hired help. Whether our tenures are brief or long term, our purpose as managers is to provide the best local government possible, and that does require a certain amount of professional detachment. It can become very difficult to navigate the politics of personality, but it is important to stay above the fray as much as possible.

My other realization is that I am still passionate about being a professional local government manager! I believe what we do is necessary and important, and it is gratifying and humbling to know I help to make a difference in the communities where I work.

And this thought brings me back to my conclusion about the value of the relationships I have formed through my career. Whether it is a chance meeting with a motivational guru who convinces you that you have time to write a chapter in his next book when you absolutely know you do not, or colleagues who readily and cheerfully share ideas and information, or residents who go out of their way to thank you for your work in their town, or the ones who welcome you to their community, the tie that binds us to our profession is the people we work with and serve. Because there is only one manager per community, or at most a small administrative team in larger communities, managers have unique relationship opportunities. It is a privilege to play the roles we do in the communities we serve, and it is very humbling to realize the potential we have to impact the lives of those we serve.

So now I am energized and enthusiastic about moving into a new phase in my local government career. But I am still not unpacked!

Appropriate Quote

> "It's not your position in life; it's the disposition you have which will change your position."
>
> Dr. David McKinley

Key Insight

Buford Watson, former ICMA President and long-time City Manager of Lawrence, Kansas used to advise all of us young Kansas professionals to seek out those folks in each of our communities that could live anywhere they wanted, and had chosen that town and ask them why. Buford admonished us that while we were in that city "to see it through the eyes of those that love it most."

As we found those folks in our communities we almost always heard, "It's because of the people" that they chose to live/stay there. Sure, natural beauty, an amenity such as a university, or even the presence of family would make the list, but more often than not it was "the people." Connecting with them while you are there allows you to love it as much as they do.

Melinda (Mindy) Moran is the County Administrator for Mathews, VA. She is the previous long-time Town Manager for Clarksville, VA and Montross, VA. She has her BS and MUA from Virginia Tech and is the recipient of the 2010 Conference Assistance Scholarship.

Story Forty Two

Past Time and Only Fair

As told by Melissa Byrne Vossmer

WHEN I started my career in local government, there were very few women in our profession. I remember my first conference when I was an Intern with the City of Leavenworth, Kansas and then City Manager, Joe Pence, took me to the annual state conference – there were two women there and I was one. The other was in my class at the University of Kansas and was working for the City of Topeka as an Intern. They didn't know what to do with us! That was 1981 – over 30 years ago. As my career moved forward, so too did my experiences as being the first women manager in every position I have ever held. For most women, I hear this continues to be a similar experience though it doesn't seem to be quite as unique now as it did years ago but still presents difficult challenges.

Over the course of 30 years, I have worked for six different communities – as the first woman in each. For years, I followed the career path of progressively larger cities until I ended up in San Antonio where I worked for over eight years. During the time I was focused on my career, I dragged my uncomplaining (for the most part!) and totally supportive husband to these communities, forcing him to start over each time. As a professional educator, certified to teach three subjects and a football / wrestling / track coach, he was extremely marketable for the classroom but in his profession of coaching, he always seemed to be starting over....there are "pecking orders" that you wouldn't believe in high school athletics – at least there are in Texas. When I left San Antonio, he left what was his favorite position in his entire career and he did so without making me feel guilty about it. It was important to us to try and be as close together as possible and so he followed me to New Mexico where I had taken a position in a ski resort / vacation home community. I want to share our experience over the last few years which has been tough on us both and brought new insight.

Upon moving to New Mexico, he took a job with the school district in Santa Fe. I should state right now that working in public schools in New Mexico was like working on another world as far as my spouse was concerned. He disliked it intensely and wasn't happy. Combined with living two hours apart, getting together only on the weekends and being unhappy, I think you can see how this was not a situation that was going to work. Next he tried substituting at the Taos School District which was only 27 miles but during the winter, just getting to Taos out of the snow and ice packed Southern Rocky mountains was a major challenge. To make matters worse, since he was only substituting he could not coach. As a result, he left teaching and coaching all together and was miserable for our last year in New Mexico.

Now my spouse – Mark – is a very strong person. He will make the best of any situation, has a long fuse before getting frustrated and is generally very easy going and laid back – I am the worrier and organizer in the family. That easy-going Mark wasn't present and it was a difficult and unhappy time while he worked a job that was totally beneath his education and skills. We decided that we needed to get back to Texas. So, in May of 2009, I informed the Mayor that I would not be asking to renew my contract which ended in November. In May of 2010, we moved back to Texas where I was City Manager of Angleton. We bought a house and prepared to settle in to our "Texas groove" again – thinking it would be that simple.

It was not meant to be. Fate and the economy conspired against him once again. In the fall of 2010, he could not find anything close to home and finally settled into a full-time substitute position in Pearland ISD – about a 45 minute drive. Again, coaching was not available. In January of 2011, the Texas Legislature began making massive cuts to school funding. Given he holds a Master's degree and was at the top of all the pay scales in school districts he applied for, it was tough to find a position for the 2011/2012 school year. Finally, he was fortunate enough to find a full-time position that included coaching junior high (!!) in the Brazosport school district which was very close to home in Angleton. Once again he started at the bottom of the coaching pecking order. But we were together, had a home we liked and friends and family in the area. Life was good – for about three months. No sooner had he got settled in, my contract was severed by the Angleton Council leaving us in limbo.

Flash forward five months later. We have had several long conversations about where we want to be and what we want to be doing. While he wants to continue teaching and coaching, I am flirting with the private sector in the hopes it will bring some options to our lives. I have had a successful career – not without its potholes (big ones!) – and I am still pursuing jobs in city management as well but have decided greater flexibility on my part is warranted at this point. I didn't make this decision lightly and it is difficult as I have so enjoyed my public service – even with the potholes. But, we have the future to think of and I still have a good 15 years in me before I decide to retire.

We have also decided he needs to go ahead and apply for positions that he is interested in now and not be limited by my location since we don't know where I will be in 3 months or what I will be doing. The only thing we do know that it will be in Texas. It has been years since he has been happy with his job – almost four years – and it is past time and only fair. This may necessitate being apart again and we will make it work though we won't like it. Lots of people do it successfully and so shall we! If I am successful in getting a local government position in a larger metropolitan area, chances are good he will find something he likes and once again we will be in our "Texas groove." As a result, I am only looking at jobs in metro areas in Texas which are significantly limiting my opportunities out there right now. We have the private sector exploration that I am involved in which is proving very interesting. I am also going through a process of re-tooling myself for future positions in local government as well as constant improvement and professional development is an on-going requirement. The future will unfold itself when it is time and I will just have to be patient and wait which sounds easy but it isn't – not for me.

During our 33+ years together I don't think we have ever truly regretted the choices we have made and it was agreed upon that we would follow my career in local government. In fact, he always joked that my positions in local government made it possible for him to teach and coach without worrying. Joking aside, the constant moving made it difficult if not almost impossible to grow his own career in coaching the way he wanted – he is a truly gifted coach. It is our time now – not just mine - and we will go forward on equal footing as we look for our next Texas experience.

Would I have done it any differently? In looking back I would say yes. I would have been more thoughtful about the need to move so many times and the communities I selected – not because they were the wrong communities for me but did they offer my spouse a comparable or rewarding career experience? I would have been less eager to look for that next challenge and learned how to appreciate more what I had. Despite the fact we may well be apart in the coming months, it is, at this stage of our lives, important we are both happy in what we are doing and that we are both fulfilled. We will get our "Texas groove" back in the coming months and until then, we will keep searching.

Appropriate Quote

> "Our deepest fear is not that we are inadequate. Our deepest fear is that we are powerful beyond measure. It is our light, not our darkness that most frightens us. We ask ourselves, 'Who am I to be brilliant, gorgeous, talented, fabulous?' Actually, who are you not to be? You are a child of God. Your playing small does not serve the world. There is nothing enlightened about shrinking so that other people won't feel insecure around you. We are all meant to shine, as children do. We were born to make manifest the glory of God that is within us. It's not just in some of us; it's in everyone. And as we let our own light shine, we unconsciously give other people permission to do the same. As we are liberated from our own fear, our presence automatically liberates others."
>
> Marianne Williamson, Spiritual Activist

Key Insight

Being a modern day Paladin (sing "Have Gun, Will Travel" if you are old enough) often requires sacrifice from families as well as from ourselves. Just as Richard Boone was often asked to "move on" after he cleaned up a town or enforced some measure of discipline, so are local government professionals. When "move on" means uprooting family – who may have put down pretty deep roots – it can be especially painful. The price paid for Democracy by those we love can be as high as ours.

Melissa Byrne Vossmer most recently served as City Manager in Angleton, Texas. Over her 30 year career she has served in Angel Fire, NM, the City of San Antonio, TX, the City of Waco, TX, Lawton, OK and Leavenworth, Kansas where she started her career. She has served as President of the Texas City Management Association and as Regional Vice President for ICMA. She is an ICMA Credentialed Manager, and has her MPA from KU.

Story Forty Three

Big Girls Don't Cry

As told by Janice Baker

EARLY in my career, professional development sessions targeted to women taught you consistently that crying in the workplace was a fatal mistake. You would be branded as weak and unprofessional – unfit for leadership. So in tough situations one of the things I expected from myself was "no tears."

In 2009, while attending the first day of our Canadian Municipal Administrator's conference, I received a panicked phone call from my Communications Director. The media were about to break a story of "hazing" in our Public Works facility, supported by a cell phone video that showed two employees, handcuffed by duct tape rolling around on a desk.

This incident had occurred months earlier, and had already been investigated by an independent party at the request of Human Resources. The investigator had concluded that no abuse had occurred, that the employees had willingly participated in the inappropriate conduct as a "birthday prank."

Discipline and sensitivity training had already been meted out to the parties involved, the entire team who witnessed it and their supervisors. However, as is often the case these days when someone feels the punishment hasn't fit the crime, the media can help turn up the heat. In this case it was an unhappy employee who decided that more needed to be done and turned the video over to a national news outlet.

The story broke that night and to use modern terms "went viral." In addition to responding to our Mayor and Councilors who were less than pleased, I spent most of the next day doing interviews on camera with local and national news outlets, live radio talk shows and meeting with print journalists. My job was to ensure the facts were known and to assure the public that as soon as we knew about the incident, we had taken all necessary steps to properly respond. Our reputation as a city that had been recently recognized as a Canadian Top Employer was being challenged at every turn, and I needed to contain the damage.

By mid-afternoon I was exhausted, but I still had one more group to talk to. That was the staff team at the centre of this storm, a group of about 16 all male employees and their supervisors who worked in our Traffic Maintenance division. By all accounts this was a tightly knit, well performing team who had been caught doing something silly and juvenile. They were now bearing the brunt of "duct tape" jokes from co-workers, friends and family members as the video played and replayed on national TV.

We had to pull them back to the shop that day to protect them from the TV cameras that tried to find them on the street. They were frustrated and felt betrayed by their former colleague who had released the video, but mostly they were embarrassed.

When I arrived at their work location, they were sitting or standing in their work area. The toll the day had taken on them was visible on their faces. The damage they had done to themselves and to the city's reputation was not lost on any of them. I needed to find the right words to support them without minimizing what they had done.

As I talked to them about the significance of what had happened, about my responses to the media, about our values as an organization, and how we valued them as a team, I guess the cumulative impact of the day washed over me.

And I started to cry.

It wasn't a deluge - just those few tears that roll down your cheek and for a few moments stop you from speaking.

A box of tissues magically appeared, and I composed myself. I apologized and made a joke about being a girl to try and cover. I finished up, not sure how the tears had affected the message, and already mentally kicking myself for my moment of weakness.

Until the applause came. Then a number of them rose to speak, to apologize, to thank me for being there in person and for what I had done that day to support them. They said I showed why the City was a great place to work.

I realized then that the tears had not been seen as a sign of weakness, but as a confirmation that I was truly in it with them.

That day, I learned that showing genuine and sincere emotion can impart a powerful message equal to the most eloquent words. I still like to keep the crying to a minimum but I now know it is perfectly ok to show that leaders are human.

Appropriate Quote

> "Tears are God's gift to us. Our holy water. They heal us as they flow."
>
> Rita Schiano, Author

Key Insight

"Your people don't care how much you know, until they know how much you care" is a John Maxwellism that rings true irrespective of your gender. When you care enough to reveal your own emotions your credibility soars.

Janice Baker has served as the City Manager and Chief Administrative Officer (CAO) for the City of Mississauga, Ontario, Canada since 2005. She is a Chartered Accountant and brings with her an extensive background in both the private and public sector. She has 25 years of municipal government and fiscal administration experience, serving as Director of Finance and City Treasurer for the City of St. John's, Newfoundland and Commissioner of Corporate Services and then Commissioner of Public Works for the City of Oshawa, Ontario. She joined the City of Mississauga in 1999 as Commissioner of Corporate Services and Treasurer.

Story Forty Four

From Modest Beginnings

As told by Karen Thoreson

GROWING up in the Midwest the 50's and 60's, surprisingly, I didn't feel defined or constrained by the fact that I was female. Looking back, perhaps that is because I was blessed with parents who told my sisters and me that we could do anything we worked hard to achieve. (I think none of us had a true sense of what could really be possible for girls and how dramatically things would change.)

That said, I remember my first professional aspirations then as 1) I wanted to be a the head majorette (leading the band with baton gleaming) and 2) an A&W girl (roller skates, perky skirts and an apron full of money) and 3) when my 4th grade career aptitude test said that I was bright, ambitious, compassionate and adventurous – it was recommended that I become a stewardess! I guess those early images of what a girl could become left more of an impression than I knew at the time.

I got to college in 1970 at the University of Minnesota and two experiences steered me on a path of public service. The first, was meeting Dr. Tom Walz who had opened a student centered place called the *Living Learning Center* in an abandoned church near campus. There I met other students who wanted to make a difference in the world NOW – not waiting until we had graduated. The *Living*

Learning Center brought us into contact with adults who were also passionate about making change – in the schools, in challenged, segregated neighborhoods and in local government. Through the *Living Learning Center* and its sister, the *Minneapolis Community Design Center*, I was able to work in community settings and take part in events most undergraduates never dreamed of.

The second revolutionary event for me was discovering the excitement of community based co-operatives. In the 1970's in the upper Midwest there was a powerful movement of initially food co-ops and later bank, bicycle, farm, health clinic, hardware, clothing – you name it – co-ops. The idea that we could organize commerce and social services ourselves, literally govern ourselves and provide for our communities was mind boggling and that idea has continued to influence my 30 years of work in the public sector.

During those early working years, I was firmly committed to working in the non-profit sector until (following the financial demise of the non-profit women's co-op that I had been working for) then Boulder's Department Director of Housing and Human Services, Melba Shepard took a chance on me. I had been labeled a bit of a hot head in the Boulder community during those earlier years. I was passionate about serving low income communities and viewed local governments as one of the perpetrators of the wrongs that kept people poor. Melba told me later that she liked the passion she saw in me and against others' advice, decided to give me a chance to help others from within the government, rather than challenging it from the outside. I quickly learned through her tutelage and observation how much more could be accomplished inside a progressive government than from the sidelines.

Thirty-Three years later, I am grateful to these two individuals and all the others who I have worked with and known along the way. Great friendships occurred and many community changing activities were undertaken. I got a chance to help build what are now community institutions: Great child care centers, shelters for battered women, beautiful affordable housing, and help neighborhoods literally sliding into an abyss change their future and their community.

Some of what I learned as a *manager* along the way can be summarized in these four observations:

It is not about me – it is about we. As a young professional, I thought that what **I** was working on was what everyone should care about. **My programs** were important and could change the world, if only more resources were applied. It took time for me to understand local government and communities are organisms that need all parts to properly function in order to make a sustainable difference. Help your passionate young professionals understand the totality of a city or county – and how their contribution is to make the parts and the whole more successful.

Lay down your pencil. As I progressed and came to manage a mid-sized staff, I prided myself on work ethic and efficiency. Thus in weekly one-on-one meetings with my direct reports, I got briefings and updates while I signed bills and contracts, or took "important" calls. During my first annual 360 degree review, the most consistent feedback was that I didn't listen to my staff – I was indifferent to their needs. Well, that hurt – and I went back to those direct reports and asked how they could think that – as I met with them regularly and acted on their advice. Each noted to me that I was always doing something else while I met with them – not really paying attention to *them.* I listened then, and still remember today to lay down the pencil or pen (now PDA or computer) when talking to someone who really wants your attention and to listen and acknowledge them.

Take time to think. Everyday *stuff* can consume all your time. For instance, email, meetings or clearing out tasks due sometime feels like it is the work we do, rather than *how* we get things done. So I challenge the readers: "Where and when and with whom do you get your best ideas?" Pre-dawn thoughts, dog walking ideas, co-worker driving (some of my staff would say – "Oh, no – they are going to be in the car for a couple of hours together! What will be the next project they have us working on?") Make time to explore and think about "what if........" There is no need to work out the details right away. Dream big dreams and some of them will come true.

Remember that everyone you touch will somehow remember you. Busy days mean that you come in contact with lots of people in routine and non-routine encounters. What might surprise us as we rise through the ranks is that routine meetings for you can be very non-routine for others. (I think of one of our interns who said in awe "It was wonderful. I got to sit next to a budget director!") Every person you encounter on the job will likely associate you with either a pleasant or unpleasant memory. You may not remember it, but the citizen needing help, potential job seeker, new employee on the job could take away something very pleasant simply through the fact that you were authentic, respectful and a human being with them. Just like we all now recognize that the Internet has an infinite memory, the people you touch over your career will carry impressions of you long into the future.

The stereotypes that dominated the mid-20th century about women's work have long been shattered. Men and women alike have created new opportunities for sexes which have less to do about gender and more about contributing passion, new approaches and camaraderie into the workplace. From modest beginnings I have been given a chance to help develop great communities. I am honored and humbled to have been chosen to be in the ranks of local government public servants.

Appropriate Quote

"We were frustrated, but we did not have any quit in us."
Pat Summit, Basketball Coach

Key Insight

Passion is a prerequisite for service in local government. The pay won't keep you there, accolades are few and far between, and the demands on time and energy far exceed the available resource. When the chips are down, believing in "the cause" matters most. Service. Community. Democracy.

Karen Thoreson is the President/Chief Operating Officer for the Alliance for Innovation, a national non-profit organization which promotes innovation and best practices for local governments. Prior to working for the Alliance, she was economic development director for the city of Glendale, Arizona. She also served as assistant city manager of Tucson, overseeing downtown revitalization, and as director of the community services department, which managed the city's affordable housing programs, human services, and neighborhood revitalization. Ms. Thoreson began her career in local government in Boulder, Colorado and has been a trainer and a speaker on public-private partnerships, community revitalization, innovation, and strategic planning. She served as national president for the National Association of Housing and Redevelopment Organization from 1999 to 2001; and is currently active in local, state, and national groups. She has a bachelor's degree from the University of Minnesota and a master's degree in public administration from the University of Northern Colorado.

Story Forty Five

Standing Up the League of Women Voters

As told by Charlene Stevens

WILLMAR is my first time as City Administrator. I am also the first female City Administrator for the City. In my nine months on the job, I've been welcomed in the community and particularly felt welcome and support from women business and civic leaders. So, when the League of Women Voters called and asked me to speak at their regular meeting of March 12th, I readily agreed. The topic was to be my career path and "particularly the highs and lows of being a female leader of predominantly male department heads and Councilmen" – is what the follow up letter said. If only I had read the follow up letter in a timely fashion!

When I spoke with the President-Elect, Andrea Carruthers, of the local chapter, I flipped open my electronic calendar and put in the meeting date, time and location. I had entered it for March 14th! Yep, I stood up the League of Women Voters!

I received the nicest message on my answering machine on the night of March 12th from Andrea. She was so polite and gave me a perfect out by saying, "I am quite certain something came up with your family and I hope we can reschedule." How gracious! But, no I had to call back and to my horror confess I was all set and prepared to come on Thursday not Tuesday.

Who stands up the League of Women Voters? Especially as the newly minted and first female administrator for the city? Apparently, I do. In all, I apologized at least three different times – via phone, letter and finally in person. Each time, Andrea was gracious.

In fact, Andrea even invited me to the annual dinner the following month in April as her guest. The day of the event, she called me at 3:00 p.m. just to confirm – who can blame her? I was on time and again, apologetic. I am now scheduled for the September program – it's marked in red on my calendar. I know, the date is correct, because I asked my administrative assistant to do it. She also put it on her calendar – just to be sure. The pressure is certainly on to give one heck of a presentation, but I think I am up to it. I plan to arrive at least 15 minutes in advance, maybe 30.

The best lesson was how gracious Andrea was and also from a friend who reminded me, "Be kind when people make mistakes, even if it's you."

One has to laugh…really – who stands up the League of Women Voters???

Appropriate Quote

> "The thing that is really hard, and really amazing, is giving up on being perfect and beginning the work of becoming yourself."
>
> Anna Quindlen, Pulitzer Prize Winning Journalist

Key Insight

Despite our best intentions, and even best efforts, we sometimes make calendar mistakes. It is harder to forgive ourselves than for others to forgive us.

Charlene Stevens has worked in local government since 1996, beginning as a Neighborhood Assistant for the City of Wichita, Kansas. Prior to that, she worked in the non-profit sector. She has broad experience from urban to rural and city to county government. She has worked in five different local governments in three different regions, currently serving as City Administrator for Willmar, Minnesota. Charlene has held leadership positions at both the state and national levels, serving as Vice President for ICMA from 2003-2006. Charlene and her husband, Dave Paulsen, are the parents of three young boys whose antics provide welcome relief from the day to day challenges of local government management.

Story Forty Six

I Still Value Parks

As told by Charlene Stevens

EARLY in my career, I was assigned responsibilities for parks and recreation. I was working for Lower Gwynedd, Pennsylvania and when I started the job, the community was just finishing development of a major park, Penllyn Woods. The community was very passionate about the park, having raised about a million dollars in private funds to develop the three million dollar park. I planned the ribbon cutting ceremony, which turned out well and moved on to the next project.

During my seven years with Lower Gwynedd, I had the opportunity to develop or redevelop two more parks. I became fairly proficient at planning the ribbon cuttings.

One tip I learned....you can never have too many scissors at a ribbon cutting!

However, it wasn't until the final park I worked on, Pen-Ambler Park, where the meaning and value of parks really sank in for me. Pen-Ambler was a joint park with a neighboring community and its planning and development had its share of headaches. But, at the ribbon cutting, my 18 month old son was able to play on the playground and that is the moment where I really felt pride in what I had helped accomplish.

Seeing my own child coming down the slide and laughing, really made an impact on the value of parks to me and on the value of what I do in local government. I still value parks to this day.

The standard I have for community parks is whether I would want my children to play in them and I can regularly be seen picking up litter in parks when I am playing with my children.

When I left Lower Gywnedd, instead of the traditional plaque, I was given a wonderful framed collage that showed all of the parks I had worked on with the inscription "In Appreciation for Making Lower Gwynedd Township a Better Place."

Exactly.

Appropriate Quote

"Be faithful in small things because it is in them that your strength lies."

Mother Teresa, Humanitarian

Key Insight

In the crush of meetings, crises, and life altering decision making, it is easy to forget the joy of a child on a slide. When that slide is there because we are there it becomes even more meaningful. A better place. Exactly!

Charlene Stevens has worked in local government since 1996, beginning as a Neighborhood Assistant for the City of Wichita, Kansas. Prior to that, she worked in the non-profit sector. She has broad experience from urban to rural and city to county government. She has worked in five different local governments in three different regions, currently serving as City Administrator for Willmar, Minnesota. Charlene has held leadership positions at both the state and national levels, serving as Vice President for ICMA from 2003-2006. Charlene and her husband, Dave Paulsen, are the parents of three young boys whose antics provide welcome relief from the day to day challenges of local government management.

Story Forty Seven

A Tale of Elk Pens, Municipal Bonds, Chickens and Parks

As told by Maureen Zamarripa

EACH of these factors have played a part in the public servant I am today. In hindsight, I started public service as a teen and that desire to contribute, participate, be a part of something that mattered has been a motivator throughout my life.

My cousin reminded me recently that we used to deliver Meals on Wheels together when we were in high school. It was a small town in Wyoming and we didn't have to drive too far but our trips delivering warm food to people in our community were gratifying and fun – we helped if even just a little.

Growing up in Wyoming, I learned that it was important to help others, to be there if asked while maintaining an incredibly high degree of independence. At least in my family, you always helped but didn't ask for help yourself. Not sure if that's a Wyoming trait, a Midwest trait or just a family trait but it was certainly a not-so-subtle message in my family.

My small town had religious groups, civic groups, community groups and the Chamber of Commerce. Each group helped in their own way. I remember the Altar and Rosary Society helping to maintain the church and to provide the dinner after funerals. Experience tells me that the presence of just such groups makes a huge difference in the quality of life of a community.

I watched the projects that people took on to make the town better, many of which survive today. They still have Frank Prosinski Park which was named after a gentleman who worked really hard to improve the baseball fields in town.

I hope that at the end of my career, when I ponder the impact I've had that I'll be able to point to just such projects and remember the people I worked with, the challenges and successes we had and the improvement our efforts had in the lives of others.

But I'm not yet at the end of my career so I'll start by telling you a little bit about who I am and what my career in government has been. My path was not linear but it has fed my desire to keep learning each day, try new things, do something that matters and have some fun along the way.

Youth Conservation Corps

When I was fifteen I spent a summer working for the Youth Conservation Corps on the National Elk Refuge in Jackson Hole, Wyoming. It was a magical summer. My first time away from home, on my own-of sorts, working with eleven girls and 12 boys from all over the state. We hauled hay, built elk pens, cleared ground and learned about environmental stewardship, conservation and life. We learned how to contribute to something larger than ourselves. We earned a minimal wage but they also provided room and board. We built elk pens so the elk could be studied for disease. We dug holes and set fence posts with rocks and dirt but without the aid of concrete. We stretched wire fence by hand and at the end of each day we hopped back on the bus and returned to our cabin on the Elk Refuge.

Every day was an adventure. Every day I learned about myself, about living and getting along with others. At the beginning of the summer we were tested on our knowledge of conservation measures, water sheds, and other topics I don't now recall. I knew very little of those subjects but by the end of the summer, I believe I passed the conservation measures test as well as having learned much about work and people.

The variety of the days was energizing to me. I learned to respect the land, the creatures that inhabit that land and the measures government takes to protect wildlife and habitat. I don't believe I understood that government was a possible career path then and I certainly did not expect to spend my life working for government. But this I think was the spark that set me on the path.

That desire for variety in my days remains with me. I moved to California just out of high school to attend college. I was the first person in my immediate family to obtain a degree so I had to learn the ropes of class registration, minors, majors and the numerous study fields available. Originally, I intended to major in International Business and eventually did minor in business. However, after much searching and trial and error that comes with taking a variety of classes, I settled on public administration. In hindsight, I think I believed a career in government and public service would be an opportunity to be in "the middle of things," to be part of a community, to contribute, to do something that mattered.

I started my career in County government as an intern while still an undergrad and quickly learned that there were all kinds of issues and services to learn about like budgeting, finance, public health, mental health, civil service, voting, jail services, courts, environmental health, environmental review, development services, drainage, sewer, water, transportation, drug and alcohol treatments, and many other services. My hunger for learning and variety could be satisfied there while still making a contribution to my community.

Early in my career, I didn't get to spend as much time working with the community outside County government but rather spent most of my time working with the internal community that was County staff. After my internship, I was hired as a budget analyst, which required that I review budgets for municipal services, general government services, health services, and criminal justice over the years. My skills and knowledge grew as my assignments became more complex.

Municipal Bonds and Finance

From budgeting, I transitioned to land based financing putting together financing programs for facilities (water, transportation, libraries, parks, drainage, parks, transit, landscaping, etc.) so that areas of the community could develop. Using the public financing tools available like special assessments, special taxes, municipal bonds, impact fees, etc. we solved the financing puzzles. I worked with developers, bond counsels, special tax consultants and other County staff assembling pots of money for facility construction and then administering the finance programs to make sure that facilities could be constructed. Eventually the facilities served homeowners and businesses that would reside and operate in the area.

The variety of projects, the financing puzzles and the high energy people (my own staff and other members of the team) were all a draw for me. We would sit around a table with finance experts and developers and talk about the various projects, legal constraints and policy considerations of using one financing method over another. It was a great challenge matching wits with such bright people and still incredibly fun. I built relationships with staff from outside agencies, other County departments, finance experts and land developers. Most of the work was performed under significant pressure and time constraints as the area was developing so fast. The discussions were exciting and educational as I worked to understand municipal finance and development in California.

Also during this time, my career in local government provided me the opportunity to have a regular and manageable schedule so that I could be a mother to three young daughters. Raising a family while working full time is challenging for anyone but especially the moms who are trying to have it all. Being close enough to pick the girls up from day care if they became ill or manage doctor appointments was very doable with this career. As the girls grew, the flexibility of an alternative work schedule was priceless when it came to volunteering for field trips, correcting papers and helping out in the classroom. I even had a stint as the class art docent. Without the flexibility my career afforded, I would have had difficulty doing any of that and would have missed some important and enjoyable experiences with my daughters. I should also acknowledge none of this could have worked had I not had very understanding bosses who were always supportive of family priorities.

Parks and Recreation

Fast forward a few more years, near the end of the real estate boom, my daughters have grown older and I transitioned to working for special districts in the region. My first assignment was for an agency that provided parks, recreation and fire services. We didn't know it then, but many of the parks we were trying to get built to serve the new homeowners that were coming, would get used, but the demand for all the new parks would drop significantly as the real estate boom ended.

At this point, I learned lessons about providing services and living a life of visibility in a small community. Not all experiences were pleasant but all were educational. I worked with many terrific people committed to providing the best services possible with the resources available. We operated parks, provided recreation classes, events, summer concerts, emergency medical services and fire response.

One of my absolute best days ever on the job, I participated in a fire training day when I got to suit up in the whole protective suit and after much instruction and assistance, enter a burning building next to and under the supervision of a fire captain, hold the water hose (it was heavy) and move through the building watching the fire climb the walls before me. It was scary and exhilarating at the same time. It helped me to understand, if only just a little, what it must be like for those that do firefighting for a living. To learn from others and work closely with the community in a high visibility position provided many, many lessons.

And now, present day, when my daughters have grown into young women demanding less time and attention, I serve as the Administrator for another special district that provides parks and recreation to a community of 29,000 residents. It is an eclectic community with traditions and history to be honored.

Here I work *very* closely with great people including an elected Board who really only seem to care about doing the best we can for the community, a committed community made up of caring people, and creative hardworking staff. Together, we have improved the look and feel of the parks, increased and enhanced the recreation services provided, and changed the way we operate to maximize the limited staffing and financial resources available.

Now for the chickens.

The community's village area is inhabited by feral chickens going back as far as the 1970s. Many a day you'll see people stopping their cars for the proverbial "chicken crossing the road." During a performance in the outdoor amphitheater last summer just steps from the office, I watched a friendly chicken perch on the back of the bench right next to a man watching a play. Neither the chicken nor the man took much notice of the other. The chickens belong to no one in particular and have managed to eat, drink and survive in the small village area for decades. People come to the parks to feed the wild chickens, while kids and dogs sometimes chase them. To some, the chickens are a valued part of the village but to others they are not valued as highly. I remain neutral but do wish they would not poop on the stoop in front of the office.

In this assignment, I've had the opportunity to build community *with* our residents not *for* them. I work closely with civic groups, teens, business, the local Chamber of Commerce, the Moms club and many others. I work with other park districts to cross-promote recreation activities and good health and work with the school district as opportunities occur.

This past year I had a chance to be Principal for a Day at a local elementary school. After my day, I walked away convinced the community is lucky to have such terrific educators. I especially liked the principal as he is totally committed to the children at his school. The school was recently awarded the "Distinguished California School" designation which came as no surprise to me after spending time with them. That designation is quite an honor and recognition of the great work they accomplish each and every day.

One of my favorite days of the year is the annual It's My Park Day. Community members volunteer their morning and help to spruce up their local park by planting, weeding, painting, shoveling bark and sand, removing rocks, and any number of other maintenance activities that make such a difference in the look and feel of the park. At the end of the morning, all volunteers are treated to an appreciation BBQ that is prepared, cooked and served by the local Theatre Festival members and Lions Club. During the BBQ, the volunteers are entertained by a rock band who also volunteers their time. The goal for this day was to bring people together in the parks, engage them in the stewardship of the parks, and encourage their return through the work they accomplished that day. Each volunteer can look at their parks all year and say, "I did that!" It is a terrific day building community with our residents. I am especially lucky to work in and with a community where people will show up and participate. They make all the difference.

Finally, I will share a story, because for me it is the essence of what we do in government, the subtle contribution of our efforts.

Every summer, our district along with the Chamber of Commerce and the Foundation for Leisure and Arts and many others sponsor free summer concerts in the park. Each week people of all ages, all walks of life, some on four legs and the rest on two, come listen to the free music. They sit on blankets, or in their beach chairs or just on the grass cross-legged. Some bring picnic dinners, others just themselves. They gather with their friends and families to enjoy an evening under the stars. Some even come extra early just to stake out their spot in front of the outdoor stage.

But I digress, the point of this story was the family I watched last summer. A mom, dad and two little boys no more than five years of age, were sitting eating their dinner while listening to the music. After dinner, the boys laid back on the blanket staring at the sky listening to the music seemingly without a care in the world. Just watching them warmed my heart because that's what life should be like for little ones.

No, I didn't do it alone, but the sponsorship we provide for the concerts, the extra care we take for the parks so people only see it as clean and green and the community we help to build through such programs are what government can do that is good. I am really happy to be a part of these efforts and proud that my work, and the work of others, helps to make this a quality community in which to live and work. That is why I continue to do what I do, in my small way, to make things better and contribute to something larger than myself.

Appropriate Quote

> "There came a time when the risk to remain tight in the bud was more painful than the risk it took to blossom."
>
> Anais Nin, Author and Feminist

Key Insight

Taking risks, trying new things, and in the process giving to others is part of the journey of many local government professionals. It all becomes worthwhile when others, with no clear knowledge of the sacrifices made on their behalf, enjoy the fruits of our labors.

Maureen E. Zamarripa was born and raised in Buffalo, Wyoming. She attended California State University, Sacramento graduating with a Bachelor of Science in Public Administration and subsequently with a Masters of Public Policy and Administration, specializing in local government services with expertise in land secured financing, development services, program management, staff development, parks and recreation. Maureen is the mother to three beautiful daughters, Marguerite, Madeleine and Marissa and loving partner to Raul, her husband of 30+ years.

Story Forty Eight

My Life Became a Circus Act and I was Center Stage

As Told by Meg Mullendore-Cluckey

MY career as a City Manager certainly is not what I thought it would be. There are things you can be taught and others that require on the job training. My first community was certainly an eye opening experience and came with challenges no one is ever prepared for but with the love and passion I have for this field I navigated my way through in one piece, a huge accomplishment with what I faced.

I started my municipal management career in my mid-thirty's and as a single mom of two daughters. Not only was this my first charge but I was the first female to be hired in this community, the county, and that corner of the state which made the press very interested in me. In fact, my father received a fax of my press announcement (two pages long) on my getting the job from a former colleague that resided in our neighboring state before I even had the chance to start telling people of my news. What I didn't realize was that I would learn more from this experience than I could or had ever been taught and knew I would have to share this at some point if for no other reason than to mentor those who came after.

Being in the spotlight, literally, was something I thought wouldn't be a bad thing. Oh, how wrong I was!

Because I was seen as a novelty by some (there were wagers on how long I would last) the press was at every meeting and I was routinely in the paper weekly with this or that. Further, the TV crews started calling and wanting interviews. This was outside my comfort zone but I realized I had to learn that it comes with the job and that I would have to choose my outfit and words carefully.

I did experience a lot of frustration at reporters' inability to succinctly and correctly quote what I said. Of course it came to a boiling point when words were misconstrued and taken out of context and damage control had to be done. So here it was, my turning point – rise to the top or put my tail between my legs and pack it up.

I had one wardrobe malfunction that I was unaware of until the piece aired and I was mortified. My blouse had shifted and my bra was exposed in all of the shots. Fortunately, this news station was not one our community watched regularly and there wasn't any scolding. I was embarrassed and learned that I needed to pick my clothing more carefully in the future and do a "once over" prior to filming as I realized I wasn't about to be clued in on something showing that shouldn't be.

For me, failure had never been an option in my life, I had battled too long and hard to come that far in my life to turn back of my own volition. So I picked myself up, dusted myself off and realized the "war wounds" would fade over time and they did.

The press continued to be relentless in its endeavors but I just learned it was one of those things that came with the job, kind of like the resident that no matter what you do or say you can't make happy. Amazingly enough I was able to turn two of them in this small community into fans, with one giving public kudos and the other sending roses, no small feat in that tough little manufacturing town. Still, you continue to do your best anyway simply because you won't be beaten.

As a female, we are "hard-wired" differently than our male colleagues. As much as I hate to admit it, it's the truth, and as such we cannot act, behave or speak like they do as it often draws negative connotations towards us as I quickly found out. Growing up with an alpha male role model, I made the assumption it would be acceptable to act like he did and just assumed that I could behave that way in a work environment. How wrong I was! A lesson, painful at that, was about to be learned.

We all know that women at times are referred to as the "B" word when we act a certain way. I hadn't a clue that my being "firm, fair and consistent" with everyone would land me with that title with words both in front and behind; but oh boy it did. In fact it did so publically in council meetings which invoked the wrath of the Mayor who took up my cause and defended me vehemently against those who would try to tear me down (thank you Joe, for that I am forever grateful.)

To further complicate matters, since I believed I had to be this tough woman, I was a bull in the china shop when I started and did some needed house cleaning. Being called the hatchet lady was the least of my concerns. Of course when one of the employees I terminated ran for council, won and became my boss it certainly tested what I was really made of and determined if I could rise above it all.

Yes, of course I did, as any professional would. This presented its own set of issues that NO one had ever prepared me for professionally. I knew, other council members knew and a lot of the community knew that this individual was doing this solely for reason of a vendetta and to be malicious and spiteful in nature and ultimately the goal was to have me taken out of my position as the last payback. At least knowing this allowed me to strategize and formulate a tactical approach as to how I would handle the situation for the next four years.

What happened then was probably the longest two and half years of my life and no, I did I not go grey, I went WHITE! Due to the stress of the situation there were several times I wanted to pack it up and move on out. I often times fought with myself and wondered if I was a glutton for punishment due to the daily "beatings" I took.

Council meetings regularly became tennis matches watching the lobbing of balls my direction and me hitting them back. Not only did I have to make sure that I had back up material for them but additional for myself because I knew everything, and I mean, everything, was going to go under the microscope; and it did. I spent countless hours on petty issues relative to how I was overseeing the administration of the organization even though it didn't fall under their purview and defending and taking the heat for my staff as they often became the target when coming after me backfired.

When it became obvious that what this individual wanted wasn't going to happen any time soon they didn't let up and the attacks became more frequent and more personal and life became harder. I started receiving phone calls during the day over any little thing and being publically chastised in council meetings over things that didn't exist and complete fabrications simply to make me look inept. My life became a circus act and I was center stage.

What all of the above meant is I had a lot of rebuilding of bridges to do as this individual tried relentlessly to discredit me and ruin my reputation. I tried numerous times to work out an amenable and amicable resolution with her, even going so far as to try to "clear the slate" and to acquiescence to her at times, yet these went unnoticed and no resolution could be found (though not due to a lack of trying on my part.)

I resorted to seeking counsel from my colleagues as a mechanism in which to deal with these incidents and attacks. Since there are so few women in this profession, finding a female mentor was nearly impossible so I had to turn to my male colleagues and just started to listen to them and how they handled situations and in turn tried the same.

Yet I will revert to what was said before, men and women are different, so how we each handle things cannot be in the same manner. It doesn't work. We as women must speak and respond differently and as I found out, the end result was not what I expected – not even close. (What's the current buzz phrase? Epic Fail; and yes how I handled this originally was an epic fail.) My only saving grace was that this wasn't in the public's view; it was between the two of us so if there is a silver lining, that's what it was.

Also, during this time frame the City lost its Downtown

Development Authority (DDA) director and I assumed those responsibilities and literally was working over 80 hours a week. I was never home, was always in the office and I had this regimen for approximately ten months and my physical health was starting to feel the heat. My daughters were frustrated as mom was never home. I missed all but two of my oldest daughter's softball games and realized that my family and life had been put on the back burner. I alerted our DDA board that I could no longer do this and that they needed to hire someone to assume this position.

Physically I knew something was wrong as my body started acting as though it was broken. I was losing control over my muscles and was experiencing pain like I had never before (having birthed two kids and played sports nearly 80% of my life I knew pain) and was hypersensitive to everything, sight, sound and touch. I had developed migraines that would leave me helpless and in so much pain even my hair hurt. Amazingly enough my body continued to march on until a new director was in place. Literally the day the new DDA director started, my health issue reared its ugly head and turned out to be very serious and scary.

I was at work having a staff meeting and was actually sitting on my couch in the office because nothing else was comfortable. I realized that my body had basically contorted into a weird position where my head was pointed down and the left side of my body was curling inward. I was in an ungodly amount of pain. I called the staff meeting to an abrupt end, asked my chief of police to take me to my doctor's office immediately knowing something wasn't right and was amiss. I needed help walking in and was sent to the hospital for X-Rays, I was unable to drive, as it appeared that something was out of whack in my spine due to the contortion.

The results of that proved all was well but my pain intensified and my body wouldn't respond to my brain. Eventually I had to be knocked out by a morphine drip, as my body was shutting down on me and the pain was so severe that even the weight of a sheet caused pain. I spent the night in the ER being poked and prodded (thankfully I was out and didn't know what was happening) while they were looking at my blood and testing me for everything blood tests could reveal. A big fat nothing came back. I was discharged with muscle relaxants and pain medication to lessen the burden my body was fighting.

At this point my doctor literally went into a frenzy trying to ascertain what was going on with me and what mysterious illness had taken over my body. The end of summer of 2009 proved to be the most challenging for me professionally, personally and tested every belief I had. The council member who had it out for me wanted weekly updates on my status medically and bordered on violating all privacy acts in place as well as HIPPA. Further she was out in the community talking about my illness openly.

She also had "spotters" who literally were watching my house and tracking the comings and goings at my address. I was incapacitated and literally had difficulty walking and needed assistance. I was scheduled for several medical tests including an MRI which was at a location several miles away. Since I was still unable to drive I had a friend take me who also worked for a municipal owned agency. He inadvertently used that vehicle to pick me up. He took me for the MRI and brought me back. This council member then went on a tirade with the other council members regarding who had picked me up and when.

Needless to say a couple of the others put her in her place because they didn't believe that someone just happened to drive by when I was being picked up. My doctor was also sending confidential progress reports to the council as I was literally on bed rest. He would not allow me to drive, go to work or leave the house without supervision. He still hadn't ascertained what I was plagued with and until he did, he was concerned that other ancillary affects could occur such as a seizure or blackout occurring while driving. Since he was unsure, he felt it was best to play it safe rather than sorry.

Since the confidentiality had been broken and news of my unknown illness was spreading fast, my doctor started providing only the Mayor with that information. They could only convey my status as to whether or not I was ready to return to work to protect my situation and to lessen any negative impacts from the council.

My life had become a living hell and continued to be one for the next six weeks, that's how long it took for a diagnosis. My ability to breathe was impaired, I couldn't hold onto anything (I was unable to take a soda from the kitchen to the living room without assistance) and I wasn't able to bathe or shower without the help of my children. A boding sense of helplessness was consuming me and I was still waiting for a diagnosis. No one could say what was going on; we weren't sure if I was dying, or what exactly medically was going on. I was baffling everyone and didn't want another trip to the ER, ending up on another morphine drip.

My pain averaged well above a ten daily and finding a comfortable position was nearly impossible as any pressure anywhere hurt immensely. At this point I thought the end had to be near (yes, I was extremely melodramatic at this point in my life with all that was going on) and started planning for that life event and preparing my ex-husband to take over and raise our daughters.

However, what I was still doing that most didn't know was that I was working every day. Either the clerk or my secretary would bring me the mail, what I needed to get done and I would spend approximately 4-6 hours a day on the couch doing office work. When my doctor found this out he was extremely upset and he fervently rejected my pleas to allow me to continue working and issued a "stop work order" to the council so that I would have to rest and to remove work related stressors for a period of two weeks.

It was the longest and loneliest two weeks of my life, granted I had my family but I didn't have my other family, my work family. I had no idea how wrapped up and consumed I was in my work, but I noticed that my body was responding positively to not working and that's when the diagnosis came. I was sent to two rheumatologist's whose diagnosis ended with Fibromyalgia. This disease is permanent, but not fatal, where you live in pain EVERY day and that's where I was, pain everywhere, every part of me hurt.

The shocker that was discovered is that my new found disease was brought on by the stress of my job which finally took its toll on me and took me down for the count. The cure, no more work, was unrealistic to say the least. As a single mom of two with a mortgage to boot, not working was not an option. I love what I do; it was highly unlikely or probable that I could live my life not doing what I was doing.

After my diagnosis I had three doctors medically advise me that I needed to stop working in my field as the stress was literally "killing" my body but I was bound and determined to stay a public servant. You see, this is my calling. It chose me, I didn't choose it. There was no way I was going to abandon something I loved so much even if it was medically murdering me. Even though I was advised that my disease could progress and become extremely debilitating, it didn't change how I felt nor did it sway me to think differently and consider not working. However, after what I had just been through I doubted it could get worse than that. The doctors said that I would not be able to do anything professionally that came with stress. "How unrealistic is that?" I asked them. "Every job has some element of stress therefore what you are saying means that I can no longer work." The response I received was, "Exactly, that's what we are trying to tell you."

I spent three months in physical therapy (aqua) to build up the muscle tissue that I lost during my "episode," which is what they call a full blown flare up. An episode which incapacitates you can last from anywhere from two to eight weeks. I lost over 60% of my muscle mass and have never fully recovered. The battle has and continues to be an uphill one daily, fighting off the pain and the symptoms of another attack coming. In my first charge some tried to use it against me being in the position and that I wasn't "competent." I had to remind them that it affected my physical state in regards to walking and pain tolerance; it didn't affect my cognitive region of the brain. They were walking a fine line of infringing upon ADA as well as harassment/hostile work environment issues, especially with the weekly prying into my physical state and how much I was/was not in the office.

At this point I had in excess of 800 hours of leave available to me. It became a frustrating routine of the "curious" probe into "how's your health?" to my having my doctor provide another letter regarding my condition and that my health fell under HIPPA and confidentiality regulations. Therefore I rescinded my authorization to keep them apprised as some were trying to use that information against me anyway that they could. It made the situation at work much more challenging and difficult.

At one point I considered leaving the public sector completely due to the lack of anonymity but my senses came back and I realized that it's okay. I am not Wonder Woman and I am human and allowed to suffer from sickness regardless of what I think I should be able to handle.

Since the initial diagnosis I have had two flare ups, one extremely severe, the other manageable; though as I type I am trying to struggle with another flare up attempting to overtake my body. That being said, the doctors control and add or take away various medicines trying to medicinally hold it at bay. In addition, I struggle with my coping mechanisms to ward it off.

What has this taught me? Two major things: first, stop taking everything so seriously and internalizing it; see it for what it is and leave it at that. Second, define your stressors, and how to address them and how you can use your body to ward off stress through relaxation, breathing and massage. Generally following these rules keeps the worst at bay. I still suffer minor to major inconveniences but can still function normally.

Additionally, Gloria Gainer's "I Will Survive" often times becomes my mantra at the office knowing that "with this, all things shall pass." I just continued on, but I recognized that I needed to change and adapt to my surroundings; not the other way. The statement of "thy will be done" no longer applies to me. I started throwing everything out the window and realized that how I handled Joe wasn't how I could handle Jane. I learned that adaptive behavior on my part was going to become mandatory in order to survive in the workplace.

Not only the challenge of working with men and women but having various personalities as well as ages demanded that I reassess how I was doing things and to act accordingly. This speaks to management style (you know that question they always ask you in an interview.) I have come to realize that there isn't one specific style; each person is different and will respond differently. You have to be willing to step out of your comfort zone and adapt to how they will best respond to you. This means that my management style depends upon whom I am dealing with because one may want more oversight while another greater autonomy.

Probably one of the biggest mistakes I ever made was at a Chamber function. It was the annual golf outing and I inadvertently dropped the "f" bomb after a horrible shank. It was subtle and not very loud, but someone heard it and oh, did the lecture from my Mayor Pro-Tem come after that. What I was firmly admonished for was because in a small community, where everybody knows who you are, you are not seen as who you are as an individual, you are the city manager regardless of where you are. This is the reason I never go to the grocery store in my p.j. bottoms as my kids do; it just wouldn't be proper for a taxpayer to see me looking that way.

I have also learned that I head home, five counties away, when I want some down time and the ability to let loose. There's nothing worse than hanging out with those you think are your friends only to find out that after one too many drinks everyone and their sister thinks you are an alcoholic. It's always better to play it safe than sorry.

I remember growing up with my father sticking a finger in my face saying, "Everything you do is a direct reflection upon me." I use that as a guide every day for what I do, say and where I am seen, thinking: "What is that reflection going to be? Positive? Negative? Will it create a buzz, or will it illicit nothing as that's what I am aiming for: the big nada." I now find myself doing and saying the same exact phrase to my girls. Instead of becoming my mother, I have become my father – which isn't necessarily a bad thing as his philosophy has saved me a countless number of times. That whole thought process of

"If you think you shouldn't be doing it then you shouldn't" has come in handy many times as I often tell key employees in those positions the same thing. They understand that the tax payer often views us differently and doesn't humanize us unfortunately.

What can I say is my life lesson after my first charge in municipal management? I honestly think it was that it's okay to be feminine, it's ok to be human, and it's ok to be Meg; in fact it's a good thing. I spent so much time trying to be like my male counterparts that while I dressed like a woman I acted just like a man and found that allowing the feminine and maternal part of me to come out bodes well. The employees embrace it as well as the businesses and public. What was the life lesson learned? I could still be firm, fair and consistent but by allowing me to be me and not trying to be my male counterpart, I fared much better. So much in fact that when I tendered my resignation I had staff coming to me asking me not to leave and to reconsider. Others asking if I landed close by and a position was available to consider them for the spot.

But what really caught me off guard was the one employee who literally hated my guts my first year and a half and did all he could to try to have me eliminated turned a corner as I did and he became my staunch advocate. When I told him I was leaving, he asked me to reconsider and that in his seventeen years with the organization, I was the strongest and greatest leader he had ever worked for. He appreciated that I knew my employees, their families and took time to joke with them and talk with them. When he told me this, it nearly brought me to tears as I had no idea I had made that type of an impact. It was my turning point in knowing that I could be me, be respected and still get the job done.

I have to say that I love what I do and believe that I am very good at it. My first community had roughly a quarter of a million dollar fund balance when I arrived and when I left just shy of five years later, one million and eight hundred thousand and I had completed over seven million dollars in projects. In this economic downturn this was a huge feat to be able to accomplish and one of which I am most proud. What I know is that Gandhi says to "Be the change in the world you want to see" and that's how I look at each organization. As the change agent, to make things better for the one who follows me and to make sure bridges crossed are not burned.

I am pleased to say that all the members of my former council are close friends that have been there for me in a bind and support me vehemently through letters of recommendation and word of mouth. While it was a rocky start, I have been blessed and am forever grateful that public servitude was my calling. I can't see myself ever doing anything but this in my life.

Appropriate Quote

> "If we don't change, we don't grow. If we don't grow, we are not really living. Growth demands a temporary surrender of security."
>
> Gail Sheehy, Journalist

Key Insight

At the end of the day, a "please don't leave" comment is a nice thing to remember as you watch the city limits sign get smaller in your review mirror.

Meg Mullendore-Cluckey has been in the municipal arena for over a decade. She started as a planner and worked her way to a CAO/CEO. She is married and the proud parent of two daughters. She believes that public servitude is a calling and that it's something innate that allows her to do what she does even in times when the job appears thankless. She sees her role as a change agent and always leaves a community better than when she found it. She anticipates another two decades in this vocation and enjoys mentoring both women and men in her profession.

Story Forty Nine

Lessons Learned by a City Manager (who happens to be a woman)

As told by Paulette A. Hartman

"YOU can be anything you want to be in life, even the President." As a little girl growing up I remember my mother and father telling me this frequently. Of course, it wasn't until I was older that I understood what a privilege that was, or how many people (both men and women) still felt that there were certain jobs that were not appropriate or "proper" for women, or that career women could not/should not also be family women (moms.) I also came to understand how the women who had gone before me endured a great deal to make it possible to have the career I have without enduring the prejudices and discrimination they did. Don't get me wrong, I have experienced some prejudice and some discrimination, but it is very infrequent.

I have been a City Manager for 8 years now. In 2004, I accepted my first administrator job as Town Administrator for the Town of Copper Canyon, Texas. I had the pleasure of serving as the Town's first Administrator. In 2007, I was hired by the City of Joshua, Texas and have served in Joshua ever since. My career started in the City of Fort

Worth, Texas in 1995 as an Administrative Assistant. I first worked in the Department of Engineering, then in the Cable Communications Division of the City Manager's Office. In 1999, I was hired as a Management Assistant in the City Manager's Office of the City of North Richland Hills, Texas and was promoted to Assistant to the City Manager in 2002. Looking back on all of this I can see how each position prepared me for the next. I can also see how the opportunities I have been given as well as the experiences I've had resulted in "lessons learned" that helped develop the traits necessary to lead an organization and manage people.

The first lesson learned was "Just act normal and be yourself." In the City of Fort Worth my direct supervisor was a man named Wilson, and his supervisor was a woman named Julia. Julia was our division head, and she was very involved in the day to day operations. I looked to her as a mentor. She was well respected in the Engineering Department by both her superiors and subordinates, and was also well liked. What I learned from her was to be myself. Don't try to be a man or act "less than" for being a woman in a man's world (remember this was the Department of Engineering,) but don't walk around with a chip on your shoulder or an axe to grind either.

The second lesson learned was "Live your life, not the life someone else thinks you should live." As I moved up in my career, married, bought a home and got a dog, it was time to think about whether having an actual human child was something we wanted to do. Many questions came to mind including how this would impact upward mobility in the organization I worked for at the time as well as my ultimate goal of becoming a City Manager. I didn't know of a female City Manager with young children. All the women managers I knew at the time didn't have children or their children were grown. Would my manager question my commitment to the organization and to the profession if I had children? Ultimately I decided that if I felt called to have children, then I should have them and leave the rest to fate. I knew myself well enough to know that having children would not impact my commitment to the profession nor my work ethic, and that was probably something I would have to prove through actions after having children. I now have three of the most precious children in the universe. Two of them were born while I served as a City Manager. It's important to find organizations with leaders whose values align with your own. I have been blessed to find organizations whose leaders value strong work ethic, but also value family and understand the importance of that with employees. Also, flexibility is possible more than ever in today's world. Thanks to technology, you can virtually be in two places at the same time.

The third lesson learned is "Forget about the men, it's the women you really have to worry about." One of the hardest lessons for me is that there are many women in the world who believe 1) the advancement of women decreases their own opportunities, 2) women do not make good leaders, or 3) "If I can't have it then she can't have it." Along the way I have been and continue to be shocked by women at all levels of organizations that actively prohibit the advancement of women through their own actions. From executive assistants who do not give the female employees as much access to the boss as the male employees, to the female supervisors who work hard to ensure that other females in the organization stay at least one level below, to females at any level of the organization who believe at their core that women are not capable of being leaders. In my opinion, this is worse than any prejudice or discrimination I have or will experience from a man. Ladies we need to remember the saying "A rising tide lifts all ships."

The fourth lesson learned is "Their prejudice is their problem" … at the end of the day they still ultimately have to deal with me whether they like it or not. The best example I can think of for this lesson is working with (or attempting to work with) an older, male developer on a big, mixed use project that was a public/private partnership. To be completely honest, I'm not sure if it was my gender or my age he had a problem with. Either way, after every meeting with him I was so frustrated and stressed out because he refused to listen to anything I had to say. He refused to hear suggestions to help the project flow smoothly through the City's planning process, and was quick to criticize any comment or concern I had. Finally, it dawned on me, it didn't matter what his issue was, at the end of the day I was the person he would have to deal with. I was the person he would have to convince in order to keep the project moving forward in partnership with the City. In other words, I realized that I could not change or control his preconceived, outdated notions. I could only change my reactions and hope that he eventually realized, regardless of his personal opinion, I was the leader of the organization he was trying to partner with, thus, working with me instead of against me was in the best interest of the project.

The fifth and final lesson is something I heard early in my adult life that has helped me tremendously in all areas of my life. It's a quote from Maya Angelou, "People will show you who they are, believe them." Whether you are male or female, young or old, this lesson will serve you well. Watch a person's actions and closely listen to their words to get an understanding of their character. Once the person has shown you who they are through their behavior, believe them and act accordingly. Do not make the mistake of believing you will change them. Do not tell yourself they are who you want them to be instead of who they have shown themselves to be. One can waste precious time and energy trying to change someone that would have been much better spent accepting what is and moving on.

So, the last fifteen years of working in and moving up in this profession have so far taught me at least these five lessons. Although I am still learning, I reflect on these five thoughts often and especially during trying times. More importantly, I lean on those women and men who are supportive, and there are many more supportive people in this profession than there are unsupportive people. Connect with your colleagues often and in any way you can because the people in this field are the reason I consider it a privilege and an honor to be part of the City Management profession.

Appropriate Quote

> "How many cares one loses when one decides not to be something but to be someone."
>
> Coco Chanel, Fashion Designer and creator of "Chanel Number 5"

Key Insight

When the City Council hires you, they are hiring you. You bring your self along with your skills, training and expertise to the position. It is important to remember that self as you accept a title.

Paulette Hartman is the City Manager of Joshua, Texas. She was previously the Town Administrator for Copper Canyon, TX and has worked as Assistant to the City Manager in North Richland Hills, TX and as Administrative Assistant in Fort Worth, TX. She has her BA from Stephen F. Austin University and her MPA from the University of Texas at Arlington.

Story Fifty

Lesson in Changing Council Members (And in Suspicion)

As told by Cynthia Seelhammer

THE method I used to cope with town elections every two years was to assume that I would be changing jobs.

Regardless of the temper, or temperature, of the election, I arranged my life, and my expectations, on the assumption that the election would lead to a change in managements, and that I would be moving on. By doing so, regardless of the actual outcome of the election, I knew that I and my family would be safe and relatively comfortable.

My longest tenure with one town was 12 and a half years. This means I survived six town elections. The first one was the most difficult because I had met and worked with all the candidates and had a very clear impression and expectation about which of them would be "good" council members, and which would be "trouble."

It turned out that I was completely wrong in my assessments.

That was a very humbling experience, to find that I had misjudged the candidates so completely. The candidate I had labeled "difficult" in my mind, assuming he would be opposed to any changes or progress in the growing community, turned out to be the most reasonable, caring and professional of council members. While it was true that both he and his wife had caused heartache and confusion on a task force the year before, he did none of that as a council member. Instead, he used his professional expertise, patience learned as a father of a big family, and his network of contacts in the community to gather support for the town government, and ease communication with residents.

I was equally wrong about the candidate I had assumed would be an excellent council member. He was bright and friendly as a citizen seeking ways to volunteer. He even undertook the planning of the town's anniversary celebration. But once elected to council, staff began to see constant suspicion from him. He would ask questions in a manner that seemed aimed at trapping whoever answered him. He clearly suspected there were hidden agendas, under-handed actions, and unsavory motivations in all proposals and actions of the town.

Because he so clearly distrusted others, the staff and fellow council members began to distrust this council member. When he found his answering machine had accidently recorded part of a conversation from the Mayor, a sentence or two recorded after the Mayor thought the phone was hung up, he chose to share that conversation with those it would irritate the most rather than merely delete it. The hurt feelings that resulted proved to be irreparable and damaged the ability of the council to work together ever after.

Toward the end of his first term, this difficult council member chose to resign in order to run for Mayor against the incumbent. A couple of the other council members supported him in this, although entirely behind the scenes.

The election proceeded, as small-town elections do, with flyers and campaign signs. Then, the week before the election, all of the challenger's campaign signs disappeared. His wife called to say that he was withdrawing from the election. A fax signed by the candidate soon followed. There was no explanation as to why this was happening.

The news broke in the paper later that week when it was discovered that the challenger had secretly been doing things that were illegal and unsavory in the extreme. He had been caught red-handed in a sting operation in a different state. Instead of going through the election, he went to jail and eventually to prison.

From this situation I learned to be far more humble about judging who might, or might not, make a good council member. But I also learned to be more aware of how other people approach the world. Could it be that those who are most suspicious of others are the people who themselves have things to hide? Do people with hidden agendas, or seamy undersides, assume that all other people do as well? Even if that is true, city staff must find ways to deal with all members of the public in positive ways if the government is to be successful.

As a result of all of this, which happened so early in my city management career, I became a believer in the importance of city council retreats where the council members come to know each other and build trust through stronger understanding. Council members who know each other, trust each other, and understand what is important to each other, are more likely to work together successfully. And the same is true for a manager working with a council.

Appropriate Quote

> "It's never too late - in fiction or in life - to revise."
>
> Nancy Thayer, Best Selling Author

Key Insight

New elected officials all come to the Council Dais with their own backgrounds, experience, knowledge and assumptions. Even one new addition to the Council by definition constitutes a new Council Team. Giving them a venue to learn about good governance, the value that only they can add, and each other early in their tenure is perhaps the greatest gift we can provide them – and their colleagues!

Cynthia Seelhammer is a semi-retired City Manager who helped to start two new town governments in Arizona (Queen Creek and

Tusayan.) Cynthia's first job out of college was as a newspaper reporter where she learned to make complicated information understandable so readers could make decisions about what was best for their community. She completed her MPA while working for the City of Mesa, and later worked in both California and Minnesota. She retired as Deputy City Manager in Phoenix in 2010. She won the Outstanding City Manager award from the Arizona City/County Management Association in 2012.

Story Fifty One

Trudging a New Path – Incredibly Rewarding

As told by Polly Hulsey

I began my career as a City Administrator in 2006. I have always been an outgoing, can-do type person. I was the first City Administrator ever appointed in Kimberly, Idaho. My professional background was in banking and accounting, so professional management was certainly a stretch. I was trudging a path that was brand new for me and my community. I thoroughly enjoyed it and continued to try and find ways to improve myself and my service.

It was interesting as I continued to pursue my career; most every meeting I attended was comprised of men. The majority of the time, I was the only woman in the room: our engineering meetings, construction meetings and even our Idaho City Manager's Meetings. I did not give much thought to it initially, until one day my Mom and I were speaking about several meetings I had attended and she asked me if it was awkward being the only lady in the room.

I began to pay attention as I continued to attend future meetings and noticed for the most part, I was always the only lady in attendance. Being a female leader in a male dominated profession has certainly been challenging. At times it seems that men are accustomed to overlooking and undervaluing women's input; not by intention, but rather by pattern. During some meetings, I was not given the time-of-day by some of the "gentleman" participants. I believe it takes a strong personality and sense of self-worth to be taken seriously and given the appropriate credit for the knowledge and expertise I am able to bring to my position.

My responsibility was to continue to learn and be able to add value and knowledge to the conversations. I take my responsibility very seriously and am not hindered by lack of recognition; however as I began to participate and demonstrate that I was knowledgeable and capable, they began to include me into "their" world.

Being a female City Administrator has been incredibly rewarding. I believe through hard work and dedication, I am respected and appreciated within my community. I am extremely proud of my accomplishments and cannot wait to see where the future takes me. I am a life-long learner and would like to pursue further higher education. I am a positive person and always look for the "possibilities" for our future!

Appropriate Quote

> "It was we, the people; not we, the white male citizens; nor yet we, the male citizens; but we, the whole people, who formed the Union."
>
> Susan B. Anthony, feminist

Key Insight

Lifelong learning is indeed a mantra for all in local government management. Technology alone dictates that we must continue to learn in order to be relevant. More important is continuing to learn to ensure our place at the table.

Polly Hulsey is the City Administrator for the City of Jerome, Idaho. She earned her Master's Degree in Business Management

Organizational Leadership from George Fox University in 2003. She is a member of ICMA and the Idaho City Managers Association. Polly and her husband Gary have been married for twenty-six years and have two children, Katelynn (21) and Brock (18.)

Story Fifty Two

New Mayor, New Manager - Not Necessarily

As told By Vola Therrell Lawson

I was appointed Acting City Manager in Alexandria, Virginia in February, 1985 by a popular, long-time incumbent Democratic Mayor who four months later was defeated by an even more popular Independent in a very bitter contest. The Council had just begun a professional national search for a new city manager. I had heard the old saying "New Mayor, new manager", so I had not decided whether I would apply as I already had a job as Assistant City Manager for Housing which I really enjoyed.

I was counseled by the old Mayor, who I suspect felt somewhat concerned about the situation I was in. He still encouraged me to apply, but his advice was very practical: "If you're going to be Acting City Manager, then ACT. The last Acting City Manager was indecisive, showed little initiative and the City all but came to a halt. Don't do that. Be a City Manager. If you are a finalist, you will certainly be the only woman. You will need to show them that you are a decisive, strong manager with proven financial and budget skills. Those are the reasons you were selected to be the Acting Manager, as well as your proven ability to work effectively with all the various neighborhoods in the City, and your strong ties to low-income and minority communities. Show them your commitment to that."

On his advice, from day one I acted as if I were the City Manager. I presented the city budget to Council and scheduled seven budget work sessions, went out to neighborhood associations at their invitation to talk about the budget and other city issues. I reviewed and edited all staff memos that were going to be on the Council docket, acted on all personnel matters, handled numerous briefings with Council about police and regional issues, minority community concerns, planning and zoning issues – basically anything they might call me about.

I met with the Urban League and the NAACP, the Chamber of Commerce and numerous civic associations and with representatives of employee groups. I seldom went home before 8:30 p.m., even later if I had a meeting with Council, or with a civic association, business groups or a neighborhood. Weekends usually found me in the office or at events in the community. It was the right time of my life to be this involved, as our older son was in graduate school and our younger son was in college. I also had a very supportive husband who was interested in what I was doing and, although a busy clinical psychologist and the director of a large mental health facility, he always found the time to encourage me and to be a creative listener.

It took the national search group almost six months to bring ten applicants, including me, to be interviewed by Council. There had been 68 applicants – 67 men and one woman. I was the last applicant to be interviewed by the Mayor and council. My interview lasted three hours, longer than any of the others I was later told. The new Mayor called me the next day and told me the good news – I had been unanimously selected to be the new City Manager. One Council member told a local newspaper that on a scale of 1 to 10 they had scored me an 11!

I will always deeply appreciate the Mayor and the City Council's confidence in me when they appointed me City Manager in 1985. That was 27 years ago and I was the third women in America to be appointed City Manager in cities over 100,000; the first woman manager in the D.C. Metro Area and the first woman in a Virginia City.

I had an excellent working relationship with the new Mayor and the new City Council and we went on to redo the City's Master Plan; achieve Alexandria's first ever Triple A bond rating from both of the bond rating agencies; and to complete a multi-million flood mitigation project that opened up the Eisenhower Valley to residential and commercial development. We hired more qualified women and minorities – from the Police Department to Department Heads and other managerial positions; and we vastly improved relations between the Police Department and low-income and minority communities.

None of this would have been possible without the strong support of the Mayor and City Council and a very talented and hard-working City staff, who shared their ideas, their energy and their professional expertise. They had a strong commitment to making the City of Alexandria a place where you would be proud to work and live. We also shared a belief that public service was a noble professional and a rewarding way to spend your life.

In thinking back over my life, I realize I didn't follow a traditional path to being City Manager, certainly not back in the early 1970's. I like to tell people that I began my career with the City the same way that President Obama began his in Chicago, as a community organizer – and it's true! I was called by a friend back in 1971 who said she had seen an ad that I might be interested in. The Economic Opportunities Commission (EOC), the City's Poverty Program, was advertising for an Assistant Director of EOC, who would be in charge of community organizing and grant writing.

I could see why she called me. I was very committed to social justice, I had several years of supervisory experience as well as experience in community organizing and I had been an Assistant Editor for a national magazine. At the time in 1971, I was doing editing at home and watching my young sons. If I decided to apply for this job I knew it would be a drastic career change for me. I did apply and was selected and it was the job that profoundly changed my life.

I served as the EOC Assistant Director for four years and helped organize public housing tenants as well as several low-income target neighborhoods citizens associations. We wrote grants that were funded for the City's first treatment program for low-income alcoholics, for the City's first pre-primary program and the first Head Start program run by the Campagna Center. We helped people get jobs and learn how to budget, and take their children to public health clinics. Those were exciting years and they left me with an indelible memory of why it is important to involve all segments of the City in running the government.

In 1975, the City Manager promoted me and appointed me Director of the City's first office of Housing. My primary responsibilities included implementing the City's Community Development Block Grant and completing two large scale urban renewal programs which the City had taken over from the Housing Authority for their failure to implement in a timely manner.

The two urban renewal projects would reshape the face of downtown Alexandria – the commercial Gadsby Urban Renewal Project covered 12 blocks in the heart of downtown and the 14 block Dip Residential Urban Renewal Projects which was a low-income minority neighborhood that straddled Route One. These projects, which totaled hundreds of millions of dollars, gave me extensive financial development experience as well as an opportunity to work closely with the residents, the businesses, the developers, the banks, surrounding communities and HUD.

Residential urban renewal projects had a reputation for displacing low-income residents. That didn't happen here. ANCIA, the civic association for the low-income DIP residents, gave me an award for working very hard with them to insure that every resident had an opportunity to come back to either a subsidized rental unit or to buy a subsidized home.

I loved my 15 years as Alexandria's City Manager, from 1985 until

I retired in 2000. I was the longest serving City Manager in the City's history and still, the only woman. When I retired, the Mayor and City Council renamed the City Hall historic Cameron Street Lobby to the Vola Lawson Lobby.

I have stayed very active in my retirement. I was appointed by then-Governor Warner and ratified by the Virginia General Assembly to serve on the Virginia Commission on Local Government which I chaired. I served on the Board of the Animal Welfare League which operates the City's Vola Lawson Animal Shelter, named by the Council for me in 2000.

While recovering from breast cancer, I founded the City's Annual Walk to Fight Breast Cancer and have served as the Chair of its Fundraising Committee since its inception. As of 2012, over 5,500 low-income and uninsured women in Alexandria have received mammograms and follow-up procedures through this program and we have raised almost $2 Million dollars. I have served on the Vestry of Grace Episcopal Church and as the Treasurer.

I was of a generation that believed a woman had to work twice as hard to succeed and you should always do your best because you need to set an example and make it easier for the young women who would someday follow you. I hope I did that.

Appropriate Quote

> "The woman who can create her own job is the woman who will win fame and fortune."
>
> Amelia Earhart, Aviator

Key Insight

In the annals of local government public service, naming things after living public servants is singularly rare. To have multiple such honors is testimony to the words, "service and servant."

Vola Lawson served as Alexandria City Manager, from 1985 to 2000, the longest tenure in the City's history and still the only woman. She received the prestigious National Public Service Award in 2000 given jointly by the National Academy for Public Administration and the American Society for Public Administration. She was named the Outstanding Public Administrator in Virginia in 1995 by ASPA and received the NAPA's National Award for Innovative Leadership in 1997. In 1994, while recovering from breast cancer, Vola founded the City's Annual Walk to Fight Breast Cancer. She has been inducted into the Virginia's Women's Hall of Fame in the State Capital. In retirement, she has chaired the Virginia Commission on Local Government. The City Hall historic lobby was renamed The Vola Lawson Lobby. The Council also named its new animal shelter for Vola, a life-long animal lover.

Story Fifty Three

Where in Roswell is Kay Love?

As told By Kay Love

AS City Administrator for the City of Roswell, I quickly realized that to meet employees and to find out what was going on in the City of Roswell meant I needed to get out of the office and venture into the field. What better way to get unfiltered information and understand the processes, practices and challenges in delivery high quality services to our residents than to go directly to those who deliver the services in the work environment!

After discussing this concept with our Community Information Manager, "Where in Roswell is Kay Love" was born. The program consists of one site visit to the City department to spend time getting a crash course of their job duties and performing those duties on a limited basis during the time in the field. The Community Information staff accompanies me in the field each time and shoots photos and video on site. When we return from the field, they narrate and edit the video and post it along with the photos on the Intranet for all City employees to view.

The phrase "walk a mile in my moccasins" took on a whole new meaning; when on recent department visits I donned fire turnout gear and entered the training burn building with firefighters; I stood next to Police recruits and shot a handgun and shotgun at the firing range;

I rode on the back of a garbage truck collecting residential garbage with a sanitation crew; I changed the oil in one of our fleet vehicles with our mechanics in the garage and I changed out an old water meter with one of our crews in the Water Resources Department.

I was not in favor of taping my field visits in the beginning because I thought it would overshadow or somehow take away from the experience. I wanted the focus to be on the employees and not on taping me out in the field. Boy was I wrong! What I failed to realize at the time was that by taping the visits to departments and posting them on the intranet, everyone could share in the experience and learn about what other departments and their coworkers.

Employees have approached me after each video has been posted to the Intranet to let me know they have enjoyed it but also that they learned something about the department featured they didn't know. That has been a welcome benefit I didn't anticipate when we began the program.

While my initial purpose for doing "Where in Roswell is Kay Love?" was two-fold, meeting with employees and understanding the delivery of services, I have come away with much more. Through this experience I have renewed respect and admiration for what our employees do each and every day for our citizens. I have discovered that there are a lot of exciting things going on in our City and much to be proud of. I have a real understanding of the challenges we face and am better prepared to make recommendations to elected officials about viable solutions. I have gained a knowledge base that is invaluable in setting priorities and understanding departmental needs, in improving employee morale, and finding ways to be better tomorrow than we are today. I consider it to be one of the most rewarding experiences in my career.

Appropriate Quote

> "I like to help women help themselves, as that is, in my opinion, the best way to settle the woman question. What-

ever we can do and do well we have a right to, and I don't think anyone will deny us."

Louisa May Alcott, Author

Key Insight

A local government is a complex and diverse endeavor, crossing multiple lines of business, many of which operate 24 hours a day. Understanding the complexity is in itself a challenge and educating others about it even more so. Technology allows us to do this more comprehensively than in times past.

Kay Love is the City Administrator for the City of Roswell, GA. Before joining the City of Roswell in 2003 as Deputy City Administrator, she worked for 10 years in local government financial management for the Columbus Consolidated Government and ten years in public education financial management. Kay was appointed City Administrator in 2007. She holds MBA and B.B.A degrees from Columbus State University. She is a member of the International City Managers Association (ICMA), Georgia City-County Management Association (GCCMA), Government Finance Officers Association (GFOA), and is a past president of the Georgia Government Finance Officers Association (GGFOA.) She is a member of the Roswell Rotary Club and serves on the Board of STAR House Foundation.

Story Fifty Four

What Exactly is a Budget?

As Told By Diane Stoddard

WORKING with the media is always interesting; working with the media in a college community is particularly interesting.

I have a great amount of respect for the media and understand that they have an important role and job to do. I learned early in my career to be very responsive to the media, making responses to their inquiries a top priority, and being particularly sensitive when they were on a deadline.

However, admittedly, sometimes my patience has been tried when dealing with college reporters and journalism students. Many seem to have their eyes on winning the next Pulitzer Prize. I think that a number of them are convinced that their investigative savvy will land them the Prize even prior to graduation! When working in local government in a college town, the number of inquiries about current events skyrockets just before finals. Journalism students are busy putting their final stories together for class.

My former colleague, Jason Hilgers, the Assistant City Manager in Manhattan, Kansas, always fielded more than his fair share of these calls. He led the major redevelopment efforts that the city was undertaking in the community. Of course, this was of great interest and a perfect subject for a good story. The problem was, typically these students would call with absolutely no background on the subject whatsoever. They wanted Jason to start at the beginning, covering multiple years of background and dedicating his entire afternoon to helping them write their paper. Needless to say, sometimes this was frustrating! We began to get wise about these inquiries and would usually lead our response by asking if they had read any background information prior to visiting with us. Sometimes this did the trick.

My all-time favorite college media interview was with an eager reporter writing a story about the city's recently adopted budget. The reporter began by asking some really good questions about the budget outcome and the budget process. I went on in my response for some five minutes or so, explaining the process of meetings and input involved in putting the budget together. I hit the high points of the facts and figures of the budget, being sure to reinforce how the budget reflected the priorities and goals of our City Commission.

His next question was one that I will never quite forget. He asked "What exactly is a budget?" I was so taken back with the question that I didn't know exactly how to respond! The best I could come up with off the cuff was "Well, I think that probably should have been your first question!"

Then, I told him that a budget is your financial plan – like your check book – you have money coming in and money going out and the budget is a spending plan. I still don't think that he ever got it!

Appropriate Quote

> "The real art of conversation is not only to say the right thing in the right place but to leave unsaid the wrong thing at the tempting moment."
>
> Lady Dorothy Nevill, English Horticulturalist

Key Insight

Stephen Covey teaches the "Power of the Pause" – that tiny space between stimulus and response that allows us to think as oppose to react. Buford Watson, former ICMA President from Diane's community used to say, "When it comes to the media, be a well, not a fountain!" One of the most difficult things local government professionals say is no thing.

Diane Stoddard is Assistant City Manager for the City of Lawrence, Kansas. She has served the cities of Manhattan, Ottawa and Lenexa, Kansas during her 20 year career in local government. Diane holds a B.A. in Political Science and an MPA, both from the University of Kansas. Diane enjoys spending time with her family and friends and she and her husband, Brian, keep busy enjoying activities of their two sons, Nathan and Adam.

Story Fifty Five

Those Electric Linemen

As Told By Diane Stoddard

I have never really felt isolated as a woman serving in local government. Fortunately, I started the profession at a time when there were a number of wonderful women who had forged a path for other women to follow. My MPA class consisted of 13 and 5 of us were women.

My gender has never affected my professional development. However, one time, I became strikingly aware of a lack of other women.

In the early to mid-1990s, the federal government was leading a large effort to address electric utility regulations and there were a lot of new issues. I was asked to attend a conference of electric linemen in central Kansas that would be focusing on new safety regulations. Besides the wait staff at the conference center, I was literally the only woman in the room.

I must admit it was a strange feeling!

However, I did enjoy having the women's restroom entirely to myself as the men stood in a line snaking out of the men's room!

To this day, I have never met an electric linewoman, though I am sure that some exist! I'm also sure that many organizations have likely modernized their titles to say Electric Line Worker or something similar!

Appropriate Quote

> "Because I am a woman, I must make unusual efforts to succeed. If I fail, no one will say, 'She doesn't have what it takes.' They will say, "Women don't have what it takes."
>
> Clare Boothe Luce, Congresswoman, Author and Ambassador

Key Insight

We occasionally experience those situations in life that cause us to step back mentally and look at our world in a new light. Not having to stand in line can be one – as is recognizing we are the only one (of whatever we are) in the room.

Diane Stoddard is Assistant City Manager for the City of Lawrence, Kansas. She has served the cities of Manhattan, Ottawa and Lenexa, Kansas during her 20 year career in local government. Diane holds a B.A. in Political Science and an MPA, both from the University of Kansas. Diane enjoys spending time with her family and friends and she and her husband, Brian, keep busy enjoying activities of their two sons, Nathan and Adam.

Story Fifty Six

The Good, the Bad and the... Funny!

As told by Amanda DeGan

MY career path to local government management led me through the ranks of entering our profession as a deputy court clerk for the City of Keller, TX. As I completed my related degrees, I also progressed to larger court offices across the DFW Metroplex – which leads to some interesting stories.

Most who work in the local government field do not realize the tremendous amount of stress and abuse a clerk who processes the traffic citations undergoes on a daily basis. The position takes a *'special type of someone'* to handle the repetitive questions, belligerent defendants, upset individuals with large judgments due to the court, distraught family members with a loved one in the jail facility, demanding attorney representatives, etc. But, every once in a while a defendant comes along that either makes you laugh out loud, is downright funny or reminds you why you work in this profession.

Arlington Court – Two of my stories come from an office that would be considered 'large' by state standards – the City of Arlington Municipal Court. As you can imagine a short period in this type of environment can lead to a wide variety of experiences. In the time that I worked in this office, I was amazed at the sheer volume of court cases and the long wait times for defendants in the lobby area. Having come from a smaller office, a one-hour wait was unheard of in my professional experience but this was fairly normal on a very busy day in Arlington.

The Bad – I was working as a Support Services Supervisor and normally had the responsibility of overseeing approximately 42 clerks who processed the docket settings, warrants, citation entry, and teen court. On this particular day, I was helping the Customer Service Supervisor oversee the front counter while he was out of the office for lunch. The queue line for defendants was long as we had several court sessions running at the same time in addition to the normal walk-in individuals who wanted to pay their citations or set a court date.

To set the scene, the court office had a bank of four windows that contained a customer service counter and glass windows with openings to talk through that were open at any given moment, and all of the cashiers were involved in some sort of customer service discussion. A male defendant, let's call him Mr. Smith, had been in conversation with a cashier for some time and the people behind were shifting in place and displaying their displeasure at what they felt was taking too long and delaying their time at the window.

The man repeatedly asked the cashier to reduce his citation for him as he felt the fines and fees were excessive. He loudly repeated his irritation at the $167.00 fine amount and couldn't for the life of him figure out why there would be a set fine amount from the judge for the offense and a set amount of taxes to be collected for the state – that combined to "rob him of his hard earned cash!"

Mr. Smith had turned around to discuss the matter with those standing in line behind him and by now was about to have the whole lobby in an uproar. The clerk dutifully attempted to explain his legal options and the break-out of the fines, but Mr. Smith was unsatisfied – he called for the dreaded supervisor. Now to fully understand, I hadn't been working in this office for long and still didn't have down all the procedures at the cashier window and was frankly a bit nervous to deal with a combative defendant in this type of situation. My first reaction, was "great… where is my counterpart when I need him!" I was sure the Customer Service Supervisor would know exactly how to explain all this better than I could but he was at lunch! So to the window I went.

Mr. Smith rejoined his cry for a lower fine amount and then demanded that I waive those d#@m taxes charged by the state as we were nothing better than tax collectors for the state of Texas and didn't deserve to take any more money out of his pocket. I reiterated all the same options the clerk had given to him and further explained that we didn't have the authority to waive or lower any fines once established by the judge.

To say that Mr. Smith was beyond irritated would be an understatement. By this time, the lobby security officers were attempting to help Mr. Smith see reason and usher him from the building. We had also gathered quite a crowd of onlookers – both in the defendant line and in the office – as all wanted to watch the circus at the window. To say I was embarrassed would be putting it mildly – here I was new to the job, wanting to make a good impression on the staff and provide them with a level of confidence in their leadership and I was unable to handle an irate defendant (which I had done hundreds of times before) at the cashier window.

This type of an event sets a bad tone for the entire day of customer service duties and is discussed in the break room for weeks – everyone becomes an armchair quarterback as to how they would have handled things differently. By this time, Mr. Smith had determined maybe it was best for him to leave and come back another day. I was so relieved to think this debacle was over – and was walking back to my office when Mr. Smith dashed back to the window – stuck his mouth into the round cut-out for talking with the clerks and yelled to the entire staff,

"HOW DID SOMEONE AS STUPID AS YOU - GET YOUR JOB?!"

Frankly how do you respond to this...I had to laugh all the way back to my desk.

The Good – Several months later, I had a defendant at these same customer service windows – who was faced with an insurmountable amount of money that he owed for traffic offenses. The young man was a student at the local university and was barely getting by on his student loan funding and the odd job that he could pick up here and there in the city. He owed something close to $2,000 and was in tears at the prospect of paying this and then realizing he would owe surcharges to the state for his driver license convictions as well.

I was again covering the cashier window for my counterpart, and could tell the clerk was having trouble explaining this person's options. I asked if I could be of assistance and the student proceeded to spend 20 minutes explaining all of his financial obligations and lack of work prospects. I know this time seems excessive, but in local government many times people just want to be heard – to feel like they can connect with a live human being who can empathize with their plight. I put that time in with the student and although I couldn't change the outcome for him, he was extremely grateful for the opportunity to discuss his life with someone else. A few weeks later, he went so far as to send a handwritten card that said "thank you for your assistance and willingness to listen to me – as well as lend your patience and kindness. May God show you the favor that you have shown to me."

I have kept this card for 14 years and pull it out from time to time to remind me of why we work in what is sometimes a thankless and trying environment. We are ultimately to be of service to our residents, stakeholders and fellow man – that is what makes local government worthwhile and a joy to serve!

The Funny – From Arlington, I moved to a smaller court for the Town of Westlake. When we began this office, it was housed in a small store-front setting where we did not have the luxury of glass windows and customer service counters. We had defendants walk in and sit next to our desks in order to help them with their case files. Now, this might seem trivial but those windows and counters serve multiple purposes – to keep down the illnesses transmitted through colds and flu season from some defendants and provide an added measure of security.

On this day, a defendant appeared in the office and stated that he needed to make arrangements to pay his citation. As I did not have authorization for this type of a process, I explained that the defendant needed to appear in court and speak with the judge to obtain an extension.

The defendant was polite and patient and felt I was extending him the same courtesy. In this cooperative atmosphere he apparently felt a great desire to explain all of his police/court encounters to me in great detail. He lived in the neighboring city of Southlake and had had several run-ins with the local police force. In order to fully understand the situation, you need to know that this man was not slight in build and did not seem to take hygiene very seriously.

He proceeded to regale me with an occurrence of how the police department had appeared at his home and 'took to shootin' him up on his front porch' at which point, he removed his shirt to show me all the bullet holes in his belly! This was definitely a first for me – a quasi-undressed, somewhat smelly and rather hairy, defendant had taken off his clothing to display his quite large belly to point out his 'war wounds' as he called them in the office.

It was a day that I will vividly remember and goes to show you that the next time your court clerk comes in to discuss a little issue with you – keep in mind that you can never really know what to expect in the Municipal Court. Treasure those who work in this field as their travails are long and their experiences varied!

Appropriate Quote

> "Do not let your fire go out, spark by irreplaceable spark in the hopeless swaps of the not-quite, the not-yet, and the not-at-all. Do not let the hero in your soul perish in lonely frustration for the life you deserved and have never been

able to reach. The world you desire can be won. It exists...it is real...it is possible...it's yours."

Ayn Rand, Author

Key Insight

In local government you never know what adventures life at work holds. Providing great customer service to involuntary customers is always a challenge, and in doing it you are likely to accumulate your own war wounds...but share them only with friends and family, and always fully clothed.

Amanda DeGan is Assistant to the Town Manager of Westlake, Texas. She has served as the Support Services Supervisor for the City of Arlington, TX, the Municipal Court Supervisor for the City of Bedford, TX and as Deputy Court Clerk for the City of Keller, TX.

Story Fifty Seven

Defining Moments

As Told by Cheryl Hilvert

ON April 9, 1999, a devastating F-4 tornado wreaked havoc on the City of Montgomery, Ohio and several other suburban communities in the greater Cincinnati area. The storm hit at 5:15 a.m., when families were sleeping, businesses were closed, and everything was supposed to be peaceful. Hundreds of residential and business properties were damaged or destroyed. Four people were killed.

April 9 is a date that will forever be etched in the minds of the people of Montgomery—the residents who suffered loss; businesses that were impacted; the schools, the faith-based community, civic and service organizations and everyday citizens who supported one another in this time of incredible challenge; and, the employees of the city and the many other jurisdictions who assisted in our community's time of need. April 9 will be remembered for the widespread destruction of beautiful neighborhoods; financial and personal loss; damage to infrastructure and the environment; the stress of rebuilding; and most importantly, those who lost their lives that fateful morning.

While it may sound strange, it will also be remembered as a significant moment for our city. Significant because it truly built "community" among neighbors, families, organizations, residents, and our City Council and staff. It also forged cooperative working

relationships between our city and other jurisdictions in our area that selflessly helped in our time of need. The tornado, in and of itself, was nothing more than a destructive storm. However, it truly created a defining moment for our community. . . and a community out of that defining moment.

For me, April 9th began as what should have been a relaxing cruise day through the Panama Canal with a group of family and friends. As I woke up and prepared for a day of fabulous sights, what I saw on the small television set in my cabin would literally change my life forever. CNN International was reporting on a tornado that had devastated parts of Hamilton County, Ohio near Cincinnati. A sick feeling came over me as I saw Montgomery police cars amidst total devastation that had occurred only hours before.

I was able to get home very early the next morning and at 2 a.m., one of our police supervisors drove me through "ground zero," the area of the city that was most heavily impacted by the tornado. It honestly looked like the devastation of war that we see on the news. It was hard for me to visualize where I was as nothing looked familiar. (I later learned that one of our veteran fire fighters that responded that morning said that he had worked in the City for more than 20 years, he literally had no idea where he was that morning when he searched for survivors in that once beautiful section of town.) It was dark, silent and uninhabited as the curfew put in place by the City had worked to get residents, gawkers, would-be thieves out of the area and deter looting. Only the satellite television trucks from every network that you could imagine sat watch on the hill overlooking the area. Also on that hill was the shell of our Public Works Department that had suffered a great deal of damage and equipment loss. It was the last time I saw the area in that state— total destruction, yet somehow very peaceful. The ambitious work of clean up and rebuilding would soon begin.

In the early hours of the disaster, our staff and City Council had done a remarkable job in managing the situation, and the people. Smart decisions were made as to the use of mutual aid, adjustment of employee work schedules, the imposition of a curfew, suspension of bidding and contracting requirements and an appropriation of needed funds to address the disaster. Quality information was shared with those residents impacted, the community as a whole, as well as the local, national, and international news outlets. Relationships were formed; trust was built.

In the days ahead, we continued to make good decisions as to what to do and how to do it. I like to think that our planning and training in emergency operations helped (yes, we had just completed a table top disaster response exercise 10 days before!), as did the quality of our city personnel. I really feel it was the belief in the "higher moral purpose" of the work we do—that "commitment to helping others regardless of what needed to be done"—that became pervasive throughout our community helped us to get through this disaster. We never lost sight of what had to be done to rebuild the community and assist our residents who had been impacted. As a small city with less than 100 employees, we had to build relationships and partnerships to get that done.

Offers of assistance came quickly from a variety of sources from disaster services agencies, other governments, citizen groups and organizations, businesses and the faith-based community. Those offers quickly became true partnerships and with many of these groups, we formed lasting relationships that benefited our community from that point forward. When these groups showed up, the work somehow became easier. All of a sudden, we weren't alone anymore. . . and that was a great feeling!

As with any natural disaster, the community was the recipient of assistance through such organizations as the Red Cross and Salvation Army. Each of these disaster assistance agencies helped to provide assistance to residents in the form of housing, food and other needs. Additionally, they provided food for the recovery workers that were present in our community for months after the tornado. It wasn't always the best tasting stuff, but it certainly helped after a long day of cleanup.

The County's Emergency Management Agency was extremely

helpful to our city as well as the three-to-four other jurisdictions that were impacted by the storm. It helped us to navigate the confusing FEMA assistance process as well as disaster declaration requests to the State of Ohio. While the State came through for us, fortunately or unfortunately, we received no FEMA disaster declaration because we had more than 99% of our affected residents that had insurance on their properties. It was a tremendous amount of work and something that we had to do. Every time I hear now of a FEMA declaration, I have a special appreciation for the people who completed all the paperwork and documentation. It is funny how, as government employees, we learn so much about things that the typical citizen knows, or cares, very little about.

The State of Ohio came through for us in a big way. When FEMA did not designate our city as a federal disaster area, the State made a special appropriation to assist us financially with the cost of cleanup and repair of public facilities. They basically filled the financial "gap" created by the lack of the FEMA disaster declaration and anticipated funding. With city clean up and repair costs associated with this disaster totaling nearly $1 million, the State funding really helped. The State also made available cleanup assistance through Ohio Department of Transportation personnel and security through the Ohio National Guard. The Ohio Attorney General's Office, assisted by our local Bar Association, created a Contractor Registration Program that helped to protect our residents against the unscrupulous contractors that always show up in these disasters. These folks, and all those representing the State of Ohio were truly wonderful partners for literally months after the tornado struck.

One of my favorite stories dealing with State assistance was when the inmates from Lebanon Correctional Institute a nearby state prison – showed up, along with their armed guards, to help with clean up. The inmates were dressed in hideous orange jumpsuits with "LCI" stamped across their backs. The guards were the biggest human beings I had ever seen and were fully armed. They were not the typical visitors to our upper-middle-class community to say the least, yet they were willing to help with almost anything. Because we were unable to assist directly on private property with cleanup (we did provide for collection for all the debris, we just couldn't go onto private property to do the work), we decided this assistance would be great for property owners and took a real risk in letting them help in the community. In spite of hot weather, our Assistant Fire Chief decided to put safety vests on the inmates to cover up the LCI stamp on their backs and no one knew the difference! In fact, one of the residents said later, "I don't know where you found those nice young men, but they were such a help to me. I would love to have them over for dinner to thank them." We all just laughed a little under our breaths when she said that.

The unsung heroes of the April 9th tornado were the employees from more than 35 different government jurisdictions that came to our aid in the weeks and months to follow. From police and fire personnel to public works staff, we literally had help from everywhere. . . and for as long as we needed it.

The public safety assistance roughly lasted for several weeks as, after the initial emergency response, we moved to providing some level of security for the impacted area. The public works personnel were with us for months assisting in debris removal. I mentioned earlier that our Public Works Department was impacted by the tornado, so these people brought tools and equipment and strong backs to assist our staff who were doing the best they could with what they had left.

We used the Public Works facility as a staging area for debris removal. There were weeks when we were processing more than 150 trucks per hour through that facility loaded with debris. All colors of trucks with the names of all the cities, villages, townships and other agencies that were helping. They were happy with a good lunch and lots of Mt. Dew and coffee. They worked hard and always had smiles on their faces for us and for our residents. I truly loved those guys.

The faith-based community also stepped up in a big way. While that old separation of church and state rule has probably prevented some of us from fully working with the faith-based organizations in our day-to-day work, we quickly found that they were excellent partners in our recovery efforts. And, those good quality relationships have continued long after the tornado was but a memory. They were there to offer comfort and counseling to those impacted by the tornado—residents and workers alike.

After more than 3000 volunteers showed up on the weekend after the tornado to help (some in flip-flops and some with baby carriages!), it became readily apparent that our staff could not manage this large influx of well-meaning, yet not-always-prepared volunteer labor. One church stepped up and hired a full-time volunteer coordinator who assisted us for a year and a half in various volunteer efforts.

Other churches prepared and delivered meals for all the recovery workers and did so for months. They didn't have to follow all the rules and regulations that the Red Cross had to with its packaged meals. I commented earlier in this story about how the quality of the packaged meals was sometimes lacking and they were never really very "interesting." That was never the case with the church workers who set up a make-shift kitchen in our damaged Public Works facility or the pastor who regularly drove his own truck to deliver delicious home-cooked meals to the workers in the field. The expression, "Eat Out of the Red Truck!" quickly became well known by all of us working in the field during the cleanup efforts as a way to get the best food out there.

In addition to the local church support, we learned that there are many faith-based disaster relief teams who came to assist. They came with workers and equipment in an almost military fashion. They wanted no compensation and were hard workers and, like the inmates from LCI, we were able to put them onto private property to assist residents. They were wonderful!

One of my favorite stories of these helpers came very early in the cleanup and recovery effort and was our first experience with a faith-based disaster relief team. All of us were tired and were desperately trying to manage the situation and all the helpers. A call came over the City band radio from the Police Department and said, "there is a team of Mennonites here to help. They have chain saws and equipment and appear ready to go. Where should we send them?" A frazzled voice from "ground zero" answered quickly saying, "I don't care what they have on (thinking the dispatcher said 'men in tights'), if they have equipment send them to me." We have laughed about that for years.

The residents and businesses of our community were rocks of strength through this disaster. They helped one another through volunteering, donations and just about any kind of support that you can imagine. The residents and the home owners association in the area that was directly hit by the storm were unbelievable. They created phone trees and remained in contact with those who lost their homes and moved elsewhere. They served as our communication link to those who were most impacted. They offered help to those in cleaning up their properties and worked tirelessly to help their neighbors.

They also had a weekly dinner for anyone who wanted to show up. Sometimes they would have an inspirational speaker, other times they would have a prayer service, and sometimes they would just talk about baseball or whatever else was going on around town. We made it a point to have at least one city staff member in attendance at these dinners so that we could answer questions. It quickly became something we all wanted to attend regularly as we got much more than we gave from these meetings. This was community building in the truest sense of the word.

I purposely saved the true heroes for the end of this story and they are the City employees and City Council members that gave of themselves in those weeks and months following the disaster. It was amazing to see what they could do. Everyone in our small organization stepped up and worked more hours and in more ways than they ever thought they could. They saw things they never thought they would see. They made tough decisions and said no when they had to. They worked beside total strangers, including inmates, volunteers, and staff from other cities, in service to our community. They cared for and supported another. They were proud of what they did. I was extremely proud of them. Mere words and stories can never explain what they faced and what they did that day in April of 1999 and in the weeks and months to come.

I related earlier in this story how my day began on April 9, 1999. What should have been a relaxing vacation day quickly became one filled with feelings of fear, inadequacy, and concern for our staff and our community. What I learned in the days and months following the tornado was the importance of relationships as well as how it feels to be part of a community where people truly care about one another as well as how powerful relationships and community can be when overcoming obstacles.

The April 9th tornado, while a devastating natural disaster, was truly nothing more than a destructive storm that was over in a matter of seconds. It destroyed property, created fear and took lives. But, what it didn't do was take away the human spirit or that driving force that made many of us enter public service—that feeling of a higher moral purpose to the work we perform. In all its destruction, that tornado made public servants out of a lot of local government employees. It built teams, partnerships and relationships that stood the test of time and made our city a community in the truest sense of the word. It taught us to see the possibilities in a bad situation and also proved that, in spite of how hard things can be, you can still find some humor in your work. It bonded citizens together and enabled them to help one another and proved that the human spirit can overcome most anything.

The F-4 tornado that wreaked havoc on Montgomery that April morning will be remembered for many things. Perhaps most importantly. . .it created a defining moment for our community. . . and a community out of that defining moment.

Appropriate Quote

> "Normal day, let me be aware of the treasure you are. Let me learn from you, love you, bless you before you depart. Let me not pass you by in quest of some rare and perfect tomorrow."
>
> Mary Jean Irion, Poet

Key Insight

In the quest for growth, for economic health, for more, for bigger, for faster, for better for our communities and organizations we often forget to cherish today. Then an "April 9th" happens and we realize what a gift a normal day is.

Cheryl Hilvert is a Senior Consultant with ICMA. She has served as City Manager in Montgomery, Ohio and Fairfield, Ohio. She is on the Board for the Alliance for Innovation and is a past Regional Vice-President for ICMA. She has her BA and MPA from Eastern Kentucky University, and is a Credentialed Manager.

Story Fifty Eight

Women Leading Government and How the Legacy of Women Supporting Women Began

As Told by Dr. Penelope Culbreth-Graft

IN June 2006, Sarona Vivanco, a bright, young Management analyst from the City of Santa Clarita, California emailed me on behalf of the Municipal Assistants of Southern California (MMASC), inviting me to serve on a panel to prepare emerging leaders for promotions. I remember my trip to Palm Desert just one month later for the conference because the temperature gauge on my care hit 126 degrees. Even more memorable was the time in between sessions and after the panel when young female managers pummeled me with questions about my career path, work/family balance and tips for success. Their hunger for information on how a female can succeed in the profession astonished my sensibilities.

Just a year earlier Frank Benest recruited me to join Cal-ICMA's Preparing the Next Generation (PNG) team. Ken Pulskamp and Frank poured their hearts into the effort and invited managers across California to answer the call of strengthening the pool of future leaders by developing the younger generation. Grim national statistics suggested that over 50 percent of all city jobs would be vacant within five years with few qualified candidates to fill the positions.

In 2006, PNG met with the California Municipal League annual conference in Sacramento, California. Unable to attend the League conference, my calendar allowed me to attend the pre-conference session of the PNG meeting. That day, everything changed for women in our profession.

The two PNG co-chairs reviewed a list of activities underway that already revolutionized the preparation of future managers. These included Don Maruska's labor of love – coaching conference calls, pamphlets of career tips, workshops, mentoring and publications. As the dialogue continued, several female city and county managers filled empty seats around the corner where I was perched. On a break, we talked about the success of PNG efforts but lamented over the lack of focus on women.

Reconvening, I took the bait when Frank asked, "Does anyone have other suggestions of how we can develop our future leaders?" "Several of us," I began, pointing to the small band of female managers, "feel there is a tremendous need to offer special assistance to young women. We want to help." I shared my experience from the recent MMASC Conference. Several women spoke of similar experiences emphasizing the need to engage this special population in our field.

Frank wasted no time. "You've got the lead Penny. Tell us when you make progress." He asked for volunteers and appointed Robertta Burns, County Administrative Officer for Imperial County, to co-chair the effort. Robertta accepted the assignment eagerly along with several other women, who would become founding members of the effort, later designated Women Leading Government (WLG.)

I do not remember much more that day other than wondering what I had gotten myself into. My work schedule already topped the ridiculous, how much more could I ignore my family range. My City Council had expressed concern that my adjunct teaching schedule at

USC distracted from my 24-hour availability. Nonetheless, everyone involved agreed – helping women in our profession ranked high on the priority list.

Our impromptu committee met briefly after the PNHG meeting. "Don't worry. We're all in this together," they said. I had no idea those women would become an immovable support base for the remainder of my career or that together we would build a national organization – the first to develop female city and county managers.

Women trail blazed the ranks of city and county management long before WLG. What astonished us was a report provided by founding member, Jan Perkins, that less than ten percent of all county managers and less than 21 percent of all local governments were headed by females at the time. With women comprising over 50 percent of the US population, these statistics confirmed that substantial work needed to be done. Women needed to be ready to step in as leaders in our communities if the local government profession was going to fill vacancies projected through the next five years. As well, representational democracy demanded that the abysmal statistics of female managers embrace and promote females to reflect the demographics of the communities we served.

The Disneyland Hotel offered our newly-appointed team free conference space, treats and resources for our first meeting. To connect our geographically-challenged group, our host arranged for a lengthy conference call. Using complementary notepads of mouse ears, we sketched out and recorded our first plans. Nine members became the founding membership to include: Robertta Burns, Penelope Culbreth-Graft, Jenny Haruyama, Irma Hernandez, Nancy Hetrick, Tamara Latourneau, Jan Perkins, Debra Rose, Cathy Standiford and Sarona Vivanco.

Accessible, affordable and inclusive. Those we the goals cited four our initial efforts. That afternoon, we agreed upon our name, identified our target membership, defined the population of women we wanted to serve, planned our first event and created a mission statement: **To help women succeed in public service by enhancing**

career-building models that develop leaderships skills and by networking professional women in government.

In December 2006, the City of Huntington Beach, California approved funding of $5,000 for the work of Women Leading Government. Within 30 days of our first meeting, our planning group included nine women with promises of more, committing to help at our first event. Energy from these outstanding women convinced me to learn to be a webmaster and launch a website. With my husband William, standing with me, he plunked down the cash for a Go Daddy website under our womenleadinggovernment.org name. Within just 30 days, over 5,000 queries navigated the multi-page site that hosted stories of women managers, a calendar of events and links to other websites to support young female managers in their careers.

In March, 2007, Pam Easter, Assistant City Manager of Rancho Cucamonga, California hosted our Inaugural Round Table at her city's Victoria Gardens Community Center nestled in the foothills beneath Cucamonga Peak of the San Gabriel Mountains. Twenty-five women participated and set out a plan for meeting the needs of young women in local government. Wanting to take our support to local governments throughout the State of California, we planned our next round table for an Orange County location.

Jack and Susan Simpson had just begun their innovative, TRACKDOWN Management Services newsier, dedicating their second edition to WLG and California's Women City Managers. Providing detailed biographical sketches on 44 California female city managers, the newsier provided exposure throughout the state to WLG's efforts. They lauded the commitment and contributions of WLG and female city managers to the profession. Other recognition of the work began to flow, bringing sponsorships for many of the activities to come.

Following our October 2007 Roundtable Luncheon at the Bower's Museum in Santa Ana, our membership list had grown to over 130 women. WLG joined with several other groups and events that supported women in management, including a Women's Leadership Summit sponsored by the Municipal Management Assistants of

Northern California (MMANC.) Women expressed excitement about the support they were now receiving and about how WLG and other efforts brought them together in a caring, professional way.

A small group of female students in my USC MPA class chose WLG for their class project. Using results from a survey carted for our members, the students identified the needs of females in our profession, explored the potential for dues, and summarized a list of the most popular program ideas. Their findings encouraged us to put forward and expand the agenda to bring services to our future leaders. Development and networking remained our two priorities. As a bonus, two of the female students decided to pursue city management as a career, as a result of working with WLC city managers.

The network continued to grow, as WLG formed its' first official Board of Directors in November, 2007. An oceanfront meeting at the newly constructed junior lifeguard headquarters at the City of Huntington Beach became the backdrop for the first strategic planning session of WLC. Offices were named for 15 positions. I became the first Chair of the group with Tamara Letourneau, City Manager of Yorba Linda, California, agreeing to serve as Vice Chair. Women from cities and counties all over California stepped into roles of support for the organization. In addition for formalizing our financial status as an organization, we named representatives for regions of the state and liaisons to various organizations such as the County Administrative Officers Association, California Association of Counties and the League of California Cities and to Special districts. WLG's first work plan included creating a national charter to support women in other states.

As the groups' efforts reached new heights, I took the City Manager position in Colorado Springs, Colorado. Facing a $90 Million shortfall in my new city, my ability to continue leading the WLG effort waned. Tamara stepped up as Chair and continued leading the effort through a job change of her own. The group remained unified and committed to helping women. By the time I resigned, member rolls topped 260 and new technology was needed to coordinate the growing group of professionals. ICMA pitched in by taking over responsibility for the website and integrating it into the national organization's data base and website. Nationally recognized by ICMA, WLCG had made it as one of America's top professional organization for women in government.

Many of the original founding members are still involved in WLG today, as scores of women continue to join the effort. Adding a new goal, Jennifer Phillips, 2011-2012 Chair , stated, "Our goals is to build not just a professional organization with a roster of quality individuals, but a network of active women that mentor and support each other in a purposeful way."

As I look back on my 32 year career in municipal management, I can attest that this group of amazing women had an impact on my life, helping and supporting me on my journey. Today in retirement, many of these women remain friends.

To the extraordinary women of local government leadership, I commend you and thank you for the contributions you make to our communities, our country and our profession. To our future leaders, I encourage you to go boldly and share your new found skills and strengths with the next generation.

For more information about Women Leading Government, visit http://icma.org/en/ca/program/wig.

Appropriate Quote

"Not knowing when the dawn will come, I open every door."

Emily Dickinson, Poet

Key Insight

Although extraordinary professionals make an extraordinary difference in the communities they serve it is often the extra-curricular volunteer activities that add the most satisfaction to a career. To be a part of founding a group of such import to so many is an especial joy.

What can you do to serve the profession?

Dr. Penelope Culbreth-Graft is a retired, credentialed City Manager. She served in public agencies for over 32 years in 11 cities and one Indian Reservation. Her positions included City Manager and Assistant City Manager in cities, ranging in population from 12,000 to 1.2 million in California, Arizona, and Colorado. Dr. Culbreth-Graft taught for five universities over 18 years in the Masters' programs in Public Administration and Criminal Justice. She has a Doctorate in Public Administration from the University of La Verne; a Master's of Public Administration from the California State University Consortium; and, two Bachelor's degrees from California Polytechnic University, Pomona.

Story Fifty Nine

Adventures of an American Girl

As Told by Dr. Penelope Culbreth-Graft

MY first memory of public service was as a Brownie in the Girl Scouts in the late 1960s. My mother was a troop leader for my older sister's troop. My Brownie troop edged its way into many of my sister's big-girl activities. For several years, we volunteered for Santa Claus Incorporated and Head Start, cleaning old toys and making new ones for impoverished families.

In those days, an adventurous life for a girl was a camping trip. We aspired to be mothers, teachers, and nurses. An accomplishment included learning proper etiquette for a dinner party and typing 80 words per minute on a manual typewriter.

After completing two bachelors' degrees, the realization that I could not find a job that paid enough to move out of my mother's home left me desperate and in search of any job I could find. I landed in a city, working as a secretary in housing and redevelopment. The prescribed dream for a girl was accomplished.

It did not take long for boredom to set in. Working on my master's degree gave me an opportunity to conduct research projects for my employer. I wrote staff reports for my boss, attended council meetings, and asked for more responsibility. My boss assigned me as liaison to the mobile home rent review board. This began an adventure that led me into unusual places and on a journey that pushed the boundaries for an ordinary girl from Indiana.

A new city job took me to Los Angeles during the 1984 Olympics. The swimming venue was located in a city facility near city hall – a place where I ate lunch. Lunchtime exposed me to the US Olympic swimming team and Olympic politics. Known for its large Chinese population, my city job allowed me to develop my Chinese language skills I learned a few years earlier as a foreign exchange student in Taiwan. Each day revealed a new facet of culture and athletic prowess right at the doorsteps of city hall.

My next position relocated me to a city impacted by the Los Angeles International Airport. A bedroom community, this small town complained of noise, fumes, and low property values from a neighboring operation 40 miles away. "The law is clear; your city can't change flight profiles," legal counsel advised. My assignment placed me at the side of a council member, who served as the chief labor negotiator for a grocery store chain going up against the Teamsters. Working with him, I learned never to accept "No." The adventure took me to San Francisco to work with an acoustic's consultant, into Los Angeles before the Airport Board Commissioners, and to Washington DC to lobby for a legislative change so we could alter the flight path. Against all odds, LAX approved the flight profile change that still protects that city today.

A pig farm is a gold mine. My first city as a city manager was home to a large pig farm owned by a reputable family. Mother and son cared for it proudly. No one complained about the smell or the noise because the pigs predated the beachfront cottages. The pig farm claimed ownership to the center of the two-square mile city, leaving little room for development. Having discussions with the son, I learned about a simpler way of life, down-to-earth values, and filial piety. The son refused generous offers for purchase and development of his land because, "Mama wants to stay and tend the pigs." The adventure of this city took me to the state and nation's capitols to fund a train station on the ocean-side of town. Not accepting "no," the station was funded and built, making it a rare stop along the Central Coast of California.

Coastal communities offer great adventure not just because of the eclectic cache of visitors but for the richness of resources at sea. Visiting an oil platform, hovering above the ocean presented a breath-taking opportunity. The oil company requested public officials take a day and visit a platform to observe the safety protocols. We departed on a helicopter, racing whales to our destination. Stepping on to the platform, the oil company representative advised me that I was in more danger of getting my high heels stuck in a metal plate than being electrocuted from the constant surge of the electrified platform. We observed men (no women) working in unfiltered sunlight, lifting barrels, soldering trusses, and cleaning every inch of the platform. Safety protocols impressed our group but did not alter the outcome of their preference that no more platforms be permitted on the Pacific coastline. By the time we returned that evening, our exhaustion tes-tified of the no-frills, tough, working environment of life on an oil platform.

San Diego is a destination resort town, covering 400 square miles and stretching to the Mexico border. Every day held an adventure. To name just a few:

- Ventured through underground tunnels used to smuggle people and drugs,
- Visited Mexico maquiladoras (US/Mexico manufacturing businesses),
- Talked to the world's first super computer at the University of California at San Diego,
- Met with Sol Price (Price Club founder) on his philan-thropic community projects,
- Built a homeless shelter out of an abandoned bread factory,
- Worked on major league baseball and national football league stadium projects,

- Created a 6 am-to-6 pm citywide day care program with free services for low-income families
- Toured air craft carriers, and
- Helped plan the National Republican Convention.

In this city, I watched 11,000 public servants do miraculous feats with little resources. Waking every morning to azure seascapes and marine breezes, the sting of the daily grind dissipated by the time I entered the doors of city hall.

Life reached a new level of excitement with an invitation to work as a Tribal Government Manager for an Indian Tribe. I exchanged my harbor view office for a prairie-bound trailer. I rubbed shoulders with the cows and a very large bull. The Indians I served taught me the important values of life, having struggled for everything they had accomplished. Sharing with me their sacred traditions and unwritten language, my concept of public service changed, as we worked to create programs to help tribal members graduate from high school, arranged for drug and alcohol addiction intervention, and designed a home loan program to replace substandard housing with homes that withstood the elements.

The Tribe provided the funds to build parks, water and wastewater systems, and pave roads. Tribal members opened their hearts and homes to my husband and me. They gave freely and asked for little in return.

During my three-year contract, I toured six other Indian nations across the state in search of a tribal court program that we could use to create our own court system. My medicine woman companion, traveling with her peace pipe and herbal remedies, revealed to me the difficulties of being Indian in a white-man's world.

Finally, I stood shoulder-to-shoulder with 2,000 American Indians at the opening ceremony of the National Congress of American Indians. As the only white face in the crowd, I learned for the first time what it was like to be a true minority.

Staring into a portal to Hades, my next city led me to the darkest place on earth. Just 60 miles to the north, I returned to local government and worked for a city with its own electric utility. This adventure led me to the coalmines of Utah and a coal refinery where I peered into a seven-inch opening of the coal furnace. The intensity of the blast nearly knocked me off my feet. The work to bring electricity to our communities is dangerous, volatile, and hard. I left the refinery with a sense of amazement and gratefulness for the work done by so many never named or credited for their labor.

The coalmine experience took us into the bowels of the earth. Donning body coverings, tool belt, and miner's hat, we received training on the dos and don'ts of the mine. Cautioned about the crackling coal overhead and the darkness without a lamp, our group still gasped as we descended the shaft, venturing in and out of darkness. Heavy metal walls separated the dangerous work areas from the off-limit zones behind the equipment. We watched an enormous grinder eat through the coal like cereal, consuming everything in its path. Coal fell on our heads and crunched beneath our feet. Earth-borne smells permeated the cave, as we followed behind our guide. Upon returning to sunlight, fresh air snapped us into the reality of life in darkness. We knew that many workers had tread into this place and died. What a sacrifice just to mine the coal that powers our cities.

The wealthy coastal city of Huntington Beach offered a special insight into the lives of men and woman who fought in Iraq. Adopting the 3/1 battalion from Camp Pendleton, I worked with my City Council in supporting families when the battalion deployed. Returning just one year later, the warriors marched proudly into a ballroom in their honor without legs and arms, having suffered as the battalion that fought in Fallujah. It took a devastating toll on the 3/1 but served as a turning point in the war against terrorism. Through the kindness of the elected officials of this beach city, these warriors and their families received a hero's welcome. What a privilege to be a part of this celebration.

One of my favorite adventures snatched us from Peterson Air Force Base in Colorado Springs, Colorado and flew us on the General's jet to military installations across America over five days. Referred to as the Civic Leader's Tour, Generals host local leaders at military installations to facilitate understanding of the critical role these bases play in our economy and national safety. On this trip, we visited the newly-constructed border fence along El Paso, Texas. We listened as soldiers from Fort Bliss and Border Patrol Officers spoke of the agonizing issues faced in their duty. Children posed with us from the Mexico side of the fence while photographers memorialized our visit.

On to Tyndall Air Force Base in Florida, we attended an awards ceremony of young officers and toured the facility solely responsible for "ensuring the air sovereignty and air defense of the continental United States." Departing Tyndall, flying into Key West, our jet became a *renegade* aircraft for a simulated assault. Snapping pocket cameras, we listened as Air Force jets warned us to turn back. As we ignored the warning, two jets flanked us, shooting simulated weapons at our jet. Even though we knew it was staged, chills rippled down spines as we watched the two jets close in on us and issue the stern warning shots.

An overnight stay in Key West Florida allowed a visit at the Naval Air Station and the Joint Interagency Task Force South. Responsible for drug interdiction, we spent the day on a Coast Guard Cutter. Several of us were asked to join in a mock pursuit of drug dealers on a boarding craft. Exhilarated by the speed, we felt the rush of the chase – that is until I fell off the seat in my slippery, silk suit. Two quick thinking civic leaders grabbed me by the ankles, as I hung overboard. I wore my bruises with pride, knowing that I had experienced just a fraction of what the men and women defending our borders experience daily.

Charleston Air Force Base gave us a glimpse of how a MRAP (Mine Resistant Ambush Protected) vehicle is built. Climbing inside and hanging on rails, we explored every inch of the monster machines recently adapted to protect our soldiers from IEDs. Many of the vehicle and weapon innovations came from soldiers and aviators in the field.

The last stop took us to St. Augustine, Florida where we met with the National Guard and witnessed firsthand our nation's disaster preparedness and homeland security. Overall, it was an impressive display of competence and comfort, seeing our nation's military capabilities in action.

City management is complex, difficult, and often thankless. Of course, our duty is to our citizens and Councils and not for the sake of adventure. Adventure, however, awaits us every day around every corner. When serving our communities, we are free to explore all facets – the positive and the negative. For me, serving in eleven cities and one Indian Nation has exposed me to experiences beyond imagination. Gems surfaced everywhere – in the people, the landscape, events, and the issues. When I looked at my job as an adventure, I found excitement, solutions, and people who cared.

Pondering a career in local government, I think of television commercials, enticing young people to find adventure by joining the military. The same goes for city management. Perhaps our logo should be, "Want the adventure of a lifetime? Serve your community and join the ranks of city management."

I proudly say, "City management is awesome!" Where else could an ordinary girl from Indiana soar the skies, explore the coalmines, live with the Indians, and be a part of making communities healthier and stronger?

Appropriate Quote

> "Security is mostly a superstition. It does not exist in nature, nor do the children of men as a whole experience it. Avoiding danger is no safer in the long run than outright exposure. Life is either a daring adventure or nothing."
>
> Helen Keller, Humanitarian

Key Insight

Getting out of the office or conference room is a challenge for most local government professionals. The call of duty so often seems to require labor at the desk top, on the phone or in meetings. As Penny points out, the adventure (and often the learning!) is away from City Hall!

Dr. Penelope Culbreth-Graft is a retired, credentialed City Manager. She served in public agencies for over 32 years in 11 cities and one Indian Reservation. Her positions included City Manager and Assistant City Manager in cities, ranging in population from 12,000 to 1.2 million in California, Arizona, and Colorado. Dr. Culbreth-Graft taught for five universities over 18 years in the Masters' programs in Public Administration and Criminal Justice. She has a Doctorate in Public Administration from the University of La Verne; a Master's of Public Administration from the California State University Consortium; and, two Bachelor's degrees from California Polytechnic University, Pomona.

About Mike Conduff

MICHAEL A. (Mike) Conduff is the President and CEO of The Elim Group – *Your Governance Experts*, a governance, leadership, training, speaking and consulting firm. Mike has 35+ years of leadership, management and governance experience. He is considered one of the country's leading experts in the field of municipal and not-for-profit governance, and has served as a CEO, Board Chair and Consultant himself. In his CEO roles Mike led highly commended public organizations with multi-billion dollar responsibilities and thousands of employees. His energy and enthusiasm as well as his facilitation and group process skills have earned him the reputation of being the "go to" guy for helping city councils and boards of directors look to the future and develop the processes to get there.

Mr. Conduff earned his B.S. in civil engineering at the University of New Hampshire, graduating Cum Laude. His M.B.A. is from Pittsburg State University. He is also a charter graduate of the Carver Policy Governance® Academy and is a past Chair of the Board of Directors of the International Policy Governance® Association. Mike's clients have included the International City/County Management Association, The National League of Cities Leadership Training Institute, The National Committee on Planned Giving, The Partnership for Philanthropic Planning, The Community Associations Institute, The Republic of the Marshall Islands, and many many cities, associations, and other non-profit and for-profit corporations.

A Best-Selling Author Mike has written with Brian Tracy in their book *Pushing to the Front – Front Line Strategies from the World's Leading Experts*, and with Jack Canfield (of *Chicken Soup* fame) for their book *Success Secrets*. Mike is also the author or co-author of a number of other books including *The OnTarget Board Member – 8 Indisputable Behaviors,* soon to be in its third edition, *Democracy at the Doorstep – True Stories from the Green Berets of Public Administrators, Bottom Line Green – How America's Cities are Saving the Planet (And Money Too!)*, and *The Policy Governance® Fieldbook,* a book on the practical applications of Policy Governance®.

Additionally he writes a regular governance column for **Public Management Magazine,** is a contributing author to the ICMA "*Green Book*" series and is frequently published or quoted in other national publications. Known as a "master of motivation," he is a sought after and frequent speaker at international, national, regional and state-wide conferences, seminars and events.

In addition to serving the International City/County Management Association as a Senior Advisor for Governance, Mr. Conduff is a Fellow of the prestigious National Academy of Public Administration. He has been honored with the 2006 TCMA Mentoring Award in memory of Gary Gwyn, the 2004 International Award for Career Development in Memory of L. P. (Perry) Cookingham from ICMA, and the especially meaningful Joy Sansom Mentor Award from the Urban Management Assistants of North Texas for his commitment to helping others achieve their potential. The Center for Digital Government has awarded Mike their coveted "Best of Texas Visionary Award."

A fifth generation Native American, Mike grew up on stories of his Cherokee ancestry, and attributes his love of motivational speaking and telling stories to his grandmothers. A graduate of the 1988 Leadership Kansas Class, Mr. Conduff is active in a number of professional and civic organizations. He serves on the Athletic Council for the University of North Texas. He is a full member and Past President of the Texas City Management Association. He was one of the very first credentialed members of the International City/County Management Association, and served on its International Executive Board. He also served six years on the Board of Directors of the Kansas Association of

City/County Management, holding all of the statewide offices including President of the Association. He is a Past President of the Kansas Engineering Society; a charter member of the Board of Directors of the Kansas Entrepreneurial Center, located at Kansas State University; and a past member of the Board of Directors of the League of Kansas Municipalities.

Mr. Conduff is fully credentialed by the International City/County Management Association and is licensed as a Professional Engineer and a Registered Land Surveyor in the State of Kansas (retired status,) and served eight years on the Kansas State Board of Technical Professions, twice as Chairman of the Engineering Section and twice as Chairman of the Full Board. He also served four years on the Kansas Water Authority.

Mike practices what he preaches while chairing and serving on a number of Boards himself. He says, "In my experience, people who give of their time and energy to serve on a Board or City Council are unbelievably caring individuals doing their absolute best to make a difference. My passion is to provide the leadership, motivation and training to give them the tools and insights they need to be successful."

About Melissa Byrne Vossmer

MELISSA Byrne Vossmer, ICMA-CM, completed 30 years of service in local government in 2011. Most recently she served as City Manager in Angleton, Texas. Over her 30 years she has served in Angel Fire, NM, the City of San Antonio, TX, the City of Waco, TX, Lawton, OK and Leavenworth, Kansas where she started her career.

Throughout her career, Melissa has been active in both the Texas City Management Association (TCMA), serving as President in 1999 and in ICMA, serving on the ICMA Board 2005-2008, as well as most recently serving as a member of the Task Force to Review Recruitment Guidelines Handbook.

She received her Bachelor of Arts from St. Mary of the Plains College and her Masters of Public Administration from the University of Kansas in 1982.

She has been an ICMA Credentialed Manager since 2005. During her career she received the YWCA Pathfinders Award, the Texas Municipal Library Directors Association Administrator of the Year and the Department of Army, Commander's Award for Public Service and has served on a number of non-profit community based Boards.

She is a graduate of the Foundation for Women's Resources, Leadership Texas Program.

Melissa has been happily married for over 33 years to Mark, an educator and coach and is the proud parent of one son, Jacob.